TRAIDCRAFT

Inspiring a Fair Trade Revolution

TRAIDCRAFT

Inspiring a Fair Trade Revolution

Joe Osman

Published by
Lion Hudson Limited
Wilkinson House, Jordan Hill Business Park
Banbury Road, Oxford OX2 8DR, England
www.lionhudson.com

ISBN 978 0 7459 8104 8
eISBN 978 0 7459 8103 1

First edition 2020

Acknowledgments
Cover collage: painted dishes © traveler/istockphoto.com; tea plantation worker © tunart/
istockphoto.com; coffee beans © Tendo23/istockphoto.com; Indian bags © RuslanKaln/
istockphoto.com; Mexican fabric © korionov/istockphoto.com; cocoa pods © pierivb/
istockphoto.com
All scripture quotations are taken from the Holy Bible, New International Version Anglicised.
Copyright © 1979, 1984, 2011 Biblica, formerly International Bible Society. Used by
permission of Hodder & Stoughton Ltd, an Hachette UK company. All rights reserved.
"NIV" is a registered trademark of Biblica. UK trademark number 1448790.
The prayer on pp.190–191 is taken from *Common Worship: Services and Prayers for the Church of
England*, copyright © The Archbishops' Council [2000].

A catalogue record for this book is available from the British Library

Printed and bound in the UK, July 2020, LH26

CONTENTS

FOREWORD
BY DR JOHN SENTAMU

> "Do not go where the path may lead,
> go instead where there is no path and
> leave a trail."

Nobody is quite sure who said this – it is often attributed to philosopher, Ralph Emerson – but, whoever said it, it means that you shouldn't follow the path which is already created by others, instead you should stand out and do something new and create your own path for others to follow. You should do something unique and leave your mark in the world.

Traidcraft (the company) and Traidcraft Exchange (the charity) took that bold step and blazed a new trail some forty years ago. And Joe Osman is the best placed person to reflect on the life and journey of Traidcraft because he was there right from its inception and holds the institutional memory of the organization.

As you will see from the book, Joe Osman has journeyed with Traidcraft through its ups and downs. From modest beginnings, he worked closely with the producers as well as understanding the complexities of the route to market for the goods. He was always innovative and always thinking of new products. What motivated Joe was the issue of fairness and justice for the small and marginalized producers who stood no chance on the world stage of trade. Joe has been very candid in his appraisal of Traidcraft plc (the company) and he has not shied away from spelling out the challenges facing the organization then and now.

Although much of Joe's work was outward facing, working mainly with producers and the wider Fair Trade movement, he was keenly aware that Traidcraft would not have achieved what it has been able to do without the producers, supporters, Fair Trade voluntary representatives (mainly from churches), as well as staff, both past and present, who have been part of the Traidcraft journey.

So, not quite a "from rags to riches" story, but definitely from selling jute hanging baskets and sikas from one bedroom in Tyneside, to selling "Eat your Hat" dark chocolate. Traidcraft has come a long way. This is a journey of faith, bringing together Christian values and the principles of justice and fairness into the commercial trade.

Of course, as the guest writers have said, it remains to be seen if Traidcraft has become a victim of its own success (in that the Fair Trade practices they pioneered have now become mainstream), or whether Traidcraft adopted a "wrong" business model which did not deliver in the end, or whether a radical solution lies elsewhere.

Together with his former colleagues as "guest writers", Joe Osman has been able to chart the Traidcraft journey through the good times and challenging times and to highlight the work yet to be done. Is Traidcraft's work done or not? I am not convinced that the mission is complete. There is much more to be done to raise awareness and to campaign for trade justice to be rolled out globally.

In this global village where we all depend on each other, may I encourage people of faith and none to stick with this journey – a journey which began with a small group of individuals, driven by their Christian values and ethics, responding to the scandal of poverty through an alternative model of trade, which puts people first before profit.

Dr John Sentamu
Former Archbishop of York

INTRODUCTION

In 2019, Traidcraft entered its fortieth year – a landmark for an organization that has influenced the lives of countless people, whether producers in the developing world or shoppers around the UK and beyond. As my own journey in Traidcraft came to an end early in 2019, it seemed fitting that a record of that journey was made. Indeed, several people encouraged it, given that my time at Traidcraft covers its entire history in some way – that includes a period at Tearcraft from which Traidcraft emerged in 1979. I eventually concluded that I was probably the best, if not only, person to write something, given that I've lived and breathed the organization for much of my life.

It's not that my own personal journey constitutes a definitive history of Traidcraft – but I have tried to include most of the key events or milestones. History anyway is, in a sense, interpretive. I was, for the most part, in a relatively senior or influential role – never the captain, but for a lot of the time "on the bridge", and the account is very much through my eyes. I've managed to get access to Traidcraft documentation from the past forty years and my thanks go to those that have supplied much of this material. Inevitably there will be lots missed out. In my career at Traidcraft, I was mostly involved with the trading company, meaning Traidcraft plc, so much of the content of this book will focus on that and it will inevitably be difficult to do justice to the important and broader work of the Traidcraft Exchange.

In the course of writing, I have consulted with many ex-members of staff and beyond. The list includes everyone who led Traidcraft throughout its history and the narrative contains many contributions from these and others. My appreciation and thanks go to all those who have contributed in any way.

Two substantive works have been published about Traidcraft in the past. The first, by Traidcraft's founder Richard Adams, called *Who*

Profits? was an account of the birth and development of Traidcraft until his departure in 1988.[1] The second was a collection of essays published in 2001 to celebrate the twenty-first birthday of Traidcraft called *Markets, Fair Trade and the Kingdom of God.*[2] I have drawn from both of these publications in this narrative. Other titles about Fair Trade have been published in the intervening years and each one gives a high profile to Traidcraft. This is the first publication which gives focus to Traidcraft and is written, as it were, "from within".

For those who are not familiar with the world of Fair Trade, let me try to outline the history of Traidcraft in a few sentences. The country of Bangladesh had suffered a terrible typhoon in 1970 and was also emerging from a period of national conflict. UK Christian relief and development agency, Tearfund, was front and centre of relief efforts.[3] In partnership with Richard Adams, Tearfund financed some of the first purchases of handicrafts from Bangladesh – showcasing the traditional skills and hard work of rural producers, and providing appropriate financial reward for that hard work. Tearcraft was established as the trading arm of Tearfund, with Richard Adams as Managing Director. In 1979, Richard left Tearcraft to set up Traidcraft. Over the next four decades, Traidcraft's partnerships with producers and suppliers all over the world were blessed with extraordinary growth. Traidcraft developed into two separate entities – a business arm (Traidcraft plc) and a charity (Traidcraft Exchange) – which worked collaboratively and constructively in providing an alternative model of trade, putting people before profit. Some of the key moments in Traidcraft's history – as I perceive them – are listed in Appendix 4.

I've reflected on the last forty years and have chosen to divide Traidcraft's history into four parts, or eras. The first era covers the birth of Tearcraft and the development of Traidcraft and its first ten years (from the mid 1970s to mid/late 1980s). This was a time of newness, discovery, pioneering, developing the principles and practices that would become Fair Trade, but in very much a "do it yourself" style given that there were few contemporaries and fewer rules to follow. It

---

1   Richard Adams, *Who Profits?* Oxford: Lion Publishing, 1989.

2   Peter Johnson and Chris Sugden, eds, *Markets, Fair Trade and the Kingdom of God: essays to celebrate Traidcraft's 21st birthday*, Oxford: Regnum Books, 2001.

3   Tearfund was formerly known as TEAR Fund (The Evangelical Alliance Relief Fund).

was also the period when consumer awareness began and the book *The Green Consumer Guide* was published (Guild Publishing, 1989).

The second era covers much of the late 1980s, the 1990s and through into the new millennium. It was a time of consolidation and evolution, and one in which Traidcraft was finding its identity in a much bigger Fair Trade world. This is the world that Traidcraft helped to pioneer – it was involved in the development and formation of what is often referred to as the "Fair Trade movement". Many of the global institutions of Fair Trade became established and Fair Trade became "mainstream" in this era. It was a time when Traidcraft wasn't "the only show in town". It also marked the period in which terminology like "ethical" began to be used more widely and when greater scrutiny of claims were starting to be important. The separate, but mutually compatible, identities and activities of Traidcraft plc and Traidcraft Exchange began in earnest but it was also an era of uncertainty, some dark times, and times of change.

The third era, I would call the financially prosperous years – from the late 1990s up until around 2010 – where growth in the business happened every year. Sales doubled in that period, profitability was maintained and there was increased product innovation. It was also a time when Traidcraft became (dare I say) a bit more professional and was hugely influential in the world of Fair Trade and beyond, through both Traidcraft plc and Traidcraft Exchange. These first three eras are covered in Parts One to Three.

The fourth era is covered in Part Eight and I would call this a period of decline and uncertainty, certainly for the plc. Sales dropped, clarity of commercial strategy and role in the world of Fair Trade began to erode, and continued losses meant that Traidcraft plc's very existence was under threat. Traidcraft Exchange continued but with less synergy in their work in relation to the plc. Each of these four eras were probably defined by the leadership and governance in place at the time. Much like any organization, leadership plays a pivotal role and defines its activities and culture. This was very much the case for Traidcraft.

In addition to the historical narrative, Parts Four to Seven contain chapters around a specific theme. For example, Traidcraft's role in the development of the wider Fair Trade movement, its Christian origins and practice, and some more specific narrative about how Traidcraft became involved in particular product areas, and how it pioneered the development of these products. These themed chapters will tend to span the entire forty years and it might seem that I switch from one era to another quite seamlessly or even to duplicate things written elsewhere. My apologies if this is confusing, but I found it quite difficult to be entirely chronological.

In preparation for writing this book, I analysed the four passports I have possessed in my lifetime – just to remind myself of where I travelled and when. Given that my role at Traidcraft was mostly "producer-facing", I've had the privilege of visiting twenty developing countries on three continents, some of them on numerous occasions. I have met inspirational people linked to the producer organizations we worked with and beyond, some of which I feature. All of this means that I will inevitably give more focus to the overseas part of my activities and, again, I will not do enough justice to those parts of Traidcraft I wasn't involved with, like sales and marketing, or those incredible supporters that we called voluntary representatives and then Fair Traders. Without their commitment, the last forty years of Traidcraft would not have happened.

I name many colleagues; indeed, many have contributed in their own words. Many more colleagues are not named and that is largely due to the focus I give to the narrative, and my apologies to any who may feel excluded. There have been hundreds of staff who have passed through Traidcraft throughout its history. All contributed in their own way and all were part of this important journey and I thank them all.

I will invariably use terminology which may confuse. For example, when I use the term "Fairtrade" I will mean the system and organizations that manage the certification of products and producers administered by Fairtrade International in Germany and the Fairtrade label awarded to licensees as administered by the Fairtrade Foundation in the UK. For simplification, I use "Fair Trade" for everything else which means the non-certified world or the so-called "movement" to which many organizations purport to belong.

Given that my passports are a reminder of the many days and weeks I spent out of the country and therefore away from home, I therefore dedicate this book to my wife, Susan, who had to deal with my regular absences.

PART ONE

The Early Years

Chapter 1

BEGINNINGS

It was a fairly ordinary Sunday morning at church in the summer of 1976, but one which was to have enormous impact on my life, not just in terms of work and career but in shaping my Christian faith. The vicar of my church in the small village of Newbottle, midway between Durham and Sunderland, casually mentioned that a friend of his might want some temporary staff for the Christmas season in the business he ran in Newcastle-upon-Tyne. I had time on my hands and was very uncertain of the future, having failed to complete year one of an engineering degree.

Ray Skinner was that vicar and he would go on to be the first Chair of Traidcraft, and Richard Adams was that friend and he would go on to be founder of Traidcraft. I didn't take much persuading and I started working for Tearcraft along with another member of the Newbottle youth group who would turn out to be my future sister-in-law. The next few months were a complete joy. Even though I was merely packing mail order parcels, I couldn't wait to start work each day. Here was a small organization in which everyone was valued, everyone was part of the team, and everyone was made to feel involved in something that was certainly more radical and mission-based than even I imagined at that time.

The story of the birth of Tearcraft has been well told by Richard Adams in his book, *Who Profits?*, which documents his journey from greengrocer to managing director of a limited company selling mostly jute hanging baskets, and describes the application of his Christian faith to a business which would put the principles of love and justice into practice through commercial activity.[4] Tearcraft emerged from Agrofax Labour Intensive Products, which was Richard's initial business, and later became a subsidiary of Tearfund, which had financed some of the first purchases of handicrafts from Bangladesh.

Over the next year, a seasonal job turned into a permanent one as the possibility of continuing the degree course receded and I found myself involved in general warehouse duties, as well as starting to get to grips with the technicalities of importing products. In a small organization this principle of "learning on the job" became part of the culture since it's not always possible to hire the experienced or the qualified. Moreover, as the organization grew it remained an important principle and, in later years, when I was in a position of recruiting staff myself, I would pay as much heed to an interviewee's "heart" for the organization's mission and objectives as I did to their experience and qualifications.

Tearcraft at that time was based in central Newcastle-upon-Tyne, close to a busy bus station. The six-storey India House in Carliol Square was originally the site of the Newcastle jail but now proved ideal for warehouse and office space. Seeing those first consignments delivered must have been quite a spectacle. Containerization had not yet developed as the standard mode of sea freight, so those early deliveries from Bangladesh were in huge wooden crates stacked onto flatbed lorries and the crates were unloaded by being dropped onto the road. There was no forklift truck, indeed there was no need for one given that storage was on the fifth floor, accessed by a goods lift. The age of health and safety had not yet emerged and it's highly likely that none of the ways we did warehousing then would be allowed today.

Products became familiar to us, as did the names of the producers who supplied them. There was an enormous range of jute sikas (hanging baskets) each with their own Bengali name, all of which we knew intimately. We knew the producers by name too, such as "CORR–The Jute Works" which was the first and biggest supplier (CORR standing for "Christian Organization for Relief and Rehabilitation").

---

4   Adams, *Who Profits?*.

The mission of Tearcraft was very clear in those early days. Richard Adams' vision was for something that became known as "alternative marketing" and then "alternative trade" – in other words, doing trade differently, putting people ahead of profit. It was a vision that was shared and discussed among all staff. Representatives of producer organizations we traded with would come to visit and we spent time together discussing what we were doing. The organization openly shared its Christian roots, and times of prayer and worship were integral to working life. Our parent body, Tearfund, very specifically adhered to Christian principles in its relief work.

But cracks in the relationship were beginning to emerge – both theological and philosophical. CORR–The Jute Works was a Catholic-based organization which did not fulfil Tearfund's "evangelical" requirement for overseas partners. Also, I'm not sure that Tearfund really understood the "alternative" nature of what Tearcraft was seeking to be. One example of this was an advertising campaign that used the slogan "Tearcraft depends on them" next to pictures of handicraft producers. This fitted with the principles of equity and partnership that characterized the relationship between Tearcraft and its overseas suppliers. Tearfund were upset about this advert, perhaps for reasons relating to the dynamics of the relationship between donor and recipient of aid. Traditionally, aid had been understood as a one-way benefit – from donor to recipient – rather than a partnership.

Many of the customers of Tearcraft were also Tearfund supporters. Much of Tearcraft's business was conducted through what became known as Tearcraft Voluntary Representatives, who raised money for Tearfund but also bought and sold Tearcraft products in their churches. They were supplied with materials provided by Tearcraft which contained information on producers and on the theme of injustice in international trade. In early 1979, Tearcraft started an initiative to engage voluntary reps further by introducing them to producers. In February, the first so-called "study tour" was organized. These tours were led by Jan Simmonds who was also involved in the development of the voluntary reps initiative. This was something that became an integral part of the future Traidcraft and was the forerunner of what became known as "meet the people" tours. I decided to pay my own way to join a group of voluntary reps on one such tour; this became my first trip abroad.

My experience of the tour was truly transformational and paved the way for a working life in Fair Trade. The tour covered Bangladesh and West Bengal in India, visiting some of the producers supplying Tearcraft. There was then time for a bit of tourism in Delhi and Agra in the north of India. The first place we visited was Kolkata (then called Calcutta) and I confess that my first experience was one of fear! The city in the 1970s was an absolute nightmare with what can only be described as a dilapidated infrastructure bursting at the seams with people, many of whom were refugees from the Bangladesh war of independence. Consequently, the number of street dwellers and beggars was enormous. Tourism in this part of India was in its infancy, so a young European venturing into the street for a look around caused me to be very much the centre of attention. I quickly sought the security of my hotel! I'm not particularly proud of that and I have been back to Kolkata on numerous occasions and not experienced anything like it. The city was transformed over the next couple of decades and ultimately became one of my favourite overseas destinations.

The study tour exposed us all to the realities of poverty. It included visits to urban slums and rural villages where poverty was still evident, though in a different way – urban slums are dirty, messy and totally obvious; with rural poverty, you needed to dig beneath the sometimes idyllic surroundings to see what was happening. A visit to some of the Jute Works producers involved a river trip and a long walk to get to a village called Boali where I was able to recognize the jute sikas that we sold.

The experience of this first trip overseas resulted in two overriding thoughts. First, it showed that what we were doing had the potential to make a difference, working with people of all faiths and none. Secondly, it highlighted something that one of my colleagues often said, with which I completely agreed. We were working with producers who had tremendous skills and who were very hard working, and yet were still vulnerable and poor. Purely by being born in a culture and part of the world different to ours, the dice were loaded against them. This drove my sense of injustice at the situation, and a desire to help.

At home, discussions about the relationship between Tearcraft and its parent company, Tearfund, were taking place. Tearfund wanted to bring Tearcraft more under its evangelical criteria and also under its strategic control. Richard wanted to pursue a more radical direction, informed by his interpretation of his Christian faith, and apply the principles of love and justice to international trade. Those of us not directly engaged in the debate with Tearfund watched from a distance. Fortunately, there was transparency in communications, something that would become a feature of Traidcraft and, indeed, a key feature of what would define an "Alternative Marketing Organization". Most of the staff were fully behind Richard Adams and, inevitably, he would need to move on while management and control of Tearcraft would gradually be integrated into the structure and vision of Tearfund.

Richard wanted to continue with his vision and he could only do this by being separate and independent of a parent body like Tearfund who, to their credit, were helpful when the terms of separation were agreed. When Richard founded Traidcraft later in 1979, several members of Tearcraft staff left and joined him. I stayed at Tearcraft though my heart was really with the new organization. I was still fully focused on purchasing, importing and logistics. The new staff that Tearcraft employed were great and I got on well with them, but it was a very strange time. In founding Traidcraft, Richard had come to an arrangement with Tearfund. He would purchase, at discounted rates, the stocks from all those suppliers (like the Jute Works) which did not meet their supplier or purchasing criteria (requiring them to be owned, organized or part of an evangelical Christian governance structure). Whether mischievously or because Carliol Square was just the cheapest and best place to set up, Traidcraft became a next-door neighbour to Tearcraft. Staff fraternization was commonplace – after all we knew each other well – whether on the roof over lunch or on the fire escape to which both organizations had access. In fact, the sale of those discounted goods to Traidcraft became an easy logistics arrangement since we merely had to open the fire door and hand over the stock.

Those early days must have been very confusing to customers. Some of those voluntary reps began their support for both organizations and we would cross paths in the Christian world for years to come. For example, Tearcraft would exhibit and sell at the Christian arts festival

Greenbelt which, in 1979, then became the launch event for Traidcraft. As I set up the Tearcraft stall that year, who should I discover setting up in the next marquee but Richard Adams and Traidcraft. Friendly rivalry prevailed, and I still don't know who banked the most sales!

Chapter 2

YET MORE BEGINNINGS

Tearcraft left Newcastle a few years later and most of the staff were made redundant, although a few moved to London. Fortunately, before this, I managed to get a job at Traidcraft looking after the warehouse, distribution and logistics. It was my first senior role and taken on without any experience of managing people; it was a steep learning curve. Traidcraft invested heavily in my training and I embarked on the first of several management courses soon after my appointment.

The answer to the question "When was Traidcraft founded?" will usually be 1979, although legally it was a little earlier. The alternative view, which I share, is that the journey started with Richard Adams and continued through those early Tearcraft days, into Traidcraft. It was Tearcraft that chose to take a different route. The culture that Richard had developed in Tearcraft, and which was well established by the time he had left, was transplanted into Traidcraft and flourished.

Over the years, although the two organizations went their separate ways, relationships were cordial, and we still shared many of the same customers and overseas suppliers. When Tearcraft, or "Created" as it would become known, was wound up in 2015, I had the privilege of representing Traidcraft at a thanksgiving service celebrating their work. Richard Adams was also invited as founder. It was an emotional and memorable event, tinged with a sense of melancholy. It's ironic that some of the Created suppliers were taken on by Traidcraft in 2015 and some of the Created stocks sold on at a discounted rate. We had come full circle after more than thirty years, and maybe reached a point of restoration and healing.

In its first year of trading, Traidcraft published a hand drawn, two-colour, brown and beige "album" (catalogue) just in time for the Christmas season. Most of the products were brown so it seemed appropriate! It contained over a hundred craft products, many of them from suppliers transferred over from Tearcraft. In fact, more than 50% of the products were from the Jute Works, including a large range of jute sikas together with other suppliers in Bangladesh like the International Union for Child Welfare (IUCW) who supplied the cane baskets for those sikas. In addition, a local youth job creation project in north east England made wooden brackets on which to hang those sikas and baskets. While mail order and voluntary reps were yet to develop any meaningful sales revenue, it was the wholesale channel, direct to shops, that was to bring a modest profit at the end of that year and the next.

A couple of key factors contributed to get Traidcraft off the ground commercially. First, sikas and baskets were well in demand and fashionable in the UK, with every house seemingly needing a hanging basket. The range available from Traidcraft was competitive, unique, of excellent quality, with twenty designs and sizes to choose from. Over the years that followed, Traidcraft exhibited its range at all the main UK gift fairs and many of us donned our best clothes to act as sales reps. I recall drawing the short straw for the Torquay gift fair, not because Torquay in January isn't a nice place to be, but because it was the longest drive in a transit van from Newcastle. We couldn't afford to send two people to staff the trade stand, so it was pretty full on! It was perhaps providential that hanging baskets were so popular at that time because, just a few years later, the demand for them disappeared almost completely.

Secondly, the contribution made by the Jute Works was pivotal. In a conventional supplier/buyer relationship, power dynamics exist. In an alternative supplier/buyer relationship, it's more of a partnership. In the world of alternative trade, the word "supplier" was often interchangeable with the word "partner". Jute Works was in a much stronger position than Traidcraft, so offered 120 days financial credit terms, which was a great help to cash flow. More radically, it turned on its head the principle of pre-finance, or advance payment, which is a key component of the Fair Trade model even today, but who has ever heard of the supplier pre-financing the buyer?

Traidcraft continued its radical mission, focusing on issues of economic injustice. Yes, it talked about poverty and poor producers and poor countries, but its focus was on tackling the causes of poverty. It gave prominence to the producers who made these products and to the fact that buying them was not some act of charity or a hand-out to poor people. It also continued to talk about its Christian roots. That first two-colour catalogue had a section entitled "What is Traidcraft?" which was replicated in subsequent catalogues and which read:

> Traidcraft is a company founded and run by people trying
> to put into practice some of the implications of their own
> Christian faith. We feel that there is every opportunity to
> demonstrate God's desire for love and justice in the world
> through responsible and fair trading. Traidcraft is supported
> by, and accountable to, people of all denominations who
> believe that redressing economic injustice in the world
> is part of their responsibilities. Traidcraft comprises a
> marketing company concerned with direct action and
> positive example in the commercial world, and a non-profit
> making trust engaging in educational and informative
> work.[5]

In 1979, we coined the term "alternative marketing" and later this became "alternative trading". Few, if any, referred to the term "Fair Trade" as it is widely known now. That first statement containing the words "fair trading" might be one of the earliest references in the UK to something close to it!

The 1980/81 catalogue moved to colour. This was the period that Traidcraft started to sell consumable products more meaningfully through the Campaign Coffee and the World Development Movement tea products. It's worth emphasizing that the tea and coffee that is widely

---

5   First Traidcraft catalogue, 1979.

available now and labelled with a Fairtrade Mark bears little resemblance to the products sold in those days. They were "campaigning" products and were the result of partnerships with two separate organizations, both campaigning for the rights of coffee farmers and tea workers worldwide.

Campaign Coffee was a voluntary campaign group seeking to promote a better deal for all coffee workers and producers. The group had developed direct links with a coffee "instantizing" plant in Tanzania. This "value addition" of having the coffee processed close to the farmers was something that, where it could, Traidcraft adopted as a principle throughout its history. Despite the fact that the catalogue description read "the coffee is a good strong brew comparing favourably with the best-quality multi-national blends" – it was very much an acquired taste!

The World Development Movement (WDM) was another organization campaigning for justice for the world's poor. Its strategy was more similar to the Fair Trade of today in that its tea was sourced from a specific tea origin in Sri Lanka, together with the "value addition" principle of having the tea packaged in the country.

The first half of the 1980s was a period of rapid growth and change. By 1983, turnover had passed the £1 million mark and, only two years later, it passed £2 million. A move to new premises was required so the River Tyne was crossed and Traidcraft's home became the Team Valley Trading Estate in Gateshead. At that time, the estate had seen better days, so premises were readily available and cheap. We now had over 50,000 square feet to fill and everything was on one level, so it was much more efficient.

The complexities of a larger organization meant a degree of organizational restructure and specialization. Traidcraft had always taken a "do it yourself" approach, or as Richard would say "DIY-DID" (Do it Yourself, Do it Differently). Early on, Traidcraft had its own graphics department to design catalogues and other published material. This evolved into a paper production unit when recycled paper was introduced and tens of thousands of writing pads were cut and glued in our own premises. When instant coffee arrived, a small packing unit had been created to fill and label plastic bags of coffee by hand. Later in the 1980s, with more and more food products being sold, packing got a little more sophisticated through investing in state-of-the-art machinery.

I focused on buying, quality, products, producers and logistics, and was no longer responsible for packing and distribution of finished parcels. Up until this point, Richard Adams had done most of the overseas travelling, managed relationships with suppliers and selected products but now that duty was shared. For craft products, a cycle of activities evolved where a small group of staff would source, sample and select ranges of products for the catalogue, which would be launched the following autumn. This would require them to travel to various producers throughout the world. It would be up to me to place orders by Christmas, to organize packaging, scheduling, shipment, receipt, and quality-checking in time for sale the next autumn.

It was decided that visiting craft suppliers to see the products being made should be an integral part of this process and so, in 1983, I began travelling again. This period was very different to my experiences on the study tour back in 1979. My overseas trips generally took place during March, April or May – the timing of each trip factoring in the likely size of order to be placed, the location of the producer and the degree of risk associated with the particular producers and products. India, Bangladesh, Sri Lanka, Thailand and the Philippines became frequent destinations for the remainder of the 1980s.

These were years of discovery, learning and even adventure. Before mobile phones, e-mails, and the internet age, the travel experience was relatively uneven. What was essentially business travel resembled backpacking and I would never travel without my Lonely Planet guide. I would usually travel for around three to four weeks at a time and cram in as much as possible, covering at least three countries on each trip. On one occasion, a call from Traidcraft headquarters asked me to check out a small tea estate in India to see if it was worth purchasing, and this extended one of my trips to almost six weeks. In later years, Traidcraft developed a policy which regulated both duration and content of overseas travel, taking greater regard to health, safety, and welfare, but these were days without such constraints and I never complained! Nor did my colleagues who would undertake similar and probably more eventful trips, having to contend not only with the uncertainty of transport, but with extreme weather and the occasional natural disaster. My colleague Mandy Jetter was in Mexico City during the devastating earthquake of 1985, which killed thousands – and, for a while, we were all very concerned for her safety. I always seemed to time my travel to coincide with the aftermath of political turmoil. In Colombo, Sri Lanka, I arrived in the wake of some pretty serious rioting, and in 1986 I observed the immediate aftermath of the "People Power Revolution" in the Philippines in which President Marcos was deposed. My hosts insisted that I visit the presidential palace to view the extensive shoe collection of his wife!

Those early days of travel were formative for me and for others, and only one regret occasionally springs to mind. On one short flight from Chennai (then called Madras) in India to Colombo in Sri Lanka, I looked across from my aisle seat to a lone traveller. It was Mother Theresa and the regret is that I didn't simply switch my seat to the empty one next to her and engage in conversation. She spent the entire flight with bowed head and eyes closed, seemingly in prayer. I didn't want to intrude!

Traidcraft's early suppliers – many of whom continue to work with the company today – had a common characteristic: they all had a clear mission to uplift, assist, protect, and develop the workers and producers they engaged with. The original purchasing principles of Traidcraft were short and focused, and the following is reproduced from one of its early documents.

> **Producer Partners:** In assessing whether Traidcraft can be of assistance to a producer group, it firstly considers whether the group is open to the examination of its aims, objectives and commercial practices. If this is the case, then the majority of the following criteria should be met.
>
> A producer group should be:
> a) organised for the benefit of its members
> b) concerned for the personal welfare of individual members
> c) paying wages and providing working conditions which are, or are above, the average in its locality
> d) making products which are now, or potentially, viable commercially
> e) paying no more than a service fee to agents (if they are involved).[6]

---

6 Traidcraft internal document, 1979.

Short and sweet, but containing the key pillars which would inform future Fair Trade principles. There was no certification, no formal assessment or questionnaires, but those of us who travelled carried these principles into the field. In the main, there were no key concerns because our suppliers shared these principles, but on occasion there was cause for action. One of our suppliers in the Philippines worked with many individual producer groups and occasionally they got it wrong with their own selection of who to work with. On a visit to a workshop making wooden trays, it soon became clear that it wasn't a good place to buy from, with an owner who clearly did not share our principles. A phone call back to Traidcraft headquarters resulted in a product being pulled from the forthcoming catalogue. The order was cancelled and production halted. I was forced to do this only twice. The only other time, many years later, was linked to recycled glass products and a concern about health and safety and child labour. A cause for concern might result in something positive and beneficial, like assistance to improve or training. On another occasion, on a visit to a workshop producing coir doormats, I was confronted by what looked like extremely dangerous machinery, supported by the fact that one of the operators had a finger missing. These were the early manifestations of something we would refer to later as "producer support", again something that became a key pillar in future Fair Trade principles.

I met some truly inspirational characters in those days and three deserve special mention.

Professor Shyam Sharma was the founder of Tara Projects. They coordinated the production and marketing of high-quality carved stone products and this was part of a larger social welfare programme covering health, education, and environmental issues in some of the most marginalized communities of Delhi and Agra. We knew him just as Mr Sharma. He had a heart for people and a deep concern about social injustice. At the end of the working day, I would readily accept the invitation to the home of Mr Sharma and enjoy the cooking of his quieter but clearly influential wife. Deep into the evening we would discuss the issues of the day and our work together, each from the perspective of our different faith journeys. It was never contentious and we easily reached common understanding. He was the most gentle, genial, and humble person I would come across in my travels to India.

Rakesh Kaushal was a medical student in India who recognized that many of the health problems he was training to deal with were the result of poverty. He set up Archana Handicrafts to give a better alternative to the handicraft producers of Moradabad and Saharanpur and started to supply Traidcraft with shesham wood products. Archana Handicrafts became one of Traidcraft's largest suppliers in the 1980s and I got to know Rakesh quite well, which wasn't easy because he was quite quiet and introverted. The quality of shesham wood was problematic in those days. As a raw material, the wood needed to be seasoned, otherwise the finished craft product would warp and crack. There was no guarantee in those days that the supplier of wood would provide fully seasoned materials. Traidcraft decided to enter into a partnership agreement whereby we would pre-finance two years' worth of shesham wood in bulk, giving it time to season, and then using it to make finished products which would minimize the quality problem. This would effectively commit to two years' worth of orders. At the same time Archana would set up a quality checking system in their central warehouse in Delhi for every finished product. I spent a week there working with his staff to help them understand the things to look out for and why, for example, a teapot stand needed to be stable and not wobble. This was a memorable and intensive week and Rakesh and I rewarded ourselves with a weekend trekking in the foothills of the Himalayas. In later years, shesham wood products would diminish and it was Rakesh himself who chose not to supply Traidcraft – the volumes declined and it was no longer viable for Archana. However, I always found time for a catch up with him each time I passed through Delhi for years to come.

Father Shay Cullen, an Irishman from The Missionary Society of St Columba, set up the People's Recovery Empowerment and Development Assistance Foundation (PREDA) in Olongapo City to the north of Manila in the Philippines. The local economy was dominated by the presence of a large US Navy base which fuelled prostitution, resulting in the sexual exploitation of women and children, human trafficking, health problems, drug abuse, poverty, broken homes, and crime. Father Shay and PREDA provided sanctuary and help for many of the victims of this economy, and handicraft training and manufacture was only a small part of a larger programme of activities. In complete contrast to my previous two examples, Father Shay was outspoken, a campaigner for human rights, willing to oppose the powerful and stand up for justice, often with dangerous consequences and personal risk. A truly inspirational person.

The Traidcraft Trust established the Traidcraft Educational Foundation (TEF) as a charity in 1981. An organization like Traidcraft, with the kind of supporter base it developed, will ultimately attract folk who wish to donate money rather than buy products. There are, after all, only so many jute sikas that can be displayed in a household! On occasion, Traidcraft would also attract potential donations from larger trust funds or individuals – but receiving such money into a business would be both questionable and legally difficult.

At the same time, Traidcraft had a remit beyond merely buying and selling products. It was concerned with broader educational issues and awareness-raising. The separation of these "non-commercial" activities from "commercial activities" was, to some, both desirable and legitimate. So, the establishment of a charity and dedicated staff to undertake these activities made a lot of sense. While the company would annually contribute to the charity, income could also be topped up by charitable donations. From small beginnings, the TEF grew its staff and developed activities which included the production of a whole range of educational materials. These included material about the producers that Traidcraft sourced from, research and awareness-raising on issues of justice and Fair Trade, and answers to lots of questions from supporters and customers. It later developed support activities to the producers supplying Traidcraft, including consultancy in market awareness and product development, and the activities of the business and charity were pretty much intertwined in those very early years.

In 1986, the TEF and the Traidcraft Trust were combined into a new charity called the Traidcraft Exchange. It had greater autonomy, with its own governance structure, including a group of external trustees who were separate to the Board of Directors of Traidcraft plc. Graham Young, a trustee of the Traidcraft Trust from the very early days, was brought in as Director to lead its growth and development. Included in its early description of its activities was the concept of the Traidcraft Exchange "triangle", one of several visual devices used over the years. Two points of the triangle were the seller (meaning producer organizations or enterprises in the developing world) and the buyer (meaning the consumer of products). The third point on the triangle was Traidcraft Exchange, providing a comprehensive programme of educational and information support to consumers, as well as a comprehensive range of technical services to producers, enabling them to acquire greater skills and to develop stronger businesses. While the suppliers and customers of Traidcraft plc were the initial focus, a broader objective would be to extend beyond this.

In later years, having obtained greater levels of external funding, Traidcraft Exchange developed its work through overseas regional offices. There would be occasional but manageable tension between the activities of Traidcraft plc and Traidcraft Exchange, driven in part by the need to differentiate commercial interests from charitable activities – for example, when Traidcraft Exchange was providing product development support and input to a producer group which was designed to promote sales to customers other than Traidcraft plc.

As it launched new fund raising activities, Traidcraft Exchange used the following narrative, painting the broader picture of Traidcraft. It perhaps gives some clue as to the origins of its name:

> We have always felt that Traidcraft is more than just selling
> jute angels or recycled toilet rolls! Traidcraft is about
> a vision. It's about here and the Third World... about
> bringing justice to the way we trade with each other... about
> understanding the how and the why of that. It's a vision
> enabling people to relate as equals... understanding and
> supporting each other. It's about "exchanging" in many
> different ways. Do you share that vision? Even if, as for
> most of us, it's rather dimly seen! The Traidcraft Exchange
> has been launched to kindle the vision. It is a charity
> concerned with Education and Development work around
> the issue of Trade.[7]

The slogan "more than jute angels" became something many were familiar with given that these Christmas tree decorations sold in their

---

7   Traidcraft Exchange, internal document, 1979.

thousands for several years, although I suspect few nowadays know what a jute angel looks like!

Chapter 3

BECOMING ESTABLISHED

Toward the end of the 1980s, Traidcraft's turnover had exceeded £5 million and, to fuel that growth, additional working capital needed to be found. As Richard Adams comments in *Who Profits?*, the decision to become a public limited company was not a straightforward one: "I had been strongly opposed... feeling that public companies epitomized the grasping, profit-oriented, devil-take-the-hindmost features of capitalism".[8]

But in the spirit of being "alternative", turning all these apparent negatives into positives is exactly what Traidcraft did as it turned to its growing number of supporters for financial investment. The first share issue in 1983 raised £300,000 and was fully subscribed, as were further share issues in 1986 and 1991 which raised a further £1.6 million between them. A fourth share issue some years later in 2003 was a somewhat more complex undertaking, but still raised a further £3.25 million.

This is an extract from the introduction to the prospectus for the second of those share issues which gives a sense of the quite radical nature of the offer given:

> This is an invitation to participate financially in the work of Traidcraft. It should not be regarded as an investment

---

8   Adams, *Who Profits?*, p. 116.

for personal gain or profits... Traidcraft's objective is to increase love, justice and equity in international trade. It seeks to do this principally through the creation and maintenance of better jobs for the poor in developing countries and by working for fairer systems and structures... Through this prospectus the company is inviting you to support further expansion of this work which puts people before profit... Dividends will be low, a maximum of 6% before tax and the directors do not envisage a substantial appreciation in the share price. If, however, you are interested in the well-being of the weak and disadvantaged and feel that changes in your own lifestyle and attitudes are necessary we invite you to read the following details and subscribe to Traidcraft's work.[9]

One of the biggest regrets throughout Traidcraft's history is that there were only dividends when the profitability allowed and this was only on a handful of occasions. On the other hand, even on those occasions, up to 50% of the dividends were waived and sent back to the Traidcraft Exchange as a charitable donation.

It's not quite true to say that Traidcraft was first registered as a private company in 1979. It was originally the name of a newspaper and actually registered in 1977 by a shop in Bristol who would sell products sourced from Tearcraft and others. The shop did not last long and Richard Adams took on that company and the legal entity was ready to roll once the agreement with Tearfund had been established. What was established in 1979 was the Traidcraft Trust which was to be the forerunner of the Traidcraft Exchange. This non-profit-making Trust had a specifically Christian basis, a subscription membership and a council of reference comprising high-profile figures in the Christian world. The Trust was effectively the owner of Traidcraft Ltd, holding the majority of shares, while individual founders of the business and members of staff had a minority shareholding. The stated aims of the Trust were "to provide the means for practical concern about love and justice in international trade".[10]

---

9   Traidcraft Share Issue, 12 July 1986, p. 1.
10   Traidcraft Share Issue, 12 July 1986, p. 2.

This move to a public limited company introduced a whole new world of stakeholder participation, and several hundred new shareholders. One of the complex issues in that transition was the degree of accountability that would be embedded into the organization's governance structures. It was deemed important to set up something that protected against acquisition and against the erosion of Traidcraft's mission, so a "Guardian Share" was created and held by the Trust and it had ultimate responsibility for ensuring that Traidcraft remained true to its foundation principles. The new shareholders owned so-called "B" shares with limited voting rights. Initially, that meant that they merely had the right to elect a "B" shareholder representative to the Board of Directors. "A" shares were those owned by the Trust and a handful of individuals.

While "B" shareholders enthusiastically attended Annual General Meetings and asked many questions of the directors, it was occasionally amusing to watch the formal proceedings of an AGM where only a few participants' hands could be raised among a large gathering, because only those with a right to vote could take part. In later years, greater voting power was extended to all shareholders, although the majority shareholding was still owned by what became the Traidcraft Foundation. Eventually, the number of shareholders would rise to nearly 6,000.

The Traidcraft Board of Directors comprised executive directors (employed by the company) and non-executive directors (appointed by the Trust externally). A third category of director were "staff directors", members of staff from anywhere in the business or charity, who were elected by their peers. Initially, there were two staff directors although in later years this reduced to one.

I served as staff director on two separate occasions and it was always a position which was well intentioned but fraught with conflicting interests. As the staff complement grew and Traidcraft was transitioning from a small organization to a medium-sized organization, the issue of staff representation to management became more relevant. There was no unionization in Traidcraft. There never has been – but it's important to stress that this does not represent any negativity toward the union movement. In fact, the opposite was the case and Richard Adams actively encouraged staff to join a union but there was no real enthusiasm. When Richard tried to get our print staff to be members of a print union, Traidcraft was blacklisted for some reason and had to get catalogues printed in Hong Kong for two years! Traidcraft also adopted a very open management style with a high degree of communication and participation, so problems were few. However, formal representation is important – indeed, a right – and it was to become an important pillar of Fair Trade principles in later years.

The staff directors became that representation mechanism, but the system had two flaws. First, the legal responsibility of directors was such that being in a representative role might prove to be inappropriate. In years to come, this would be highlighted when issues of organizational restructure and potential job loss through redundancy would inevitably occur. Secondly, legal directors had to be practising Christians and even had to sign a declaration of sympathy with Traidcraft's Christian basis of faith. In Traidcraft's early years, virtually every employee was a Christian because recruitment, like mine, was usually through "word of mouth" and inevitably happened through the local church network. But the Christian contingent of staff, through the years, moved from "exclusively" to "majority" and then ultimately, in later years, to "minority". This was because most jobs and roles were ones in which it was not necessary to be a Christian – indeed it would have been discriminatory to only appoint a Christian.

Since the staff director was an elected office it became more and more dissatisfying that only one group of staff could be nominated. Therefore, in the late 1980s, the Traidcraft Staff Association was born and, as one of the staff directors of that time, I found myself helping to lead that process, helping to draft the very first staff association constitution. This representative structure has evolved over the years but remained essentially the same and it was to be an important voice for the staff over the next four decades of Traidcraft's history.

Understanding and developing clarity of mission

At the same time as Traidcraft Exchange was being developed and Traidcraft plc continued its growth, and with independent but mutually compatible mission activities, there was much discussion and debate about the need to define and formalize what it was that we were doing or seeking to do, and what the ultimate goal might look like. This would be more than merely top-level mission statements or any formal purchasing policy document. In keeping with organizational culture at the time, this process involved a high degree of non-compulsory staff participation as well as contribution from the wider group of external stakeholders.

The end result was a formal objectives document, published in July 1986, which would ultimately inform short-term strategic direction and aimed to influence strategic thinking for years to come. On re-reading the document I was reminded of that process, even of some of the sentences that I helped to construct myself, and of the debate involved. Interestingly, while the term "alternative trade" was well used at the time and later "Fair Trade" would be the familiar phrase, Traidcraft chose to focus on the term "just trade". I see this document as an important milestone in Traidcraft's history and reproduce here the opening two paragraphs. The document is reproduced in full in Appendix 1.

TRAIDCRAFT'S OBJECTIVES

Traidcraft, following an extended discussion and consultation period with staff, shareholders, customers and representatives of partner production groups, sets down the following objectives as defining the main purposes of Traidcraft plc as it works in collaboration with the Traidcraft Exchange. These objectives should not be regarded as a mould within which all future developments take place but rather as a framework enabling a steady and purposeful growth. A regular review every two years by the Trustees of the Traidcraft Exchange and Directors of the company in consultation with those groups mentioned above will seek to ensure that Traidcraft tests its experience acquired in practical action for justice in trade against these objectives in a continuing process. These objectives should be read in conjunction with the basis of faith of the Traidcraft Exchange and the current purchasing criteria policy statements for food and craft products.

Traidcraft aims to expand and establish more just trading systems which will express the principles of love and justice

> fundamental to the Christian faith. Practical service and a
> partnership for change will characterise the organisation,
> which puts people before profit.[11]

Setting such objectives was not something to be used to beat oneself
up about when they weren't achieved in the short-term, given that they
were aspirational and occasionally theoretical. However, as I analyse
each one, I can see how they may have been realized in later years:
in the way that Fair Trade and some principles and standards were
established and formalized; in the way Traidcraft later developed its
human resource policies which became "best in class"; and in the way
that Fair Trade and its place in the future commercial landscape became
established.

It is a fact that, not long after this, Traidcraft saw its success
eroded by a couple of lean years. Financial and human resources were
stretched, and leadership would change and evolve over the years,
causing the document to be largely confined to history. However, it
would sow the seeds of impact measurement and the development of
social accounts in later years. After all, if so much effort is spent in
developing objectives, then surely there should be some effort spent in
establishing how we measure up to them.

---

11 Traidcraft internal document, July 1986. See Appendix 1 for full version.

Chapter 4

HANDICRAFTS AND MORE

The first couple of years of trading were dominated by jute products and baskets selling predominantly into the wholesale sector. This was supplemented by a range of gift products such as painted wooden ornaments and toys from Sri Lanka, and textiles and wooden tableware from India and Thailand. A few other products were more utilitarian, like paint brushes, selected deliberately to avoid a business wholly geared toward gifting. Already, the business was evolving into something very seasonal, driven by this high dependence on gift products but also a growing voluntary representative scheme and mail order business which meant that more than 60% of turnover was achieved in the three months before Christmas.

As everyday consumable products, the introduction of WDM tea and Campaign Coffee partly addressed this, but more and more of the product development emphasis would be upon less seasonal products. Traidcraft continued to expand its craft ranges over the next few years by introducing more diverse products directly from producer groups and with a greater geographical breadth throughout the developing world. But it also started to highlight lifestyle issues in the richer countries and how that impacted the lives of those in developing countries.

Recycled paper products were introduced around 1983 and much of the early marketing highlighted the impact of deforestation, especially on those most vulnerable, and a link back to Fair Trade products. Many of the craft producers were in Bangladesh and it was a fact that much of the periodic flooding they endured was caused, in part, by the removal of natural forest in Nepal. So, wouldn't it be good to create awareness, and to encourage UK consumers to both recycle and reuse as well as buy recycled paper products, and to buy them from Traidcraft?

The concept of recycled paper was very much in its infancy in the early 1980s and the introduction of recycled toilet rolls was met with much confusion and humour based on a lack of understanding as to what recycled paper actually was. We found a supplier making toilet rolls using recycled paper and also started to buy in huge pallets of so-called "pre-consumer" wastepaper or offcuts from the paper making industry. That first recycled paper range consisted of writing pads made at the Traidcraft headquarters in Gateshead, envelopes to match, a range of notepads and reuse labels, and three colours of toilet paper. There was even a range of what was then called duplicator/offset reams or what we would call now copier paper. Toward the end of the decade, Traidcraft would aspire to float off this part of the business as a wholly owned subsidiary called "Paper Traid" which ultimately did not happen due to the fact that recycled paper became much more mainstream. Traidcraft's recycled paper business would eventually reduce and be limited only to "household tissues".

A range of food products was introduced a bit earlier than recycled paper, with a related lifestyle theme, a link to issues in developing countries, and awareness-raising. Consequently, the first range was branded "Food for Thought" and consisted of around twenty-five "wholefood" products. The products included dried fruit, nuts, spices, grains, and pulses from a whole range of developing countries and the occasional non-developing country like soya beans from Canada. Along with the products came a variety of leaflets covering issues like nutrition and healthy eating, agricultural reform and land use, world hunger and its causes, and other food-related topics. Richard Adams writes:

> I was particularly keen to get foodstuffs into the range
> because of all the preparatory work that had been done for
> Agrofax in the early 1970s. Agrofax ran alongside – and
> in fact owned Tearcraft – for the first nine months. It had

> its reason for existence as supporting small agricultural
> producers and bringing a justice element into their trading.
> It was always with a view to getting back into agricultural
> and food products in a big and ethically structured way.[12]

None of these food products had known origins. They were merely bought in bulk from a large wholefood cash and carry business based in London called Community Foods and repacked by hand at Traidcraft. Community Foods, at that time, had a set of values with a strong Christian influence and was a natural partner for Traidcraft. Visiting their headquarters needed to be timed precisely, either to avoid or to join in with their daily sessions of worship and prayer when the entire business would close for a period.

There was a very clear Traidcraft purchasing policy for the directly sourced craft products but not for these wholefood products, so an equivalent policy needed to be devised to cover both foods and beverages which was as follows:

> Traidcraft seeks to provide small farmers and agricultural
> workers in the "third world" with an alternative outlet for
> cash crops produced in addition to their food (for own
> consumption).
> We buy from:
> 1. community-based groups of farmers and cooperatives
> 2. countries seeking justice for their rural poor through active
>   development policies
> 3. community-based groups which process and pack locally
>   grown food products.[13]

This policy was supplemented by an intention to forge more direct links with producers (point 1) and move away from merely a country focus (point 2). The key outcome was to enter and develop the food market and this good intent, while laudable, would cause problems for the next decade as food sales became dominant, individual products would become top sellers, and the resource needed to develop direct origins

---

12 From personal correspondence with author, 2019.
13 From Traidcraft internal document, early 1980s.

would be scarce. Countries like Tanzania, China, Nicaragua, Cuba, Afghanistan, and numerous others were deemed to be "acceptable" to source from but there were some oddments like apricots from Turkey which became the number one product for Traidcraft. As the policy was implemented throughout the decade, it signalled a move away from merely selling wholefoods. Other interesting value-added processed products became available such as sweets and chocolates from Zimbabwe, and chutneys and poppadums from India. Cuban peppermints became a best seller. When the product was dropped (as we implemented the direct sourcing policy later in the 1990s), it became a contentious topic at AGMs for years to come. ("What happened to Cuban peppermints and can they be reintroduced?") Sugar from Mauritius was introduced and honey from Zambia, Tanzania, and China, as well as various UK processed products like nut butters. Dominance of food products was good for me personally as I was to focus on food sourcing and product development and faced the interesting task of moving away from a country sourcing policy and into direct sourcing. This would keep me busy for much of the 1990s and keep me at Traidcraft because it was almost like taking on a new role.

That early tea and coffee would also evolve into different tea products and different coffee products. Not too much roast and ground coffee was consumed in those days in the UK, but we introduced a range in partnership with a Fair Trade Organization based in Holland, comprising a Nicaraguan blend and a Tanzanian blend. Teabags branded WDM and new variations of instant coffee followed. Encafé was an instant coffee powder made in Nicaragua, and a granulated instant coffee in a jar which was packed in Bolivia was also trialled but wasn't too popular.

In line with its mission to educate and create awareness, resources and educational materials have always been part of the Traidcraft range. Catalogues were always information-heavy in that first decade and, in the 1982/83 catalogue, it was not until page 19 that one could find any products for sale, much to the dislike of anyone who embraced a sales culture. Suffice to say that this practice diminished after the first loss-making season of the 1980s. However, there would always be a reasonable space given over to producer information (which, arguably, was one of the reasons to purchase products) and there would be ranges of books, calendars, Christmas cards, and even games for sale.

In the late 1980s, Traidcraft launched a clothing range. There had always been a textile offering embedded within the craft ranges, but this was an attempt to enter the world of fashion, and what a complicated process it turned out to be. We employed a dedicated clothing manager, Abi Garner, to put the range together. This was Traidcraft's first real attempt at designing and commissioning ranges of products from producer groups. It not only covered the manufacture of the finished article but the design and manufacture of materials, all hand loomed in India. It also involved some very complicated arrangements for shipping of the material into Bangladesh where the garments would be made. Much is written in detail about this project in Richard Adams' book. For my part, I got involved in the logistics and quality side of things and, on occasion, would link up with Abi, given that she spent most of her time abroad.

These early developments in textiles and clothing would pave the way for a more progressive way of developing, designing, and commissioning product ranges for Traidcraft. It would also prove to be a stepping-stone toward delving down into the murky world of cotton growing, the later work of Traidcraft Exchange in developing projects with cotton farmers, and the ultimate development of Fairtrade standards for cotton as an agricultural crop. Abi would use her experience at Traidcraft and continue to work in textiles and cotton, both Fairtrade and Organic, and co-found the fashion brands Vericott and Gossypium. Now Abi Petit, she writes:

> The existence of Traidcraft, this friendly, optimistic and passionate business far away somewhere on a Tyne and Wear trading estate, was a life changer for me personally. My time there was spent making contacts (thirty very different producing groups), and researching the economics of the clothing trade. It contributed to me being able to go on and add more pioneering chapters to Fair Trade clothing after leaving Traidcraft itself.
>
> In 1985, my logical career route was to go and be a buyer for the power-dressing Marks & Spencer, where

sharp suits for new career women were all the rage.
Instead, led by a route that followed E. F. Schumacher's
Small is Beautiful, I found myself amidst thirty different
clothing suppliers around India and Bangladesh.[14] With a
freedom no longer possible in the more regulated world
of overseas employment, I spent magical weeks at a time
with product groups in India, Bangladesh, and Nepal.

Traidcraft's rich address book had been created by a
range of sources. Some of the producing groups, like St
Mary's, were the work of missionaries. There were others
– such as Swallows in the north of Bangladesh, where
a women's group weaving cloth by hand and providing
stripy shirts of the kind the hippies wore – had been
started by a Swedish development organization after the
Bangladesh War of Independence in the 1970s.

Other producer groups came from fascinating
sources within India and Bangladesh. For example, the
Women's India Trust in Bombay was a block printing
outfit for inner-city slum girls and had been started
by an Indian woman, Kamila Tyabji, and her British
partner, Shelley. This avant-garde couple welcomed me
as a guest and I was served "bed tea" on a silver trolley
as if the Raj were still present!

The family Shroff, also based in Bombay, couldn't
have been more different in terms of their links to the
UK. Here, the family, who were very close to Gandhi,
were part of the Swadeshi movement established
to promote independence from the British Empire.
In spite of this, a link to a UK organization (The
Schumacher Centre for Technology and Development)
meant that they had entered the Traidcraft address
book and I found myself integrating both their Bombay
slum-based cross-stitch project in the first clothing
catalogue, as well as a dress featuring hand embroidery
from their project in the desert Kutch region.

I am happy to say that, thanks to People Tree, who
started their business based on the list of suppliers

---

14   E. F. Schumacher, *Small is Beautiful,* London: Harper Collins, 1973.

mentioned in the back of Traidcraft's first clothing catalogue in 1987, many of these groups have gone on to become successful long-term suppliers of Fair Trade clothing, and have grown with their buyers.

With Traidcraft facilitating such a blue-sky approach to working during that period, we innovated at every point possible. For example, we pre-dated the selfie revolution by showing photos of the producers actually weaving, printing, and sewing the products in the corner of the modelling shots. To see clothing actually being produced next to what was being sold was totally unknown – and, in fact, is still not often seen today. Furthermore, we invited customers to send in photos of themselves wearing the clothes, and my studio was adorned with smiling faces. Traidcraft customers were more than just customers, they were an active part of the business!

As with all grass root movements that are of their time, there were Fair Trade Organizations in other European countries, and once I'd moved to Belgium to work with a fibre multinational, I kept in touch with some of the producing groups via voluntary work at OXFAM Belgium. I designed some tea towels for the hand loom weavers of Tamil Nadu through Cooptex that were then sold across Europe and into Traidcraft. However, there was a steady decline in hand weaving from 3 million weavers to fewer than 300,000 today. Most of them weave for IKEA and the alternative we provided was most definitely significant. To illustrate the power of our involvement, I was recently invited to the wedding of two young Indian people whom I had known since they were children – one was the daughter of the dedicated hand weaving government official, her husband the son of a Tamil Nadu garment factory – two families who would almost not have met if not for my work building Fair Trade networks spanning different worlds. This marriage would not appear in any impact assessment report, but I am sure of our reach in changing aspirations among producing groups, and Traidcraft's humble mission, spread by word of mouth and deed. Meanwhile, changes in India and the opportunity of jobs in the high-tech sector around Bangalore has meant that families no longer want to be weavers to the same extent, alas! Hand weaving remains the most environmentally friendly and socially decentralized way to make cloth by a long way!

This period in Traidcraft's history was so creative and, although relatively short-lived, its standing as an organization embedded in alternative culture was profound and far-reaching. When I left, I went on to research the supply chain of a cotton T shirt for Greenpeace. It became the definitive study, shedding light on the fact that 33% of its value was at the cotton stage. I later developed this work with OXFAM Belgium, and subsequently Marks a& Spencer, to create the first known origin cotton supply chain. It was the test case for a Fairtrade cotton standard which was to have far-reaching impact.

As for a UK-designed clothing range, this stayed part of Traidcraft's offer right up until the end and the baton was passed to a series of designers who all had the privilege of creating markets for hand skills in textiles.[15]

A series of product groups were established (for the purposes of sales reporting and range management) and by the end of the 1980s, these were defined as handicrafts, clothing, cards and calendars, recycled paper products, teas, coffees, and food. Handicrafts and clothing sales – which had once dominated as a proportion of total sales – were down to just over 30% of sales, and now Traidcraft was evolving into a business where food and beverages would become dominant products.

As well as increasing products there were other business developments during the 1980s. Some would say that we were starting to overreach and lose focus when we developed a handful of retail

---

15 From personal correspondence with the author, 2019.

shops throughout the country and offered our warehouse facilities and fulfilment to others. For several years, we would manage all of the support materials, catalogues, and distribution for organizations like Greenpeace and Christian Aid. This certainly filled capacity and increased turnover, but it meant that things became fairly complicated.

The end of an era

The time came for Richard Adams to move on in 1988. He went on to be heavily involved in the founding of Out of this World, a chain of organic and ethical grocery stores, *New Consumer* magazine, Shared Interest (the Fair Trade financial cooperative providing financial services to producers, retailers, importers, and exporters throughout the world) and Fairtrade Foundation which became the UK member of Fairtrade International, licensing the Fairtrade Mark to thousands of retail products.

Richard was by nature entrepreneurial. He was never going to be the leader of a Traidcraft which was fast reaching a period where it needed to consolidate, become a medium-sized organization with structure and financial control, while still innovating and developing into new and exciting areas. The losses of 1987 compounded this and, in many ways, was a shock to the system and to the organization. Belts needed to be tightened, costs controlled, and such shackles applied to Richard were always likely to end in tears. I recall attending some very animated and challenging board meetings as a staff director and it was no surprise to some that he moved on. But it was the end of one era and the beginning of a new one and who would be appointed to lead us into it?

PART TWO

Into the 1990s

Chapter 5

A HARD ACT TO FOLLOW

Maybe succeeding Richard Adams was always going to be a hard ask. What had started very small had developed into a complex, medium-sized organization. The Traidcraft Exchange was a separate legal entity with its own governance structure and leadership, and Traidcraft plc was operating in a multitude of complicated product sectors and across multiple and diverse sales channels. In addition, Traidcraft adopted a low salary differential (the highest salary could be no higher than 2.75 times the lowest salary at that point) and a requirement that all directors needed to be practising Christians. This all meant that recruitment would involve fishing from a very small pool, something that has been a constant in the history of Traidcraft.

After a thorough recruitment process, Paul Johns joined as Traidcraft plc's new managing director with a background in management consultancy and extensive involvement in the work of CND (Campaign for Nuclear Disarmament), including holding the office of Chair both of Christian and National CND for several years. There was a need to stabilize the ship after all accumulated reserves had been eroded in one bad year of trading and, to some extent, this was achieved until another difficult year arrived in 1991. Sadly, despite increased sales of nearly 50% in three years, levels of profitability did not match that growth. It meant that this lean year and its resultant loss was something potentially terminal to the business and caused the Board of Directors to instigate a thorough review of Traidcraft plc structures and cost-base led by external consultants. It was not a happy time and what followed meant that a significant proportion of staff, around 15%, was made redundant.

The business restructured into more identifiable business units, each with more focused staff, activities, and targets, and with dedicated management for each. Greater effort was directed toward marketing. For this reason, the consultants recommended leadership with greater experience and skills in this area and so Paul Johns moved on as part of the staff rationalization process.

It should be noted that 1991/92 was a difficult time in general for the UK retail sector, with the economy under recession. The rate of inflation had risen, and interest rates spiked beyond 10%, meaning that the average consumer with a mortgage had much less to spend. Traidcraft and Fair Trade in general has never been immune to such things and the fact that it was able to ride out this recession and continue to increase turnover is noteworthy.

One of the legacies of Paul Johns was the continued affirmation of Traidcraft's Christian heritage and mission which was represented in a new corporate identity, introduced to coincide with its tenth anniversary. This saw the introduction of a new green and yellow corporate logo and a move away from the previous brown logo. The typeface changed into something regarded as more modern and the letter "T" which had always tried to symbolize the cross of Christ changed into something closer to that symbol. In the literature of the time it was written that the new logo was meant to "convey Traidcraft as alive, human and creative, with symbolism that is not only Christian, but which portrays the company stretching across the world". For the next decade and beyond, others described the same logo as resembling not Christ on the cross but a scarecrow!

During Paul Johns' tenure, Traidcraft was actively involved in the initiative which would see the creation of the Fairtrade Foundation and a Fairtrade Mark. He writes:

> I was Managing Director for not much more than two
> years. Looking back, I see the most fruitful thing I did
> was to become the representative of Traidcraft plc in

a small working party which later birthed the Fairtrade Foundation. We were just a small group – representatives of Oxfam, Christian Aid, CAFOD, one or two others, and me as convenor of the group. We saw the need to take Fair Trade into mainstream food retailing, which meant the supermarkets. I remember getting deeply involved in some tricky issues. How do you set standards, and how do you audit the supply chain when it comes to coffee, chocolate, or bananas? Will supermarket customers value Fair Trade enough to create a sustainable demand? This is familiar territory now, but it was all new then. And I'm glad Traidcraft gave me the opportunity to be part of the early exploration.[16]

Despite the Board indicating that a new leader should have marketing experience and skills, the managing director that was ultimately appointed to succeed Paul Johns came from a finance background. The same constraints as before applied with continued low salary differentials and the need for a practising Christian to be appointed. Philip Angier had joined Traidcraft as Finance Director some years earlier and he was asked by the Board to take on the role of acting Managing Director. The experience of this ultimately caused him to apply successfully to take on the role on a permanent basis and his tenure would ultimately last for more than a decade.

Meanwhile this new focus across business areas was to prove pivotal in my own future journey in Traidcraft in that it resulted in my role being mostly involved with food product and supply chain development. The Traidcraft food product range, as it entered the 1990s, included some top sellers which were a legacy of the wholefood developments of the 1980s. The food purchasing policy which allowed sourcing from "countries seeking justice for their rural poor through active development policies" was becoming outdated as Fair Trade was becoming more established and labelling or certification schemes were being introduced and mainstreamed.[17] Traidcraft was in danger of being left behind and even embarrassed by some of its products. It was not simply a case of dropping products, since that would have been

16 From personal correspondence with the author, 2019.
17 From Traidcraft internal document.

a commercial disaster. Although some minor products were dropped as a consequence, it seemed more sensible to put some resource and effort into developing a new food purchasing policy and creating new supply chains and Fair Trade products that met the requirements of that policy.

This new food purchasing policy, adopted in 1992, defined a fairly traded food product as one containing ingredients from producer organizations meeting the following criteria:

- There is a long-term trading relationship of partnership and cooperation
- A fair price is paid
- The producer receives a clear and definable benefit from the purchase of their produce. Typical benefits include:
  - a fair return for labour
  - community development
  - improved working conditions
  - participation in decision-making
  - an increased ability to make choices
  - access to advance payments[18]

Problem product categories at that time were sugar, dried fruit, nuts, rice, and honey and the next few years signalled a fruitful and innovative period for product development resulting from close working with the growing Traidcraft Exchange.

---

18   From Traidcraft internal document, 1992.

Chapter 6

A NEW WAY OF
WORKING OVERSEAS

Since its birth in 1986, the Traidcraft Exchange had grown substantially and had established development education activities in the UK as well as business and marketing support to overseas producers. The so-called "Education Unit" continued to provide support and materials to the voluntary reps who, by 1990, numbered more than 1,800. The "Development Unit" engaged in project work and the provision of business and marketing assistance to overseas producers which was now extending beyond merely those who were selling to Traidcraft plc. Indeed, it would begin work which would not even be linked to export activities and would focus on domestic trade, something that would become a feature in Traidcraft Exchange development projects in the coming years. Advice and consultancy in design, manufacture, processing, packaging, marketing, exporting, and business planning were important – as well as occasional grants for specific materials or pieces of equipment.

What emerged from the Development Unit in the early 1990s was a new unit called the Overseas Business Development Service (OBDS), later to be known for a short while as "Traidcraft Exchange Worldwide". A major grant had been won to extend this work from what is now called DFID (the UK government's Department for International Development) but was then called the ODA (the

Overseas Development Administration). It was important legally for charitable and grant-funded work to be separated from commercial activities and therefore the strategy and agenda for the OBDS was not linked to any strategic business and purchasing activity. However, Traidcraft plc would be an active client to the OBDS. We shared the same office space so it was inevitable that personal and professional links would be close.

Part of the grant from the ODA was earmarked to set up partner organizations in various developing countries geographically linked to the ODA's own development agenda at that time. Inevitably, as I looked to explore new supply chains and producer groups as part of Traidcraft plc's growing food business, linking up with some of those Traidcraft Exchange partners became a sensible option. The model of those overseas partners partly mirrored the model of Traidcraft – a business component actively trading fairly and a support component facilitating trade or offering consultancy services. All staff were recruited and managed locally rather than by UK-based staff and the longer-term objective was complete independence from Traidcraft UK. There were four initial partners: Just Exchange based in South Africa, International Resources for Fair Trade based in India, AMKA based in Tanzania, and Philippines Fair Trade Programme (later to become known as the Association of Partners for Fairer Trade Inc or APFTI). Later in the 1990s, similar partners would also be established in Malawi, Zambia and Bangladesh.

South Africa

In the early 1990s, South Africa had just emerged from its apartheid era and many development agencies were targeting that country to provide assistance. The trade embargo was lifted and a new era of export development was starting. South Africa became a hotspot for potential Fair Trade activities.

Just Exchange, the partner organization established by Traidcraft Exchange, was based in Cape Town and a scoping study and an initial visit by a consultant showed that there might be some interesting products and supply chains that could be established as Fair Trade. This ultimately meant that the producer infrastructure of South Africa fitted the requirements of our new food purchasing policy. Apart from that, products were of good quality, especially in dried fruit. In collaboration with Just Exchange, I set off for South Africa to follow up the scoping study, on a mission to develop a Fair Trade raisin and a Fair Trade apricot, and who knows what else besides?

Much of the fruit growing industry was cooperatively-based and state-controlled, so a relationship was developed with the South African Dried Fruit Co-operative (SAD), who effectively had a monopoly in the buying and processing of fruit products. There was also an equivalent organization for fresh fruit. The relationship with SAD was positive. They could see what we wanted to do and were incredibly helpful, especially in our desire to find a producer organization that we could engage with directly. All fruit growers were members of SAD, whether a large plantation or a small farmer, and we managed to locate a group of small farmer members growing and drying grapes based in the Northern Cape near a town called Keimoes. The region was ideal for vine fruit growing. It was mostly hot and dry and with an abundant source of water for irrigation provided by the Orange River, flowing westward before emptying into the Atlantic Ocean. When flying to that region, it was always easy to spot how close we were to landing. A thin ribbon of green would emerge in the distance, tracking the flow of the river in an otherwise barren and dry landscape.

The Eksteenskuil Farmers Association (EFA) was newly formed, aiming "to contribute to the social and economic upliftment of the historically disadvantaged small-scale irrigation farmers of the Lower Orange River Valley in the Keimoes area in the Northern Cape".[19] It was located on a series of islands as the river formed a kind of "inland delta" and the land was generally regarded as uneconomic. As well as that, the land had been allocated to a group of mixed-race families several decades earlier. In a country where the colour of a person's skin had historically defined them, the term "disadvantaged" was highly appropriate.

This started a long relationship with EFA. Various support activities were undertaken, including training programmes and provision of agricultural equipment. EFA would eventually transition into a cooperative called the Eksteenskuil Agricultural Co-operative (EAC) and become Fairtrade certified in their own right, becoming one of

---

19   http://www.eksteenskuil.co.za/company-history/

Traidcraft's biggest suppliers providing raisins and sultanas for a whole host of retail products, including Geobar.

We were less successful with apricots, although we had initially started to work with a group who bought in fresh apricots and dried them. It fulfilled that part of our purchasing policy which allowed us to buy from "community-based groups which process and pack locally grown food products", but toward the end of the 1990s, Fair Trade was giving more focus to so-called primary producers – those who cultivated the crop, rather than the secondary producers or processors that we were dealing with. So, for apricots, despite some small-scale trading activities of a slightly 'tart' variety of the fruit, South Africa would not provide a long term solution and we needed to turn our attention elsewhere.

Working with Just Exchange was a pleasure and, literally, bore so much fruit. In addition, it sowed some seeds of future developments as we explored things like wine and rooibos tea. Ultimately, the role of Just Exchange was as a catalyst organization and they became less involved in our work as we developed our own contacts and became familiar with working in and travelling around South Africa.

Tanzania

AMKA (named after the Swahili word for "awaken') was established by Traidcraft Exchange in Tanzania and based in Dar Es Salaam. Once again this proved a fruitful relationship for the development of Traidcraft products, particularly tea but also, significantly, honey. Honey had been introduced by Traidcraft toward the end of the 1980s and Tanzania was regarded as one of those acceptable countries under the original food purchasing policy. A direct source of honey from Tanzania was therefore desirable and AMKA started to work with the Tabora Beekeepers Cooperative Society in the centre of the country. However, the journey toward a good-quality, exportable honey was a difficult one – and one with many highs and lows.

The beekeepers would construct log hives and locate them in the forest area miles away from Tabora, the local town. Then they would collect and transport to a central processing unit in Tabora where the honey would be filtered and decanted into large steel drums for onward transportation to Dar Es Salaam for export. Much of the support work undertaken by AMKA involved managing the speed of movement from hive to port, the quality of the processing procedures, and the quality of the containers that the honey was moved around in. One indicator of quality in honey is something known as the HMF level (HMF meaning hydroxymethylfurfural). Let's not dwell too much on chemistry but the formation of this organic compound in honey is a result of age and overheating, and is not a desirable quality. It is subject to strict controls with an upper legal limit for all honey sold in retail packs, known in the trade as "table honey". It became the bane of our lives at Traidcraft for a while. A hot country, long and inconsistent transport times, and unregulated filtering (which involved a heating process) meant that it was a huge risk to buy this product, but with the AMKA inputs, much of this risk was controlled and managed and it became possible for Traidcraft to import several containers. We also became involved in facilitating trade in partnership with AMKA and found a willing buyer in the Netherlands, who liked the honey and was less concerned about the HMF levels because it would be used as an industrial honey so not subject to the same regulations as table honey.

There were a couple of problems to overcome before this could happen. First, Tanzania was not recognized by the European Union as an acceptable country or origin for honey, but we managed to jump through all the hoops, both in the UK and in Tanzania, to enable this. It took time and was a bit bureaucratic, but we got there in the end. Secondly, a more lucrative market than Fair Trade was the organic sector. It's not straightforward for honey to be recognized as organic because bees will go where they choose to collect nectar, whether or not sprayed with chemicals! Strict geographic standards need to be applied which was not really a problem for the remote and naturally organic forest area of Tanzania. Still more hoops to jump through, lots of maps drawn, and a very helpful relationship with the Soil Association – the leading UK organic certifier – resulted in a green light to import. The collective result was nearly 200 tonnes of honey imported by Traidcraft for onward sale into the Netherlands. Certainly, this was very lucrative for the Tabora beekeepers.

After this highlight came the lowlight. Problems in the cooperative caused it to collapse and the export trade diminished. But happily, several years later, Traidcraft Exchange would resurrect the relationship and attempt to develop a new project with the remnant of Tabora beekeepers, this time giving focus to the domestic market.

India

International Resources for Fair Trade (IRFT) was the Traidcraft Exchange partner established in India and based in Mumbai. It was an odd set-up due to its linkage with a large agrochemical manufacturer, Excel Industries, sharing premises and including trustees from Excel. There had already been a historical relationship with the family who owned Excel Industries, the Shroffs, through their efforts to develop various handicraft initiatives. As Abi Petit described in chapter 4, products from those producer groups – the Shroff Self Help Centre based in Mumbai and Shrujan based in the remote Kutch region of the state of Gujarat – were already well represented in Traidcraft clothing catalogues and many of us in Traidcraft had developed close relationships with several of the Shroff family members who managed them.

One of the subsidiaries of Excel Industries was Agrocel Industries, also based in Kutch. This was an organization set up essentially to sell the agrochemical products of Excel directly to the small farmers based in Gujarat through a series of small-scale service centres located throughout the state. At that time, Agrocel was developing a "one stop shop" model which also purchased the agricultural produce of those same farmers and would market them locally and, in time, nationally. I was aware through the relationship with Shrujan that locally grown organic cotton was used to make their products, that those farmers would grow more than just cotton and that one of those crops was groundnuts, more popularly known as peanuts.

Peanuts were one of our problem products in terms of clarity of origin and that outdated food purchasing policy of the 1980s. In collaboration with IRFT, a visit to Kutch was arranged to check out the Agrocel model. While not perfect in terms of the organizational structure of the farmers, which would improve over time and eventually become certified as Fairtrade in later years for organic cotton, it was agreed to develop a project which would see Agrocel becoming an export organization for peanuts. Traidcraft bought its first container in the mid-1990s.

I was not only responsible for the sourcing of food products at that time but also looked after the warehouse, storage, and quality functions. Managing peanuts was a steep learning curve and our Team Valley warehouse needed to adapt in order to store products which the local bird and rodent population took a keen interest in. While there were some losses incurred due to this, the more taxing issue on peanuts was one of quality management. Aflatoxins are poisonous carcinogens which are produced by mould that grows in soil and can potentially affect many crops if the growing, harvesting, storage, and processing conditions are not managed carefully. In the mid-1990s, there were legal maximums for the levels of aflatoxins in peanuts which were relatively easy to meet, and despite the high sampling and microbiological analysis costs, we introduced these peanuts to the food range and used them as an ingredient to develop other retail products – Bombay mix being a notable example.

Sadly, our ventures in being a peanut importer from India were thwarted by the lowering of the aflatoxin limits to levels which were just not manageable. This affected not only Traidcraft but the entire Gujarati peanut industry that exported into Europe, since the conditions there were just not conducive to reach those legal levels. However, this experience with Agrocel in Kutch was to signal a long and, on the whole, positive relationship which would last for many years.

Over the next few years Agrocel were to develop their service centre model beyond Gujarat and looked to Traidcraft as a willing and interested export customer for potentially a whole range of new products. We still had that apricot issue to resolve and there were one or two other products which could ideally be sourced from India. So, together with key IRFT and Agrocel staff, I embarked on what would turn out to be an extensive grand tour of several important agricultural areas of India. This included Himachal Pradesh in the far north looking at tree nuts like walnuts and apricots, Haryana looking at basmati rice, and Maharashtra exploring cashew nuts. Looking back, I regard this particular overseas trip as the most memorable of my career at Traidcraft, not the least because of the ridiculously long car journeys and impossible schedule that I would not even have dared to endure in later years, nor been able to as the health and safety of overseas travellers became more important!

I have a vivid recollection of driving through the rice growing region of Haryana with Hasmukh Patel, the general manager of Agrocel, with flat green fields on either side, twilight approaching and ready for a rest after yet another long drive. We decided to stop and have a wander through the rice paddy and talk to a few farmers who were tending to the crop. You never know how these "first contact" encounters will develop and usually they are merely a good source of information about the locality and what it is like to be a farmer there. On this occasion, there developed an in-depth conversation about the problems and difficulties of being a small farmer in a region where mostly larger farms operated. Not only would this brief encounter start the process of Agrocel setting up one of its service centres in the region, registering a group of farmers, and starting to buy and sell their crops, but in later years they would become certified as Fairtrade and evolve into the first independent Fairtrade small producer organization of basmati rice in that region. Apart from that, it ticked off another problem product for Traidcraft and we began importing basmati rice on a regular basis and for many years to come.

Traidcraft managed to source cashews and later raisins through Agrocel – although their primary product was still cotton from Kutch. This would become an important source of Fairtrade certified cotton in later years, used in many mainstream brands. But right now, there was still the problem of apricots to deal with.

Chapter 7

NEW PARTNERSHIPS
IN THE UK

Nick Kightley, my colleague in Traidcraft Exchange, was programme manager for South East Asia and had been instrumental in the setting up of APFTI in the Philippines. Having obtained funding from DFID to scope out the possibility of setting up additional Traidcraft Exchange partners, he recalls a venture into Pakistan to locate potential suppliers and Fair Trade products. This involved not only traditional craft products and textiles but also food products like basmati rice. The research extended into the Northern Territories around the towns of Chitral, Gilgit, and Hunza, close to the foot of the world's second highest mountain, K2. Products here included walnuts, almonds and, importantly, apricots.

The complexities and challenges of working in Pakistan would ultimately mean that Traidcraft Exchange would not progress any further work there but it did result in an introduction to an organization called Tropical Wholefoods who were more than able to face those complexities and challenges head on. Adam Brett and his partner Kate Sebag had set up Tropical Wholefoods some years earlier and were working with producers of dried banana and pineapple in Uganda, providing them with solar powered drying equipment and training to add value to their crop, then selling these products in the UK. Adam recalls being funded by Traidcraft to conduct a more detailed study on the feasibility of setting up a viable supply chain of apricots from these remote regions of Pakistan and his link up with the Aga Khan Rural Support Programme (AKRSP) in Gilgit. AKRSP funded the start-up of a new organization, to be called Mountain Fruits, and a programme of technical assistance which would see Adam and one of his colleagues, Richard Friend, spend much of their time in Pakistan over several years helping to set up the farmer's organizational structure and the drying facilities which would ultimately provide a new source of apricots for Traidcraft.

This partnership with Tropical Wholefoods would be one of the most significant for Traidcraft for years to come. AKRSP's funding of Mountain Fruits was contingent upon Tropical Wholefoods buying a full container of apricots which was something like 20 tonnes, worth a lot of money. Traidcraft made the important decision to underwrite the purchase of this first container.

Just before this, I had made contact with a Sunderland-based bakery called Fullwell Mill Bakery, whose owners were supportive of Traidcraft's mission and values. As well as bread, they made flapjacks and bars and we had found a way to use the South African raisins and apricots and the Indian peanuts in a new product which they made for Traidcraft. They were nearly called "Sunshine Bars" but in the end, they went by the more functional names of "Apricot Snack Bar" and "Peanut Snack Bar". The Fair Trade world in those days was characterized by a high degree of networking and collaboration and some years later Tropical Wholefoods and Fullwell Mill Bakery would merge to become Fullwell Mill Ltd with Tropical Wholefoods becoming their product brand. Traidcraft had much influence on the wider world of Fair Trade but, in this instance, maybe it was in being a matchmaker for a "marriage" that would result in the development of a significant and influential Fair Trade Organization in the UK.

Richard Friend writes about that early and continued development of Mountain Fruits and the fact that here was an organization similarly committed to pioneering in Fair Trade and prepared, literally, to go that extra mile to do so:

> Visiting Mountain Fruits in 2001 was my first experience of a developing country. I remember being concerned about how transferable my knowledge would be and if I would

be able to make an impact. It turned out that I was able to make an impact in more ways than I had anticipated. The conditions on the farms were basic, as was the processing site, and the quality of the apricots was poor. By the time I started visiting alone in 2002, I was quite a bit more experienced and confident about planning a new factory. I started to help Mountain Fruits to introduce the business improvement, food safety, and quality methods that we had adopted in our own manufacturing business back at Fullwell Mill.

The new factory was built, and I visited Mountain Fruits nearly every year for around ten years. The Fullwell Mill team in the UK put a lot of time and energy into tracking problems and lobbying for Fairtrade standards. Particularly in those early days, the indulgence of Traidcraft for goods which were not perfect quality, given that they were to be used as an ingredient in the Geobar, was vital. Between us, we helped Mountain Fruits to build a thriving and sustainable processing business which is still flourishing. During this period, in addition to organic certification, Mountain Fruits produced the first Fairtrade certified walnuts, almonds, apricot kernels, dried apricots, dried cherries, and dried apples and we were able to get these ingredients into a wide range of products. Particularly gratifying was Fairtrade's lobbying of Unilever, encouraging them to talk to us about using almonds and walnuts in Ben & Jerry's ice cream. Walnuts were too difficult – but we managed it with almonds, after a complicated two-year process. Sales of almonds went from 5 tonnes to more than 50 tonnes, and at its peak around 7,000 families were benefiting from higher prices and Fairtrade premium.

The work in Pakistan was not without problems. Natural disasters included a major earthquake which damaged many villages and closed the main road to Islamabad for two months in the harvest season. On top of that, a landslide which dammed the fast-flowing glacial Hunza river   created a lake 25 km long between Mountain Fruits and many of its suppliers – it had to be negotiated by boat. Being so close to Afghanistan meant that Mountain Fruits would be impacted by conflict and the effects of conflict. 50,000 refugees arriving in the region caused immense pressure on the local infrastructure as they became dependent on the locals for more than six months and, on more than one occasion, conflict and violence affected the workers of Mountain Fruits. Sadly, that included the murder of a Mountain Fruits outreach worker travelling to some of the remote communities.

The work of Fullwell Mill in Pakistan paved the way for extending our activities into Afghanistan, working on almonds and raisins, of which more could be written. All in all, having applied unsuccessfully for a job at Traidcraft Exchange a few years before all of this and then finding a way to do something more interesting and rewarding in my own business meant dream work for me. I could never quite believe it was my job.[20]

I suspect that one day the good folk from Fullwell Mill will write their own story and I look forward to reading about their own pioneering work in Fair Trade.

Cafédirect

It's unclear (to me at least) who dreamed up the idea and name "Cafédirect" but the general sense, from a commercial perspective, was that Traidcraft was not geared up for selling products into supermarkets and did not have the right products or brand to do so anyway. Perhaps we naively thought that it was some sort of impossible dream to enter the supermarkets, but I certainly recall my colleague responsible for food marketing – Michael Delamere – waxing lyrical about the subject, openly talking about doing it in coffee, and calling it "Cafédirect". Whether or not he came up with the brand name isn't

---

20   From personal correspondence with the author, 2019.

that important but it's very clear that Traidcraft played a leading role in bringing together a collaborative project which would see the leading UK Fair Trade players working together, investing equally, and creating a new marketing organization and brand. Cafédirect launched its first roast and ground coffee in 1991 and would be the first product to enter a UK supermarket owned by such organizations.

I've always been an advocate of collaborative activities between like-minded organizations and the Fair Trade "movement" would not have grown and developed without that. But there were some real dilemmas involved. How would it affect sales of our own products for example? Traidcraft had been involved with coffee since its early years and had entered the roast and ground sector in the mid-1980s with some half decent products. In fact, we had been approached by Safeway, who were one of the top five supermarkets of the day in the UK, to submit a commercial proposition for a listing, which we turned down!

After due consideration and the fact that this would be the route of entry for each of us into supermarkets, the consortium of Equal Exchange, Oxfam Trading, Twin Trading, and Traidcraft made it happen. The product needed support so Traidcraft and Oxfam would push the product alongside its own ranges in their respective markets. Equal Exchange would focus on the wholesale sector, and Twin Trading would manage the product development, coffee procurement, and producer relations.

It was a big deal at the time for a product that named "Traidcraft" on the front of the pack to go mainstream, and both Safeway and the Co-op were the first supermarkets to list the product. Ultimately, it would not impact the sales of Traidcraft roast and ground products. However, when Cafédirect instant coffee was created some years later, it certainly knocked a few nails in the coffin of Traidcraft's two instant coffees – Campaign and Encafé.

It must be remembered that Cafédirect was launched before Fairtrade labelling was established but it would go on to be the first coffee product to carry the Fairtrade Mark. It would also set up Traidcraft to be an important partner to Cafédirect when it developed Teadirect toward the end of the 1990s.

Chapter 8

NOT JUST FAIR TRADE

The period from the late 1980s into the 1990s was probably the most innovative time in Traidcraft's history in the way that it shaped, led, and influenced not just the Fair Trade, but also the wider business and commercial landscape.

Developing social accounts

In the early 1990s, and led by External Affairs Director Richard Evans, Traidcraft pioneered the concept of social auditing. The organization was trying to be "alternative" in virtually every aspect of its activities and had objectives going way beyond financial performance. Financial statements and annual accounts contained a very clear picture of how it was performing against its financial objectives but up until then there had been no systematic method of how it was performing against non-financial objectives. Shareholders had not invested into the mission of Traidcraft for financial gain and being accountable to such stakeholders for the broad spectrum of their investment interest was important to consider. Yes, there was a lot of published material – anecdotal information collected by travellers or supplied by the producers – but nothing that related this to organizational objectives.

Starting in 1993, the trustees of Traidcraft decided that it would publish a separate report to the annual financial report which would evaluate activities against non-financial criteria. It further decided that the report, once published, would be subject to external scrutiny. It would therefore be called a "social audit" and external assessors would be appointed at the annual general meeting much in the same way as financial auditors were appointed. And in the same way that the financial statements were subjected to independent auditing, so also would be the social statements. As was written in one of the early preparatory documents:

> Just as financial auditors look after shareholders' financial interests by ensuring that the managements accounts give a true and fair view of the company's financial affairs so the social auditor looks after stakeholder interest by ensuring that the company's account of its social impact and ethical performance give a true and fair view.[21]

It was fairly radical at the time and would prove time consuming and cost money. But it would also influence the wider world as the concept of 'corporate social responsibility' emerged during the 1990s. Traidcraft, in its producer relationships and evaluation of Fair Trade, was already starting to reflect on the mantra "don't just tell me, show me" which had been used in some of the networking meetings with likeminded organizations throughout Europe. We all shared the same concerns that it would only be a matter of time before tangible proof would be required against the claims we were all making. And remember, this was the period when Fairtrade labelling was being birthed.

Traidcraft actually published a document entitled "Toward Social Accounts" in 1992. It was meant to signal intentions and give a flavour of the scope of social accounts, inviting stakeholders to comment and feedback on its content before the first attempt at a detailed and audited report would be published to cover the financial year 1992/93. The concept of social accounting was not new – but here was another example of Traidcraft developing such a concept into something practical, which could be transferable to mainstream business in the years to come. The contents, indicators to measure, perspectives to gather, and methodology employed to construct the report were a work in progress and would evolve in the years to come.

For that first report, much of its preamble would explain why this document existed in the first place as follows:

---

21   Traidcraft internal document 1992.

> What is social auditing? – the assessment of a company's
> social impact and ethical behaviour in relation to its aims
> and those of its stakeholders.
>
> Who are the stakeholders? – producer groups, staff,
> voluntary reps, public and consumers, shareholders.
>
> Why do social auditing? – to determine social and
> ethical performance, to strengthen the stakeholder role
> in the company, to improve social impact and ethical
> behaviour, and to encourage others to adopt similar
> processes.[22]

In terms of methodology, the different groups of stakeholders (where possible) were questioned or interviewed either through paper questionnaires or through physical focus group meetings to get feedback on Traidcraft's performance, so much of the content of the report contained merely anecdotal information together with facts and figures.

For example, the staff perspective would contain views on what Traidcraft was like as an employer together with hard facts related to things like salary differential (which had now crept up to 3:1), gender balance, training investment, and days lost to sickness.

As another example, the producer's perspective would contain similar anecdotal information about how they regarded Traidcraft as a buyer and they would be encouraged to challenge rather than just affirm. These were combined with hard facts about purchase increases or decreases and the amount of time Traidcraft staff spent travelling or supporting producers.

These social audits allowed the possibility for Traidcraft to be transparent on its pricing policy and just how much of a product's price went to the producer. The first report chose two handicraft products and broke down the retail price into its cost components – raw materials, direct labour costs, overheads of the producer, freight, distribution in the UK, marketing costs, discounts, and VAT. Future reports would select several products including crafts, clothing, and food and do the same thing, although the exercise was not straightforward and it was not always clear how this contributed to impact. However, as an

---

22 Traidcraft Social Audit 1992/93, p. 4.

exercise in transparency it was ground-breaking in a commercial world that was notoriously non-transparent on such things.

As I look back through the social audits (later to become known as social accounts) from those early days up until the end of the 1990s, much of the format remained the same, as did the stakeholders represented. The methodology evolved – clearer indicators and targets against which to measure had developed, and questionnaires had become more systematic. And there was a greater emphasis on the inclusion of case studies, especially about producer organizations and their workers. For most of the decade, social accounts covered only Traidcraft plc. Traidcraft Exchange published something similar which was called an "annual review" but in 1999 the first joint Traidcraft plc/ Traidcraft Exchange social accounts were published as a single report.

Much of my own contribution to the social audit process involved giving focus to producer perspectives and providing statistical information but, importantly, it was decided to be transparent and open about the weaknesses of our old food purchasing policy and give an annual report on progress toward full compliance against a new policy.

Growing policy work

The legacy of the development of social auditing would be significant. It had always been an objective to encourage others to do the same and as the 1990s drew to a close, those who had pioneered the process and had developed a more formal methodology had moved on from Traidcraft and were working with other organizations on their own social accounts. Names as familiar as The Body Shop, the Co-operative Bank, and Allied Dunbar had adapted and used the methodology and published their own set of accounts, and big businesses like BP, Shell, and BT had all produced forms of social accounts. Through Traidcraft's pioneering work, the Institute for Social and Ethical Accountability (which became known as AccountAbility) had been established, which would develop into a global organization, formalizing the standards and methodology adopted for social and ethical auditing.

The Traidcraft Exchange Education Unit had evolved considerably toward the end of the 1990s. Information, awareness-raising, and the development of educational materials were still important but the development of social accounting meant that Traidcraft Exchange could play a leading role in the wider commercial and political world and could expand its lobbying work in the area of ethical business practice. It contributed to the development and launch of the Ethical Trading Initiative and would play an important advisory role to government in ethical and fair business practice. The 'Traidcraft Policy Unit' was established as part of a broader ethical business programme, working out of a London-based office, with an objective to maximize the presence of Fair Trade in international debate and to influence the ethical policies of business and government. From these small beginnings would emerge some of the most influential and impactful work of Traidcraft for years to come.

Shared interest

Right from the early days of Traidcraft, the principles which defined what Fair Trade would become were wrestled with on a regular basis. Access to affordable capital would be recognized as one of the key issues faced by producers and artisans throughout the world. For Traidcraft, on a practical basis, the solution in its day-to-day trading activities would be to offer its suppliers interest-free pre-financing alongside the order. This would, more often than not, happen up to six months before the goods would be shipped and nine months before those products could be sold. Much of the marketing of the time talked about eliminating or by-passing the so-called "middleman" who might offer quick payments but at low prices or charge high interest rates. Traidcraft offered interest-free finance, though not because it regarded charging interest as wrong (indeed, on a number of occasions the concept of charging interest was considered). Ultimately, it was concluded that it might be costly to manage and that "interest-free" was probably less expensive administratively!

Those early supporters of Traidcraft who were not only interested in buying products but were willing to invest financially in the company could do so through becoming shareholders. Beyond that, there was the sense that there were willing investors in an alternative financial institution and this ultimately sowed the seeds for what became 'Shared Interest', established in 1990 as an "Industrial and Provident Society".

Mark Hayes, an investment manager at one of the leading venture capital organizations, 3i, had been one of the early investors in the work of Traidcraft in its first public share issue. He had a vision similar to those at Traidcraft for exploring the concept of alternative finance which might have led to something called "Traidbank" and which might have been a subsidiary of Traidcraft. He would go on to be founder of Shared Interest and become its first Managing Director. Working for Traidcraft Exchange in the late 1980s, his proposals would lead ultimately and more sensibly to an entity separate from Traidcraft. For the next three decades, it would service the Fair Trade movement, providing loans and financial services to hundreds of Fair Trade businesses throughout the world.

Chapter 9

HARD TIMES AND BIG CHANGES

For the business, hard times would re-emerge in the mid-1990s. After the restructuring in 1991 and the change of leadership, there was a degree of stability – right through the 1990s, sales would increase incrementally year on year, and over the whole decade by more than 35%. There were plenty of innovative projects, exciting new product ranges, and producer initiatives throughout the decade and the work of Traidcraft Exchange would grow and broaden. But for the business, profitability was still an issue and two losses over consecutive years in 1996 and 1997 resulted in another dark and painful time for Traidcraft. There was more restructuring and more redundancies, again numbering around 15% of staff.

The concept of "business process re-engineering" was introduced and was on everyone's lips, with increased efficiency, greater focus, and cost savings explored and implemented. Greater focus meant that external retail shops were divested, and distribution for other charities was stopped. As well as the loss of staff, some of the business units changed, with the crafts, textiles, and clothing businesses drastically impacted. In the first half of the 1990s, there was a catalogue produced for virtually every occasion and every product range. Dedicated catalogues would be published for foods, experimenting with new branding which would see the appearance of the short-lived strapline

"Fine Foods Fairly Traded", as well as for recycled paper and handmade cards, and for Christmas cards and gifts. Clothing and accessories would be branded as "alternatives" and household accessories and gifts branded as "interiors". Sales had increased with this approach but came at a cost, and a cost which was too high.

This rationalization programme stemmed the losses and reached break-even, and levels of profit were achieved by the end of the decade with sales turnover passing £7 million. A more professional approach to running the business was adopted with some key appointments in operational and sales areas. There was also investment in information technology and order processing, although things were almost derailed by the difficult implementation of a new computer system.

Traidcraft Exchange had grown into a sizeable charity alongside Traidcraft plc, each with their individual governance structures, yet with a unifying mission and values. There was a possibility that the two organizations might diverge under this structure, therefore a key decision was made in 1998/99 to unify governance – one management structure, one mission, and one strategy. Another process of change emerged as well as an evolved set of objectives:

> Traidcraft is a Christian response to poverty. Its mission is
> to fight poverty through trade. It strives to:
> * show a bias to the poor
> * respect people and the environment
> * be transparent and accountable
> * show creativity and innovation
> * be the best.

Success would be measured through a set of indicators which would go on to be the framework for unified social accounts reporting (the first of which was published in 1999):

> * improving the livelihoods of "third world" producers
> * providing effective local support for producers
> * setting trends in ethical business
> * winning more customers and supporters
> * leading opinion in the Fair Trade movement.

For some, the move away from any explicit reference to "justice" in a statement of mission was a move away from some of the fundamental founding principles and with this radical organizational change came consequences.

Traidcraft's first strapline had been "Third World Trade for Practical Aid" which then evolved into "Trading for a Fairer World". This statement would not work for the newly unified plc and Exchange because the work of the Exchange was broader than Fair Trade and it didn't do any trade. So, the new strapline became "Fighting Poverty Through Trade". While I was not opposed to it, it was not something that I had any great affection for in terms of product messaging. As a result, it was never knowingly used on the retail packaging of any Traidcraft food product. I had, by then, visited many agricultural producers and most of them would not necessarily regard themselves as poor compared with others in their society. Many of them owned their own land, for example. On one memorable occasion I was visiting a rice farmer in Haryana, India. As I walked along the edge of his rice paddy field, I lost my footing and slid into the well irrigated soil. Covered in mud up to my knees, the farmer pulled me up, led me to his home, took off my shoes and socks to wash them, and then proceeded to wash my feet. In telling this story, the biblical parallels are not lost on me, and if the definition of poverty goes beyond mere economic indicators then this farmer was by no means poor! The strapline "Fighting Poverty Through Trade" was an understandable one in that it covered the work of Traidcraft Exchange and, indeed, would assist when seeking project funding which would invariably need a "poverty" focus. My personal perspective was that for Traidcraft plc, the new statement of mission was not an improvement.

A further consequence of this radical organizational change concerned the management structure. Traidcraft Exchange had its own Director, Graham Young, while Philip Angier was Managing Director of Traidcraft plc. The decision for unification would bring with it the role of Chief Executive of Traidcraft – all of it. Both Graham and Philip would be interviewed for the one job, but for the successful candidate it would bring a double-edged sword. It was deemed that the person who would lead the organization into the new millennium would only have a short-term contract and that a fresh face would ultimately be needed. For those of us watching from a distance and not engaged with the recruitment process, it was a very strange time. No one could really say there was a favourite and support for one or the other would be determined by which part of the organization you worked for. Talking to both Philip and Graham some twenty years later, the sheer emotion and pain of the process is clear. And for the decision makers, I imagine that it was just as hard, which was evidenced by the fact that it took time, was by no means unanimous, and caused some to move on. Ultimately, it was considered that the vulnerability of the trading company should determine the decision and that a degree of stability and continuity be adopted. Thus it was that Philip was appointed as Traidcraft's first Chief Executive Officer (CEO) but the search for a successor would begin soon afterwards and that person would lead Traidcraft into yet another period of change and certainly for Traidcraft plc into a period of relative financial prosperity.

Graham Young writes of his time at Traidcraft:

> The underpinnings for me were my five years working at Christian Aid with a number of overseas trips to the Caribbean and South Africa. This taught me what oppression and social and economic inequality means, forged on the anvils of slavery, colonialism, and apartheid.
>
> But my foundations in Fair Trade were built in the rough and tumble of debate and action around how we made business work for all its stakeholders. The eventual construction of Fair Trade in all its guises enabled many people to grow out of poverty and oppression and create their own futures.
>
> As I read what I have just written, I am surprised by the florid nature of my language. This stuff fired my soul. There were times in the journey when that rhetoric was necessary and useful. But for the most part it was about hard work and complex, and called for, difficult decisions.
>
> We were a group of people, first nationally and then internationally, who were committed to making business work fairly, particularly for its overseas producers. But we came with different motivations for

wanting to see that happen and from different contexts. That meant the discussions were not always easy. Good people can disagree, and we did. This was true in terms of the institutions and process which we strove to establish nationally and internationally. But it was also true within Traidcraft itself.

The decision to move into enabling purely commercial players to sell Fair Trade products, and to set up the systems to ensure that they did that in a way that was as fair to the producers as possible and enabled their ongoing development, was contentious. Not only how to do it, but whether to do it at all. Good people disagreed, and some parted company.

In the end, the principle of maximizing benefits for as many overseas producers as possible became the key principle, rather than any concerns we might have about working with those of different motivations or our ability to keep the system fair and "pure".

The other reality was the zeitgeist. A growing number of people in the business, which at some stage reached a tipping point, knew that it had to be more sustainable – economically, but also socially and environmentally sustainable. Our thinking and experience were well received, and they enabled us to be in the right place to enable the development of the tools and environments which now underpin the great push for ethical business. In those early days, they included investment (Traidcraft plc and Shared Interest), the legal framework (our work with Labour on a new Companies Act and the role of business in international development), social accounting and reporting (accountability), labelling (Fairtrade Foundation and Fairtrade International), Fair Trade brands (Cafédirect etc), non-labelled ethical trade (Ethical Trading Initiative), public policy lobbying and campaigning (Traidcraft Policy Unit).

This was a formative period in business change and Traidcraft was a key part of it. No matter how many products Traidcraft sold directly, it was this impact which will have the largest and most long-lasting effect on the lives of the poor. And, just as importantly, on the lives of the rich.

Yes, the end of my time at Traidcraft was emotional, you don't pour your life into something for twenty years without the end being significant! But it was necessary, the time for change had come and that meant making difficult decisions. And I was proud of what we had already achieved: the hard work of lots of staff, volunteers and supporters had changed the way the country did business and had changed life for the good for a lot of overseas producers. That is what Traidcraft was all about, it was about far more than the products we sold, it was about making business more evidently ethical, by giving it the tools and the environment in which that could happen.[23]

Philip Angier writes:

When Joe asked me to reflect upon my time as Managing Director (and briefly Group CEO) through the 1990s, I responded that I was more conscious of whether we could or should have done better than I was of a series of ground-breaking achievements.

That said, the 1990s were a period of rapid change and rapid development in Fair Trade, global business ethics and social enterprise – and Traidcraft played its part alongside others, often as an influential shaper and practitioner. A number of these are described in more detail elsewhere but for me the list includes the following:

- Shared Interest came into being and established itself as a leading player in the provision of finance for Fair Trade.
- the Fairtrade logo was established – after much wrangling as I recall – and the UK Fairtrade Foundation grew rapidly in size and impact.

---

23   From personal correspondence with the author, 2019.

- the Ethical Trading Initiative was launched. After the debt campaign, the UK development agencies – especially Christian Aid – put their weight behind the trade justice movement.

- a new Labour government, with Clare Short as International Development Minister, perceived a real synergy between Fair Trade and the UN's global development goals.

- socially responsible investment was becoming mainstream. A reform of the Companies Act was considering how directors' responsibilities should be reframed to take into account the interests of other stakeholders, not just shareholders.

- social accounting was being talked about – and practised – not just by Traidcraft, but also other value-based businesses such as The Body Shop and Ben & Jerry's. "Social entrepreneurship" and "social enterprise" were starting to attract the interest of business schools.

Some of the above ideas – to be fair – had their genesis in the late 1980s, but they all came to fruition in the 1990s.

Traidcraft did not make all of these things happen – but the values which Traidcraft stood for and practised certainly had an influence. Sometimes this was by having a seat at the table (for example, Cafédirect); other times, by seeding and nurturing the ideas (for example, Fairtrade Foundation, Shared Interest); by being seen as an example of theory into practice (social accounting, ethical business); or less directly, because former Traidcraft staff members or Traidcraft shareholders/Fair Traders were involved.

The power of the Traidcraft ethos and example was very evident, and the opportunity to influence led eventually to the formation of the Traidcraft Policy Unit. The influence of the Traidcraft "diaspora" – former staff members, shareholders, and customers who have been influenced by Traidcraft's values and ethos, was significant through the 1990s and remains significant today.

It's important to say – because I write this from the perspective of the MD of the trading company – that without the presence and work of Traidcraft Exchange, led by Graham Young, the list above would be much shorter. It was the example and influence of both strands of Traidcraft's work which made the difference.

If Traidcraft had a formative role in a decade of social change, shouldn't we be breaking out the champagne?

Externally, Fair Trade was flourishing. Internally the business was going through adolescence (formed in 1979 remember) and trying to become more "grown up". We inherited the "ideal" business – strong faith basis, egalitarian labour policies, home grown systems, very forgiving purchasing standards (in other words, we were in the habit of accepting poor-quality goods and absorbing the cost), volunteer sales force, shareholders who didn't expect a financial return, and so on – but was that "grown up" business?

Through the 1990s we undoubtedly made massive strides in quality control, customer service standards, order turnaround (eventually!), and we became less afraid to bring in professional skills from "mainstream" business. Something that featured in many of our management discussions was what should stay and what should go in the values and practices we inherited from the 1980s. How best should we introduce new business processes in order to become more effective and retain (with integrity) our identity as a Fair Trade pioneer?

The process was stuttering and slow – and painful, as restructuring led to significant numbers of compulsory redundancies.

Often, one of the points of challenge was the "faith basis" and the requirement therefore that directors (including executive staff) needed to declare themselves in sympathy with the basis of faith. This – together with the self-imposed limits on senior staff salaries – was perceived (quite reasonably) as restricting the pool of talent from which to recruit to help guide the company's development.

The series of essays – *Markets, Fair Trade and the Kingdom of God* – with contributions from directors, staff, and trustees capture well some of the dilemmas about what Traidcraft's mission, policies, and practice should seek to be in the pluralist marketplace of the late 1990s.[24]

Toward the end of my time as MD, I was invited to take part in the radio series *The Choice* and to reflect on the process of leading a major downsizing of the company's staff from a Christian perspective. I was asked at the end of the interview, "Any regrets?" I responded, "No, only that I did not do it sooner."

Twenty years on that response is right – some changes would have been better done sooner – for the staff, for producers, for customers. But then again, that's the benefit of looking back at adolescence from the perspective of adulthood.

Other value-based businesses have grown faster, and then gone mainstream (for example, The Body Shop, Ben & Jerry's, Innocent Smoothies). Should Traidcraft have taken that route in the 1990s?

One of the things I believe that we did right through the nineties was to "keep the faith" – literally and metaphorically. That at least ensured a good inheritance for the "noughties".[25]

---

24 Johnson and Sugden, eds, *Markets, Fair Trade and the Kingdom of God: essays to celebrate Traidcraft's 21st birthday.*

25 From personal correspondence with the author, 2019.

PART THREE
A New Millennium

Chapter 10

NEW LEADERSHIP, NEW APPROACH

Philip Angier had left Traidcraft and his successor, appointed not long after this in June 2001, was Paul Chandler who had successfully led the Christian mission agency, book publisher, and retailer SPCK for the previous nine years. This new decade under Paul's leadership would see major change and a higher degree of financial prosperity, visibility, and influence. Sales for Traidcraft plc would double over the next decade, peaking at over £16 million of profitable turnover, and the work of the Traidcraft Exchange would grow and broaden.

The commercial and social climate in the early 2000s meant that growth was, to an extent, inevitable with a growing consumer awareness about fair and ethical trade. The trade justice movement began in 2000 and Traidcraft was fully involved with its development. The "Make Poverty History" movement would shine a light on Fair Trade just a few years later. The growth of Fairtrade labelling was starting to have more impact and gained more visibility through more and more supermarket listings of Fairtrade products, and this would inevitably be helpful to Traidcraft, whether or not its products carried a Fairtrade label. Because fair and ethical trade was firmly on the agenda for consumers, it could not be ignored by the supermarkets and mainstream brands. There were few organizations like Traidcraft around, with such a broad remit, so it became one of the "go to" organizations for help and assistance to the so-called "commercial world" in all things fair and ethical. Several well-known supermarkets would approach Traidcraft for advice and we were willing and eager to engage, whether or not there were commercial benefits!

A new strategic direction emerged and with a revised mission statement and updated objectives, and this only three years after the previous iteration:

- Traidcraft is a Christian response to poverty
- our mission is to fight poverty through trade
- we respect all people and the environment
- we abide by and promote fair business practices
- we strive to be transparent and accountable.[26]

The measures of organizational success would be defined differently. These key areas which informed all strategic and organizational planning for the next few years across both Traidcraft Exchange and Traidcraft plc would be:

- direct impact on poverty
- influencing others (business and individuals) to help fight poverty through trade related choices and practices
- being more sustainable as an organization
- working more closely with our Christian supporter base.[27]

This would evolve into what became known popularly as Traidcraft's "trade, support, influence" model represented visually by three intersecting circles:

Trade: directly helping overseas producers by providing a market for their goods in the UK and practically applying the principles of Fair Trade.

Support: helping producers develop the skills they need to trade by providing training and support in the areas they need to build long-term sustainable businesses.

---

26 Traidcraft Annual Report 2001/02, inside front cover.
27 Traidcraft Annual Report 2001/02, inside front cover.

Influence: building awareness of trade justice issues among UK consumers, engaging with mainstream companies, and presenting Traidcraft as a viable business model.[28]

Supporters might have interpreted this in terms of what the different parts of Traidcraft represented – so "trade" would mean the work of Traidcraft plc, "support" would mean the work of the Traidcraft Exchange overseas programmes, and "influence" would mean the work of the Traidcraft Exchange Policy Unit in London. However, the reality was somewhat different, and the intersecting circles were there for a reason. There was some degree of cross-organizational working, although maybe not enough, and several staff would work jointly for both the business and the charity.

As part of this new direction, I would see another change of role which would bring me back into the world of handicrafts. As well as overseeing the sourcing and development of the food ranges, I would lead on applying greater scrutiny of our purchasing policy and principles and we would go deeper into the relationships we had with our overseas producer partners. I would find myself at a much more senior level which ultimately saw my appointment to the Board of Directors in 2006 and I would remain in that position until I stepped down in 2017.

In the mid-2000s, a further review of strategy would articulate a new vision statement and evolve Traidcraft's mission statement while maintaining the "trade, support, influence" model:

Vision: a world freed from the scandal of poverty, where trade is just and individuals and communities can flourish.

Mission: we fight poverty through trade, practising and promoting approaches to trade that help poor people in developing countries transform their lives.[29]

That 1990s mantra "don't just tell me, show me" took on a new meaning in this evolving Fair Trade environment. Traidcraft had pioneered and used externally audited social accounts as a demonstration of mission

---

28 Traidcraft Annual Report 2003/04, p. 4.
29 Traidcraft Annual Report 2005/06, inside front cover.

in practice, but more was needed. Formal definitions of what Fair Trade meant had been developed and agreed internationally. Fairtrade International had developed its product standards and monitoring procedures to reassure those who used the Fairtrade mark that there was substance behind it. All of these things had consequences for Traidcraft which could no longer merely rely on reputation alone, and a perception that it could be trusted to "always do the right thing".

A major decision was made in the early 2000s that the Fairtrade Mark would be used on all Traidcraft products which qualified for that mark. Prior to that, the Traidcraft position had always been "the Fairtrade Mark was developed for supermarkets and Traidcraft supporters didn't need it"!

Those known as voluntary representatives were now called "Fair Traders" and accounted for a significant proportion of sales, and it's fair to say that there was some confusion out there. It was hard to explain why Traidcraft teas and coffees did not carry a Fairtrade Mark despite fully meeting Fairtrade standards – especially when, alongside them in the Traidcraft catalogue, sat Cafédirect products. They were an integral part of the product range and, as supermarket products, they carried the Fairtrade mark. There was a fair degree of begrudging acknowledgement of this confusion, despite the fact that Traidcraft brand sales were buoyant – not least because using the Fairtrade Mark accrued substantial licence fees. On the other hand, Fairtrade International was putting lots of energy into monitoring all those Fairtrade standards, so it was only right that Traidcraft paid its fair share of costs.

Throughout the 1990s, Traidcraft had supported the development of Fairtrade labelling – even messaging supporters to look for the Fairtrade label in supermarkets. This was, in a sense, an act of solidarity and playing our part in the development of the wider Fair Trade movement but as a commercial strategy it was counterintuitive, in that we were effectively promoting the sales of other brands!

But what about all of those other Fair Trade products that Traidcraft sold? A vast range of handicrafts, clothing, giftware, and fashion accessories which could not carry a Fairtrade Mark but were still sold as Fair Trade products. Then there were the food products for which there were no Fairtrade standards like dried fruit and nuts.

So began yet another review of Traidcraft's purchasing policy. This time, it was alongside the development of a more structured and formal monitoring system to verify that products could indeed be confidently called "Fair Trade", with its own tools, documentation, and decision processes, and with dedicated staff to implement those processes.

The newly formulated purchasing policy retained the principles adopted in the early 1990s for food products but encompassed all products. It also acknowledged internationally developed Fairtrade standards, and added elements which were of particular relevance to Traidcraft's strategy and direction at that time:

Essential criteria were established as follows:

- a fair price is paid for the product.
- there is the intention of a relationship of partnership and cooperation between buyer and supplier of the product that is expected to last for at least the medium term.
- products are purchased only from suppliers where there are clear and definable benefits accruing to the producers of the product which arise as a result of the purchase.
- the working conditions for producers are safe and non-exploitative.
- Traidcraft will follow FLO (Fairtrade Labelling Organization) and other internationally agreed standards except where alternative benefits are identified.[30]

In addition, secondary criteria were established:

The following principles will be applied where possible. They are a desirable progression of the relationship that may occur as part of the continued partnership with the supplier. They are not in themselves sufficient to define a "Fair Trade" product although any one or more combined with the essential criteria should be regarded as positive:

Added Value – Traidcraft will aim to maximise the value added in country of production by processing or packaging

30 Traidcraft internal document, Purchasing Policy, 2003.

at or near to the source. Wherever possible this will be organized and controlled by the supplier. This will not be at the expense of fulfilling the essential criteria and achieving objectives. The maximization of sales, and benefits resulting from that, should not be compromised by reducing the viability of a product through lower quality or high costs

Target Groups/Regions – Traidcraft may wish to target specific types of producers or regions e.g. disadvantaged or marginalized producers in specific regions, women's groups etc. In particular this may direct choices over whether to favour one supplier for a specific product or range over another.

Sustainability – Traidcraft recognises the need for progressive agricultural practices, sustainable land management, and respect for the environment. In partnership with suppliers, this area will be monitored and developed.

Location – we will target those geographical areas in which Traidcraft Exchange partner development and/or trade facilitation are operating.[31]

This so-called "monitoring and evaluation" process was rolled out for all of the overseas suppliers we were buying from who were not themselves aligned to any other external evaluation system like that of Fairtrade International. That dedicated team of Catherine Howe and Monica Philbrick travelled extensively, and by 2005 nearly fifty suppliers had been covered. The process involved more time spent with suppliers, gathering information through in-depth interviews, covering all key components of the purchasing policy, and greater scrutiny and inspection of how and where products were made or grown.

As Traidcraft's trade, support, influence model had developed, so this monitoring and evaluation process evolved to encompass the "support" part of that model. Renamed "partnership review process", this was a time when Traidcraft was deepening its approach to Fair Trade,

---

31 Traidcraft internal document, Purchasing Policy, 2003.

embracing partnership with overseas suppliers and acknowledging that Fair Trade was developmental in nature. "Producer support" had always been an integral part of wider Fair Trade principles but here was an attempt to take it from the informal "nice to do" into a more formal, resourced, and funded activity. Financial results were strong, and budgets were increased. It was something that Traidcraft plc could afford to do and producer support became an integral part of the business of being a Fair Trade organization. So-called "producer plans" and "partnership agreements" were drawn up with suppliers which enshrined the relationship, formalizing the inputs and undertakings of each of us and with formal producer support projects included.

Our counterparts in the European Fair Trade Association (EFTA) were facing similar challenges and adopting similar practices and so it made a lot of sense to develop common monitoring tools and processes and to share the workload and expense. No point in several people visiting the same supplier, asking virtually the same questions and obtaining more or less the same information. Besides, several of our common suppliers had pointed this out as a waste of their time. As well as being members of EFTA we were also members of IFAT (International Fair Trade Association) who had been designing tools for self-assessment for Fair Trade Organizations and had developed ten key principles of Fair Trade. Therefore, we all tore up our own monitoring systems and tools and devised a new, centralized system based on those ten principles. An EFTA Monitoring Group was established which would establish a plan, allocate the monitoring duties to each member, and regularly meet to share and disseminate the findings. It also led to occasional producer support projects with shared funding.

A renamed "Supplier Support" team, led by Nicky Robinson, was established to oversee the partnership review process. This was Traidcraft going the extra mile, going beyond merely buying and selling Fair Trade products, attempting to be an example to the rest of the Fair Trade world alongside our EFTA partners, and trying to demonstrate practically the developmental dimension of Fair Trade. Objectives were defined as:

- ensuring fairness in the way we trade with our suppliers
- monitoring compliance with our purchasing policy

- building an understanding of the rights and responsibilities of workers and producers in our Fair Trade supply chains

- understanding the impact of our trading relationships and Fair Trade more broadly

- providing support to enable our suppliers to achieve greater sustainability.[32]

Some would have argued that merely buying and selling Fair Trade products would have been quite enough. Why go beyond this, given that some of our Fair Trade competitors don't? This was, after all, funded from business activities, and not from any charitable income which was quite separately managed and used by the Traidcraft Exchange. Others might have argued that it should have been funded from that charitable income, as others of our Fair Trade competitors did, but that was not an option at the time given the growth of Traidcraft Exchange overseas programmes and the consequent thirst for unrestricted funding. Certainly, the profitability of Traidcraft plc would have been much higher had what ultimately became known as the "Producer Support Programme" not existed.

Ways were found to fund the programme over and above the substantial general overhead allocation. Brand licensing was taking off and Co-op Retail, impressed with our whole approach to Fair Trade and the robustness of our partnership review process, would use our brand as an endorsement of their own Fair Trade products, initially on wine but later on other products. A proportion of that licence income would fund the programme. I even recall writing a proposal to introduce more explicitly the biblical principal of the tithe to Traidcraft. We would give away one-tenth of our profits, but to the Producer Support Programme. In reality, I suppose we were already doing this, just not in the way I had proposed.

Then there was the toilet roll conundrum! The days of Traidcraft having a tangible mission-based rationale for selling recycled paper products had gone. Every product from those early days had long been discontinued, but what was left were toilet rolls, kitchen rolls, and facial tissues. I was probably regarded at that time as the guardian

---

32 Traidcraft internal document.

of Traidcraft's purchasing policy and approach to Fair Trade and I had regularly challenged why we were still selling these products. Every supermarket had their range and, while we had a very positive relationship with the manufacturer, the origin of the recycled material was obscure. The case for "recycled" was less clear and FSC (Forest Stewardship Council) certified paper was becoming the norm. The answer to the challenge was always that they generated lots of income and profitability, were loved by customers, and were a top seller. I was always hoping that they would be less popular and that customers would choose to buy only our Fair Trade products. Also, there was always the underlying concern that maybe some of those customers thought that these tissues were actually Fair Trade products! It was a bit hard to argue against some of those commercial reasons so maybe the best way to proceed would be to turn them into fundraisers. In yet another revised purchasing policy revision, we gave ourselves permission to sell what would become widely known as "cause-related products"; products which would contribute funds to some of the "real" work of Traidcraft. Problem solved. To link to the environmental dimension of the recycled range, we developed various projects with producers which would also have an environmental dimension – things like tree planting or waste management.

Chapter 11

GROWTH AND INFLUENCE

The step change in sales growth in the early 2000s was initially driven by the supermarket and wholesale sales of Geobar which was developed specifically as a response to an opportunity for a listing in Waitrose. Launched in 1999, it became a £1.25 million brand only a year later. Further growth in all sales channels and across product sectors followed. Previously it had been a worry that handicrafts, gifts, and fashion were stagnating, and that growth would be fuelled only by food products. But this trend was reversed and even though foods represented over 70% of all sales, things were looking healthy right across the board. This growth of almost 40% required new working capital to accommodate these extra sales and funding purchases to producers, much of which was paid in advance. It was also needed to expand warehouse capacity through purchasing a new building close to Traidcraft headquarters in Gateshead and to improve information technology infrastructure. A new share issue in 2003 would raise over £3 million and was called the "Fair Share Offer". New investors were invited once again to invest in people rather than profit as outlined in the share issue prospectus:

> When you see the word "share" what do you think?
> Making a fortune on the market or investing in someone's future?

91

With your help we can:

- place more orders with hard working producers
- offer more opportunities for UK customers to buy quality products with added value
- encourage more UK companies to join us in fair and ethical trading
- behind our products are stories of lives changed for the better, communities offered hope for the future. Producers supplying Traidcraft can afford to invest in a safe water supply, a village school, a clinic or a child's education. These things won't feature on our balance sheet, but they are the real "capital assets" from our way of doing business. Why don't you buy a share in it? This is not a donation but an investment in an organization that fights poverty through trade.[33]

The success of this share offer brought many more investors to Traidcraft. A change and simplification of governance structures meant that shareholders were able to exercise more voting rights. Rather than merely nominating and voting for a non-executive director who would be appointed as a board member, they were now allowed to vote for all resolutions brought to an AGM. The guardian share still existed which protected the mission and values of the organization, but shareholders could now influence who actually ran the business. In each of the three years following this share issue, shareholders received a dividend based on good growth and profitability.

Tim Morgan, who joined Traidcraft as Finance Director in 1998 and served for the next eight years, writes of that period:

I think there are a number of key points to note alongside the financial success of Traidcraft at that time. The Company had almost trebled in size in terms of its scale as measured by purchases and turnover. It had become a leader in the field of social accounting, winning a number of national prizes for its reporting in this area. The combined success of the social and financial impact

33   Traidcraft *Fair Share Offer* flyer, 2003.

was critical to its recognition. On the back of this, Paul Chandler and I were able to meet with the corporate social responsibility team of our main banker (HSBC) in their corridors of power in Canary Wharf. The fact that we were a longstanding customer, but also successful in pursuing a social mission profitably, was very interesting and it opened doors, allowing "David to speak to Goliath" and put the case for more ethical and responsible trade. There was sufficient trust and communication with Traidcraft's stakeholders to be able to launch a very successful public share issue raising over £3 million during this period. Traidcraft also helped Cafédirect to do the same two years later when it raised £5 million from supporters in a similar offer.

For me, the period was one of great learning – both in the technical aspects of the role but also about the meaning of servant leadership. I learnt much about the concept of being entrusted with a precious responsibility to use your talents at the service of others. It is a way of leading which consciously tries to turn on its head the traditional concept of leadership, involving the accretion and exercise of power by those "at the top". It is a journey that continues for me today as I continue working in the Fair Trade space, having served as Shared Interest's Finance Director for almost ten years.[34]

Meanwhile, Traidcraft Exchange would enjoy similar momentum and growth as it aligned its structures with the trade, support, influence model and by 2002 had become a £2.5 million charity. Its largest single overseas project, part-funded by the Department for International Development, had been established in Malawi (although ended prematurely) and, over the next few years, overseas programme activity would still grow but take a new strategic direction. Regional strategies were established but centrally coordinated from UK headquarters. This contrasted with the previous approach of setting up self-governing,

---

34 From personal correspondence with the author, 2019.

independent overseas partner organizations. Those which had already been established in the 1990s had already flown the nest, some more successfully than others, and it would not be until a few years later that new overseas offices managed from the UK were established – the first two being in Kenya and Bangladesh. Much of the Traidcraft Exchange project work was themed around cotton, tea, and handicrafts and the scale of projects became much larger. This constraint, combined with a changing landscape of funding, meant that there were fewer opportunities for the overseas work of the Traidcraft Exchange and Traidcraft plc to overlap. For me, this was cause for some regret – although it was understandable, given the broader geographical reach of the plc, and the fact that much of the producer support work linked to the suppliers that Traidcraft bought from would be smaller-scale projects. On a number of occasions, I would find myself partnering up with other development agencies to deliver some of those projects rather than with the Traidcraft Exchange.

The "Market Access Centre" (MAC) was established in 2002 within the Traidcraft Exchange offering training and consultancy services. Although much of their work was directly linked to the overseas regional programmes, they would also seek additional work from other clients – whether in the Fair Trade world or beyond. They famously worked for the large tobacco company British American Tobacco to advise on the delivery of their corporate social responsibility programme, although I believe we kept that quite low key! Later in the 2000s, the MAC would undergo name changes and also combine with the producer support staff of Traidcraft plc to pool resources.

In London the Traidcraft Exchange Policy Unit would grow in size, influence, and impact throughout the 2000s. It became an important resource to the Fair Trade movement, and played an important campaigning, lobbying, and advocacy role in the development of international trade rules, company law reform, or broader corporate behaviour.

This "go to" reputation would mean that many opportunities were presented to us and very few were ignored completely. Occasionally, they would result in a new product launch and, while some stood the test of time, others would be short-lived. On occasion, these opportunities would result in Fair Trade being introduced to completely new product categories and Traidcraft's influence on those would be significant.

Fruity new products

Wine would be introduced into the Traidcraft range through collaboration with some of our counterparts in the European Fair Trade Association who had already started working with producers, initially in Chile. Very quickly we became a wine importer and retailer with the usual sharp learning curve that such things entailed. Great partnerships were established with experts in the wine trade and a range of Chilean and South African wines were introduced in 2001, with Argentinian wines following later. Fair Trade wines were not available from anyone else in the UK, so sales were reasonable. Managing wines through our warehouse and distribution departments would be a bigger challenge and, sadly, breakages and returns would be higher than desired. The upside of this was that everyone would look forward to the annual staff sale, usually just before Christmas, where bottles with label damage would be offered at very attractive prices. Eventually, selling wine just could not be done viably and, ten years after its introduction, the range was discontinued. The legacy of those early pioneering days would be the fact that wine became one of the new products introduced by Fairtrade International, and many of those early producers would go on to be Fairtrade certified and find their place on supermarket shelves throughout the UK, not the least through the Co-op, who would go on to become the world's leading Fairtrade wine retailer. We would soon be introduced to other fresh fruit possibilities.

In 1999 we had received a call from a business that imported canned fruit products from across the world and distributed them into most of the major supermarkets. They asked whether we would endorse a Tesco canned pineapple, sourced from Swaziland, as Fair Trade. At that time, the concept of endorsing any supermarket brand as Fair Trade was a bit far-fetched and the fact that it was Tesco even more so, but I was already travelling to South Africa and a detour into Swaziland was organized. Nick Peaty was the man who made that first call and we met up in Swaziland. I rather liked what I saw which was a relatively large-scale processing factory and farm, but with fairly progressive ethical credentials and with good links to the local community where most of its employees lived. Small-scale cooperative fruit growers also supplied the factory so there was already a good possibility to develop something that was Fair Trade. Maybe this was all before its time because nothing really came of it apart from a newly formed relationship; Nick and I would remain in contact after that.

A few years later, with the growing momentum of mainstream Fairtrade labelling, the question was asked again. It was now 2003, but the concept of endorsing a Tesco product was still a tricky one to deal with and now that we had a formal "constructive engagement policy", it was considered that aligning our name with a Tesco brand was a risk we could not take. However, a Traidcraft brand listed in Tesco would be very acceptable! At that time, supermarkets were jostling for position in terms of Fairtrade labelled products and eventually it was decided that the brand would be Traidcraft and would carry a Fairtrade Mark. The problem was that there were no Fairtrade standards for fresh or canned fruit, so no Fairtrade Mark was possible.

At that time, when Traidcraft products were starting to carry the Fairtrade Mark, I worked very closely with the Fairtrade Foundation. Traidcraft was one of their partners of choice to co-develop the Fairtrade standards and identify the producer groups who would go on to be Fairtrade certified. Wine, dried fruit, and cotton were other examples of this collaboration, but this initiative would fall into the fresh fruit category.

As it turned out, there was a window of opportunity to get a canned pineapple product into Tesco but the timescale for developing a new set of global product standards for Fairtrade would be longer. The product launched without a Fairtrade Mark and a Traidcraft brand would appear on the canned goods section of Tesco. We were not directly involved in the supply chain of this product so Traidcraft entered into a brand licence agreement with the importer and distributor. Sadly, it was short-lived, sales did not take off, and the listing was lost some time later. Maybe Fairtrade doesn't work so well in some fast-moving, low-value grocery categories – canned goods is probably one of those, perhaps because it's such a cheap and commoditized sector. The Fairtrade fresh fruit standards were finally completed, and the Swaziland supply chain would later become Fairtrade certified. Traidcraft would go on to sell pineapple and citrus products for years to come, which carried the Fairtrade Mark, although not in cans but in smaller, plastic pots.

This had not been the first time that we would get involved in a product where our brand would be licenced to another business, as we entered the world of fruit juice in 2001/02. Again, this developed out of Traidcraft being approached by a business interested in developing a product with a Fairtrade Mark. This time, it was a very large juice manufacturer and packer called Gerber Soft Drinks who supplied many of the supermarkets with their own brand of fruit juice.

I was fairly well networked into the world of Fairtrade International and together with fellow EFTA members we had a reasonable knowledge of appropriate orange juice producers – small farmer organizations and cooperatives rather than the large plantations owned by large private multinationals. Fairtrade International had been working on standards, and producer organizations had been identified, mostly from Brazil. Fairtrade orange juice had been launched elsewhere in Europe and we thought that it would be nice to launch in the UK and be the first to do so.

The combination of expertise in a product provided by Gerber combined with Traidcraft's expertise in the world of Fair Trade brought with it another licence arrangement which would see the brand "Fruit Passion" launched into a number of supermarkets in 2002. Looking back, it might have been regarded as a slightly odd arrangement in that the Fairtrade Mark was an integral part of the brand so could easily have been developed without Traidcraft. Ultimately, Traidcraft would look after producer relations and implement its partnership review model and provide the producer stories that would lie at the heart of the brand. In reality, Traidcraft would go on to be much more than that given that none of the producers already identified were able to provide the quality of orange juice that Gerber required. It seemed the UK consumer preferred a different orange juice taste from their counterparts on mainland Europe. In those early development days, Traidcraft would organize the sampling of juice and, on one occasion, on a flight from Germany to the UK, I found myself carrying hand baggage full of jars of frozen orange juice concentrate packed in dry ice which were duly delivered to Gerber. Fortunately, I was not asked to open the hand baggage while passing through airport security!

Finding another supplier who was able to provide the right quality of juice would take us to Cuba. Fortunately, our colleagues in EFTA were developing contacts there with both orange and grapefruit suppliers whose produce would ultimately be used in Fruit Passion.

It would take some effort to enable those producers to be Fairtrade certified but things worked out and Fruit Passion would launch and include both a Fairtrade Mark and a Traidcraft logo on its packaging.

These early fruit-based brands would pave the way for later brand licensing opportunities. The "influencing" part of Traidcraft's strategy would prevail. Traidcraft would be a catalyst for the growth of the Fair Trade sector and be the preferred route for the Traidcraft brand to be represented in supermarkets. History might dictate whether or not it was a sustainable long-term business model. Fruit Passion would demonstrate that such relationships are not for ever. Changes of ownership in Gerber meant that the organizational "fit" between us would change and ultimately the relationship ended. For Gerber, Fruit Passion continued for a while (although it ultimately failed) – but it was just one brand among the many it managed.

The beginning of decline?

The 2000s were the years when Traidcraft was probably at its commercial prime and recognition levels were at their highest. It was not too much of a boast that we described ourselves as the leading Fair Trade organization in the UK! We might not always have been the largest in terms of sales turnover, but we were most certainly the most influential. An independent survey showed us as the fourth most recognized ethical brand on the high street, behind Co-op, The Body Shop, and Marks & Spencer, and we were awarded the Queen's Award for Enterprise in the Sustainable Development category in 2007. I even got to meet the Queen at Buckingham Palace, although I have to report that her husband was less than enthusiastic about Fair Trade!

However things were about to get more difficult as sales would stagnate and decline, and there was yet another painful restructuring process with resultant redundancies. But the underlying business was still relatively healthy so there was, rightly or wrongly, no undue panic. A new strategic plan was developed in 2010 which would reflect the commercial and the developmental landscape of the day. Hopefully, its implementation would reverse the trend.

"From Fair to Flourishing"

In the climate of commercial stagnation, yet buoyant and impactful development activities right across the two organizations, a new plan was developed which was intended to set the agenda for the next decade. Some would say that it was short of tangible commercial plans which would bring Traidcraft plc back into growth but heavy on developmental plans which did play to the strengths and reputation of Traidcraft Exchange. The document was entitled "From Fair to Flourishing" and in many ways it was merely an evolution of the previous strategic plan but with greater emphasis on four things:

- **The promotion of human flourishing**: Fair Trade had always been defined by some of its core principles like payment of a fair price or producers having good working conditions. It was a bit of a buzzword, but "empowerment" was also one of those core principles normally expressed by working with producers who were part of democratic organizational structures and could participate in decision-making. In some of its previous policies, Traidcraft had expressed some of the impacts of Fair Trade in less tangible things like producers "having a greater ability to make choices" or "being valued". Clearly material issues are critical but the non-material aspects of poverty would be a focus for this next period. New ways to measure the impact of our work would be developed but more in terms of the "well-being" of producers or beneficiaries. In addition, while issues of gender had always figured in much of our work, a greater emphasis would be given to work on projects and with suppliers which benefited women.

- **Positive environmental action**: More emphasis would be placed on projects and producer-support activities which would help producers to adapt to climate change and greater efforts would be made to reduce carbon footprint in Traidcraft supply chains. Much of the impactful work of the Traidcraft Exchange overseas programme work had given focus to crop diversification and this would be built upon.

- **Innovation**: The history of Traidcraft had pioneering and innovation at its heart. The 2000s had seen this accelerate and new partnerships and developments would be explored, and new supply chains and product categories of Fair Trade developed.

- **Integration**: The previous three decades had seen different kinds of relationship between Traidcraft plc and Traidcraft Exchange. The 1980s and 1990s had seen the two organizations work very closely together but the 2000s had seen a divergence. Maybe this was the right time to draw on the developmental and commercial expertise of each organization and work more closely. This would be most tangibly expressed in the integration of the producer support activities of Traidcraft plc and the overseas programme work of Traidcraft Exchange while continuing to respect the legal and governance structures and differences of each. It also recognized the characteristics of Traidcraft's supporter base where a vast majority of them would be both customer and donor.[35]

New management structures and new ways of doing things emerged. A "Development Management Team" (DMT) and a "Business Management Team" (BMT) were formed. Some of us sat in both teams and for the DMT, both Traidcraft Exchange staff and Traidcraft plc "producer-facing" staff were represented.

For Traidcraft plc, working with and trading with an increasing number of producer organizations, a so-called "Producer Support and Innovation Programme" was established and the acronym PSIP would become commonly used. A further evolution of the way we worked with approaching 100 overseas suppliers across all product types would develop and which would categorize those suppliers based on their relative strengths and weaknesses. Producer support projects would be targeted more toward those who could benefit most from them.

---

35 Strategic Plan 2011-2020 entitled *From Fair to Flourishing* May 2011.

All of this would differentiate Traidcraft from the rest of the Fair Trade world. It would be "Beyond Fairtrade". Or so we hoped!

End of another era

Leading the development of this new strategic plan would be one of the final tasks of Paul Chandler, who had come to the end of his time at Traidcraft and would leave in 2013. His leaving was not particularly surprising given that he had always signalled his intentions and the process of appointing his successor perhaps should have started a lot earlier than it did. In the end, it would surprise and concern all of us who worked for Traidcraft just how difficult it was to recruit a new leader and this would, in many ways, determine the difficult times that lay ahead.

PART FOUR

Part of a Global Movement

Chapter 12

EARLY YEARS

In the next few chapters I will explore Traidcraft's place in and contribution to the wider "Fair Trade movement", as it has become known. As well as attempting a historical narrative covering all of the key developments in Fair Trade, I will give some of my own personal reflections. One of the things I have observed in the many years I have spent networking and representing Traidcraft in this "movement" is that Fair Trade is a broad church. There are many and varied opinions, with more than their fair share of disagreement. This is, more often than not, born out of a deep passion held by the many people and organizations involved in Fair Trade who share a common desire to see a different world and who have a heart for those who are poor, exploited, and marginalized.

My story will start in the 1980s when a myriad of seriously minded, mission-driven businesses like Traidcraft were gaining profile across Europe and the rest of the world and generally calling themselves "Alternative Marketing Organizations" which then became "Alternative Trading Organizations", or ATOs. And, more importantly, they were starting to talk to each other, meeting informally to share and learn.

Even in those early days the differences of opinion and approach would surface and Traidcraft was very familiar with that territory given that its birth was a result of such differences. There were those whose motivation was faith-based and whose key supporter base or ownership was linked to a church network or to denominational allegiances. Then there were the more politically and solidarity-motivated organizations.

There were also those who were part of larger international development agencies or charitable organizations, and there were some who spanned more than one of these.

A common goal would unify this myriad of organizations and these informal meetings would ultimately be the origin of both EFTA (the European Fair Trade Association) and IFAT (the International Federation of Alternative Trade) later to become known as WFTO (the World Fair Trade Organization).

Traidcraft was always very collaborative, and networking with external organizations was an important characteristic of those early days – and, in a sense, it needed to be. Having originated from the narrower Christian evangelical wing of the church in its Tearfund days, it would need to position itself as acceptable both to the broader church as well as to the more secular part of the spectrum of alternative traders and development organizations. While staying true to its Christian roots, and overtly Christian in its messaging, it was able to engage readily with all of those different types of organizations around the table and was invariably the one that took a leading role in coordination and organization. Graham Young, the Director of Traidcraft Exchange in the late 1980s, was one of the key people to engage at this level and he would later say that he "chaired IFAT, EFTA (and later Fairtrade Foundation) into existence".[36]

While EFTA was not formally founded until early 1990, in one sense it started a lot earlier. Its members had always been part of that informal grouping of ATOs, and some had started to cooperate and work quite closely. There were already very close synergies between the Dutch, German, Swiss, and Austrian members – largely because they had all originated out of the Netherlands as subsidiaries of the first European Alternative Trade Organization, SOS Wereldhandel. It was believed that a union of European importers would be helpful to all by coordinating activities like buying, developing products, and working with producers. In the context of wider mission, it could also have a louder voice in influencing the policies and practices of the European Union in matters relating to international trade.

IFAT was founded several months earlier than EFTA in 1989, but still emerged from that informal gathering of ATOs. The grouping was

---

36 From personal conversation with the author, 2019.

global but was still only represented by buying organizations based in the so-called "global north". This concept of the "global north" and the "global south" emerged in the 1980s to highlight the difference between rich countries based mostly in the northern hemisphere with the exception of Australia and New Zealand, and poor countries being entirely based in the southern hemisphere. There was a difference of opinion as to whether there should be formal representation from producer organizations who would argue that they were themselves ATOs and therefore worthy of membership of a global organization of ATOs. Traidcraft took the minority view that the time was not yet right for this and, as a result, withdrew from its role as chair of the steering committee. Ultimately, IFAT would become a global membership body of ATOs and those located in the global south were invited to join. And Traidcraft would choose to keep a foot in both camps, remaining an active member of both IFAT and EFTA, and continuing to network across all parts of the Fair Trade movement for years to come.

The origins of Fairtrade labelling can also be traced back to the Netherlands where the Max Havelaar Foundation was established in 1988. This had a specific focus on coffee and was linked to the collapse of the International Coffee Agreement which had been designed to regulate production and stabilize world market prices. By engaging with Dutch coffee traders and offering a label on a retail pack which would guarantee a price to small farmers in Latin America, it sent a powerful message that consumers could make a difference in their everyday supermarket shop. It was the beginning of Fair Trade emerging from a ghetto populated by the dedicated ATOs and their supporters, and into the mainstream world of retail and supermarkets where consumers did not need to step into that ghetto.

Those who were key players in the birth of the Fair Trade movement operated under the mantra of "in the end, all trade must become fair".[37] EFTA would go on to co-found Transfair International which would operate in other European countries and Traidcraft would play the leading role in enabling the same for the UK, co-founding the Fairtrade Foundation. It was a simple proposition. Mainstream businesses, if they respected very specific Fair Trade criteria for a product and opened themselves up to external monitoring, would be awarded a "seal of

---

37   European Fair Trade Association, *Fair Trade Yearbook 1995*, Maastricht: EFTA, p. 11.

approval" for their retail product. A simple proposition, yes, but the complications in practice would be something I would live and breathe for many years to come.

Lots of different label designs in different countries existed for many years: the Transfair label had different versions in different countries, the Max Havelaar label which had also spread beyond the Netherlands, and the Fairtrade Mark in the UK. A unification in 1997 created "Fairtrade Labelling Organizations International", or FLO as it became known, but still there were many different labels. The letterhead for FLO documentation was a complicated affair since all international labels needed to be represented. It was not until the 2000s that a unification of labels happened but even then, and to this day, the Max Havelaar and Transfair identities have been retained in some countries.

One other significant membership organization emerged during the 1990s – the "Network of European World Shops" or NEWS. "World shops" were small retail outlets dedicated to promoting Fair Trade and selling Fair Trade products and many would also have associated educational and campaigning activities. These shops had existed for a while and were the main route to market for many of the EFTA members. World shops also existed in the UK and some of those early Traidcraft supporters or voluntary representatives had gone on to establish their own world shop. NEWS brought all of these national initiatives together and the UK coordinating member became BAFTS, the British Association of Fair Trade Shops.

Together the four established membership organizations would join to talk and collaborate and in 2001 would establish a formal definition of Fair Trade which has remained virtually unchanged to this day. It was called the FINE (FLO, IFAT, NEWS, EFTA) definition which states:

> Fair Trade is a trading partnership, based on dialogue,
> transparency and respect, that seeks greater equity
> in international trade. It contributes to sustainable
> development by offering better trading conditions to, and
> securing the rights of, marginalized producers and workers
> – especially in the South. Fair Trade Organizations, backed
> by consumers, are engaged actively in supporting producers,

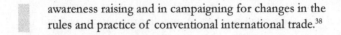

awareness raising and in campaigning for changes in the
rules and practice of conventional international trade.[38]

This definition was formally embraced into the so-called "International
Fair Trade Charter", jointly authored by World Fair Trade Organisation
and Fairtrade International in 2009 and relaunched in 2018

---

38   International Fair Trade Charter, which can be viewed in full at https://www.fair-
     trade.website/the-charter-1, p.17

Chapter 13

FAIRTRADE LABELLING

The Max Havelaar Foundation had been established in 1988 and not long after that the groundwork for the establishment of a similar organization in the UK had begun. Richard Adams, founder of Traidcraft, had left to establish *New Consumer Magazine* and joining him, also from Traidcraft, was Phil Wells who had worked in the Traidcraft Educational Foundation since 1982, having originally been a Traidcraft rep in London. Phil writes:

> I moved on to join Richard at *New Consumer* and co-wrote *The Global Consumer*, trying to do for Fair Trade what the *Green Consumer Guide* did for the environment.[39] *The Global Consumer* turned into more of a manifesto than a consumer guide and revealed just how little interest or understanding there was among consumers and in businesses about the environmental, human rights, and developmental impact in supply chains.
>
> But, in a sense, it did pave the way conceptually for the Fairtrade Mark – the idea being to develop objective ways to assess best practice, initially in commodity

---

39   Phil Wells and Mandy Jetter, *The Global Consumer: best buys to help the Third World*, London: Orion Publishing, 1991. John Elkington & Julia Hailes, *The Green Consumer Guide*, London: Victor Gollancz, 1989.

trading, and reward this with a consumer logo. It's fair to say that attitudes among the ATO/FTO community ranged from guarded to negative. The main issue for most was basically that Fair Trade can only be done by non-profit organizations – and the main point of disagreement was over the likelihood of these ever improving the lives of even a small proportion of producers. Organizations like Traidcraft decided to "ride the tiger" and make the most of the rising tide.

Richard Adams and Bill Yates, Oxfam's head of campaigns, met with the Max Havelaar Foundation and its co-founder Solidaridad and came back fired up. They started to lobby various non-governmental organisations (NGOs) and charities, and a steering committee was established in 1989 which later became the Fairtrade Foundation (FTF) with Richard as founding director.

I started working for two days a week for FTF, working with Richard, initially as "standards manager". The project developed slowly with little traction amongst food retailers. The issue with the supermarkets was that any Fairtrade products raised a question about their own product provenance, so our strategy was to work with supermarkets to develop their overall approach to supply chains in the developing world, at the same time as encouraging them to provide shelf space for the likes of some of those early Fairtrade labelled brands like Clipper, and Green & Black's. I became the chief executive of FTF, with only one other member of staff, and worked closely with the Co-op and Sainsbury's to develop their code of practice. This approach then dovetailed well with the social accounting work pioneered by Traidcraft and the organization that was established from that – Accountability – and we worked together to launch the Ethical Trading Initiative. It worked, and allowed these two retailers to break ranks – and the rest is history![40]

---

40 From personal correspondence with the author, 2019.

For those of us working at Traidcraft in those days, it was a case of watching with interest and continuing to be supportive, with the Traidcraft Exchange holding a position on the board of FTF. But a label was not for Traidcraft products. I suppose we could easily have been first with a Fairtrade label. Many of our products would have qualified because they met the standards, but we retained the position that this was designed for supermarkets, for mainstream businesses. In other words, not for those who were dedicated FTOs, unless they happened to want to sell into supermarkets, which we did not want to do at that time. This would cause some confusion among Traidcraft supporters and customers for several years.

It was not until the early 2000s that things changed and that there was support and a compelling reason to use the Fairtrade Mark on Traidcraft products. This paved the way for a very close working relationship with the Fairtrade Foundation, whether sales and marketing initiatives, campaigning, or product development. It was this latter category that caused me to get quite involved in standards development work and, for a while, Traidcraft was either a kind of guinea pig for the development of new approaches to Fairtrade or was the catalyst in the development of new product standards for Fairtrade.

Composite products

One example which stands out is in the development of so-called Fairtrade "composite products", meaning a product containing more than one ingredient. Before this, FLO had only a few product standards – and most of those products were very clear. A pack of tea or a pack of coffee carrying a Fairtrade Mark meant that the content was 100% Fairtrade tea or coffee. Other products had emerged like honey, but only honey sold in a jar could carry a Fairtrade Mark. Other products like dried fruit, nuts, and sugar were emerging and all of these new products could easily be used as an ingredient. In fact, the bulk of their consumption was as an ingredient, for example in biscuits, but there was no scope for the Fairtrade Mark to be used on such products.

Traidcraft had, by then, obtained a supermarket listing for its Geobar, created to use more honey and more dried fruit. It could not carry a Fairtrade Mark because it was neither a 100% dried fruit product nor a 100% honey product. Apart from that, with the development of

Fairtrade sugar, a light was shone on Fairtrade labelled chocolate bars which, hitherto, had not required Fairtrade sugar to be used. In fact, a chocolate bar was regarded as a cocoa product and the fact that it was also a composite product was conveniently overlooked. Geobar had been launched without a Fairtrade Mark in one supermarket but there were opportunities to grow and extend into other supermarkets and, to do that, a Fairtrade Mark was regarded as essential.

Geobar became the testing ground for a new composite product standard which was eventually adopted by FLO and rolled out globally, and today all chocolate products, biscuits, cakes, and more which carry a Fairtrade Mark need to comply with that standard. Some of those early formats of the Fairtrade Mark can be seen in pictures of the original Geobar packaging, with all manner of "percentage content" illustrations bolted onto the now familiar mark. It had to be acknowledged that there might be a need to use ingredients which were not Fairtrade. Milk in chocolate and flour in baked products are good examples. For Geobar, it was oats and rice and it would only be several years later that Fairtrade rice emerged. We tried a minimum percentage content by value of Fairtrade ingredients which proved difficult to monitor, and settled for a minimum percentage content by dry weight of Fairtrade ingredients, and a principle that if an ingredient could be Fairtrade then it should be Fairtrade. Various tweaks to this standard have occurred over the years but the essential principles, as trialled through Geobar, remain the same.

For the first few years of FLO's existence, cooperation like this was commonplace and extended throughout Europe. After all, the EFTA members and other FTOs provided a decent slice of the FLO income through the licence fees they paid to use the Fairtrade Mark. In fact, we were quite lucky in the UK and enjoyed much lower fees than our EFTA counterparts. All of us engaged in the work of FLO, exchanging information on producer partners, contributing our experience and knowledge, and even doing some of the standards development work. I recall that the early dried fruit standards of FLO were written by Traidcraft and Tropical Wholefoods and I was even commissioned (and trusted) to set some of the minimum prices for South African dried fruit on one of my regular overseas visits. In those early days, FLO operated product registers and product committees where standards development, monitoring against those standards, and inspections, were all fairly integrated. Later on, the standards development and the certification process would be rightly separated. EFTA was fully informed of what was happening in FLO and even entered into a formal partnership agreement covering the scope of cooperation.

Fair Trade standards

The FLO International Forum, started in 2001, brought producers and traders together in one place to discuss all things Fairtrade and it was interesting to observe some of the cracks starting to appear. There are lots of passionate people involved in Fair Trade with a common goal to see a changed world, but there are lots of different opinions on the ways to achieve this goal. One of those differences of opinions revolved around whether Fairtrade should even allow plantations into the system and this was especially expressed by the Latin American contingent who mostly represented coffee cooperatives. They had seen at first hand the negative effects on their organizations of coffee grown on plantations, which they regarded as unfair competition. This smallholder versus plantation issue would continue for years but be managed through most of FLO's product standards being restricted to smallholder producers. However, it would ultimately be the reason for the USA to split from FLO International and create its own system which incorporated more plantations, and controversially that included coffee.

Being quite involved in Fairtrade standards work led me to be proposed by the Fairtrade Foundation to join the FLO Standards Committee and I was duly appointed in 2003 and would serve in this capacity for the next nine years. All of the committees of FLO ensured that all stakeholders were represented – traders, producers, and those, like the Fairtrade Foundation, who awarded the Fairtrade Mark within a region. I would represent FTOs on this committee and would renew my acquaintance with Phil Wells who chaired it for a while. This was all part of Traidcraft's "influencing" strategy of the 2000s and I was released to do this although, in reality, it probably had many commercial benefits to Traidcraft as I attempted to influence the way standards were developed throughout that time.

Being part of that FLO Standards Committee enabled me to experience the breadth of the Fair Trade movement and some of the tensions involved. Supermarkets, large traders, and big brands were entering Fairtrade, and agreeing the monetary value of something like a "guaranteed minimum price" or a "Fairtrade premium" would have a major influence on their degree of support and participation. The balance between keeping those prices at "affordable" levels for the traders, yet still being "fair" to producers, would sometimes cause much debate and disagreement, more often than not between the trader representatives and the producer representatives on the committee. This was not a new scenario to Traidcraft and even in its one-to-one discussion with its own suppliers, defining exactly what a fair price looks like was occasionally a complex task, especially for handicrafts. The default position would always be to accept the price that was offered, but if that would compromise whether or not the product could be sold, then entering into what I sometimes described as "fair negotiation" would commence. Translating this principle into a global Fairtrade system would ultimately mean that not everyone would be happy with the outcome.

The Standards Committee would usually meet in Bonn twice a year but on one occasion it was decided to take the meeting to one of the producing countries. FLO has occasionally been described as a neo-colonial institution despite its producer membership and participation, and maybe a bit too Eurocentric, so we all descended upon the Lake Naivasha region of Kenya, with its multitude of Fairtrade certified flower farms, to conduct a Standards Committee meeting. There were at least more African observers present than European observers this time and it was great fun. In principle, it was a progressive thing to do but hugely expensive and probably not something that would be attempted too often.

People have occasionally asked me, as someone who has been part of an organization that pioneered approaches to mainstreaming Fair Trade, what I think of FLO and the Fairtrade Mark. My reply has always been that I both love and hate it and I know that many of my contemporaries who lived and breathed Fair Trade through their experiences of working for a dedicated FTO would share that view. Someone once said to me that the worst thing that happened to FLO was that it became a system of certification regulated by ISEAL (International Social and Environmental Accreditation and Labelling) which is the global membership association for credible sustainability standards. Lots of things changed in those early 2000s and words like "compliance" and "non-compliance" entered the language of Fair Trade. Producer organizations and traders started to pay to be certified by FLO and this was in addition to the fees that licensees needed to pay for their brands to carry the Fairtrade Mark. Relationships became different, more formal, and words like "partnership" diminished and were used most frequently by the dedicated FTOs. The retail sector called for such certification so, in some ways, it was a necessary direction of travel to achieve the volume of Fairtrade sales which would result in impact at scale for producers.

This would have consequences for Traidcraft and for many of the Fairtrade certified producer organizations we imported from. The cost of compliance, both financial and human, would be burdensome for many of those producers. Several of our suppliers were suspended and occasionally decertified and we and they would feel somewhat aggrieved by this, especially where the "non-compliances" were more technical than material. On one infamous occasion, one of our Indian suppliers was suspended for exceeding the Fair Trade standards in a way that producers benefited to a greater extent than the standards prescribed. This meant that they could not trade under Fairtrade conditions until the issue was resolved. I was so angry that I confess that I wrote a very uncomplimentary letter of protest to FLO, although to no avail.

Later on, FLO would give more strategic priority to what they called "major products" like coffee, tea, or cocoa and less to what they called "minor products" like dried fruit, nuts, or spices. This would mean that, on occasion, Traidcraft might be the only customer for a producer organization and the question of viability arose. As the 2010s wore on, Traidcraft would need to consider whether or not it would be forced to remove the Fairtrade Mark from some of its products.

Then FLO introduced the concept of single ingredient certification which meant that some brands could carry Fairtrade messaging but not be required to meet the composite products policy referred to earlier. At the time, they called this new approach their "Fairtrade Sourcing Programme" or FSP. For many in the Fairtrade Movement, this was met with huge negativity. It was "selling out" and threatened a dilution of Fairtrade standards. Undoubtedly, it would also mean greater impact for some producers as big brands would commit to buying huge amounts of their raw materials, particularly cocoa, on Fairtrade terms. Traidcraft would always be asked for a view on these developments and, as a measured organization, would present a balanced view. I recall writing a website piece in 2015 which would sum up our approach when Mars started to use Fairtrade cocoa, and painted a picture of what Fair Trade meant to us as compared to these initiatives to mainstream Fair Trade. It still feels relevant enough to reproduce, and can be read in full in Appendix 2.

I think that FLO had always struggled with how to deal with the dedicated FTOs like Traidcraft and our EFTA colleagues. While the relationship that we had with their national labelling member, the Fairtrade Foundation, was positive, in other European countries it was not so healthy. Were we all really part of "one movement'? Most of our EFTA colleagues began to remove the Fairtrade Mark from their packaging while still retaining their status as Fairtrade certified traders. They would say that such a label detracted from their own brand and that their approach to doing Fair Trade was at a higher level than, for example, a supermarket who used the Fairtrade Mark. Traidcraft would think or say the same things but continue to apply the Fairtrade Mark to its products. The good collaboration in the UK did yield positive discussions and, at one stage, there were serious proposals to create a new Fairtrade Mark just for the FTOs – a kind of "gold standard" recognizing that the FTOs went beyond merely complying with a set of standards. In the end, this never happened. It was the same story. Lots of people and organizations passionate about Fair Trade, but with lots of different opinions and approaches and there could be no consensus. By the 2010s, other Fair Trade certification systems were emerging; they would start to interest the FTOs, and Traidcraft was no exception.

Fair Trade standards were being developed by some of the organic certifiers. One of them, Fair for Life, covered the Traidcraft palm oil project, although we never chose to use that label. I regarded the most interesting alternative labelling system as one developed by producers themselves. Emerging from the Latin American and Caribbean Network of Small Fair Trade Producers, it became known as the "Small

Producer Symbol" or SPP (its Spanish acronym) and was restricted only to smallholder producers, harking back to that early "plantation versus smallholder" conflict of opinion. A certification scheme wholly owned by producers was surely something that Traidcraft should seek to support, so we aspired to support its use in the UK.

Chapter 14

WORKING WITH EFTA

I was a fairly active participant in the workings of the European Fair Trade Association over the years and represented Traidcraft in several of the working groups. The transition from Alternative Trade to Fair Trade was happening in its early days and we would begin to refer to ourselves as Fair Trade Organizations (FTOs) rather than Alternative Trading Organizations or ATOs. The emergence of Fairtrade labelling was also happening and there was an acceleration in development of more and more Fair Trade food products. Therefore, foods and handicrafts had their separate working groups called PPC–Food and PPC–Handicrafts. PPC stood for "Product and Producer Committee" and met at least twice a year to discuss common producers and look for opportunities for joint product developments. For handicrafts, it was harder to do this joint product development because markets were so different and what worked in the UK was not always reproduced in other parts of Europe. Consequently, the PPC–Handicraft group would focus more on common producers and would eventually phase out as a useful committee in later years.

PPC–Food was much more productive and, over the years, the sharing of workload became commonplace. The word "supplier" was never used in relationship to producer organizations. They were referred to as "partners" which absolutely signified our common view of Fair Trade. Things formalized such that a member might propose themselves to buy everything from a single producer organization on behalf of another member and also to provide information about that organization. This worked really well for coffee and by the mid-1990s there were literally dozens of coffee cooperatives selling into the collective EFTA membership, with regular buying and selling between members. Buyers were known as "partner attenders" and there were formal EFTA trading agreements which meant that pricing was totally transparent and there would be no need for any negotiation. Traidcraft played into this partner attendance activity and we became the source of things like dried fruit for much of the EFTA group.

For example, Traidcraft did not need to work directly with producers or import any coffee beans despite being significant coffee retailers because someone else in EFTA did that on our behalf. Our natural EFTA partner for coffee was Oxfam Fairtrade in Belgium who bought everything we needed for a complete roast and ground coffee range. For much of the history of Traidcraft, neither I nor any of my colleagues would set foot overseas anywhere near a coffee cooperative represented in that range, yet we were equipped with lots of information about each cooperative, were fully informed about the impact of Fair Trade on them, and indirectly contributed to producer support projects conducted by Oxfam Fairtrade.

The other early success in EFTA was the development of a chocolate bar called Mascao. Other product initiatives were less successful and would reflect market differences in each of the European countries. For example, there were lots of initiatives between members in tea, but there was little to align the tea drinking habits of the UK and those of mainland Europe where tea is almost a completely different product. Consequently, Traidcraft always needed to do its own thing for anything tea-related. Similarly, instant coffee was, and probably still is, a pretty alien concept for the rest of Europe yet dominated the UK market, so there was little collaboration on this product.

But there were lots of other differences between Traidcraft and the rest of the EFTA members – and maybe there were some parallels between our membership of EFTA and the UK's membership of the European Union. Our "island nation" mentality sometimes meant that we stood alone in EFTA. For example, we would display a degree of pragmatism when it came to products containing more than one ingredient which was Fair Trade. Virtually every other EFTA member would refuse to compromise below an ingredient content of 50%, yet

Traidcraft was developing products where this was just not possible – mueslis and snack bars, for example. As time passed, most EFTA members took an organic focus and some even switched to only Fairtrade *and* organic certified. This was one of the key reasons that the first Fair Trade chocolate bar, Mascao, was also organic.

PPC meetings were occasionally adventurous affairs. In those early days, when money was tight (or maybe it was a natural affinity to frugality), the venues and locations of meetings were rather hit-or-miss. Dormitory accommodation and remoteness were the order of the day. In fact, for a while, it was deemed important to meet well away from urban areas in order to focus the mind and to meet where managing to find the meeting venue would be regarded as a success, whether a remote vineyard in Italy in the summer or high up in the Swiss Alps in winter! In fact, despite my many years of travelling to developing countries, one of my most worrying experiences in travelling was trying to locate a remote Swiss conference centre, past midnight, in a blizzard!

We would share our various product development projects, the new partners we were working with, and telling the tales of overseas visits, but ultimately it was a place to do business. Many of the products which Traidcraft introduced through the years originated from those experiences. Later on, things became a bit more professional. Locations for meetings would become more accessible and we would begin to meet at the headquarters of the host member. We would even stay in hotels and could choose a single room!

Other EFTA working groups were established. The leaders of each member would meet as the EFTA Managers, overseeing strategy and purpose, and there would be other groups meeting occasionally, covering such things as marketing or quality management. During the 2000s, EFTA would certainly pay greater attention to developments in FLO, especially relating to the PPC–Food group, and there would be regular joint meetings of FLO staff and EFTA to discuss standards, new initiatives, and producer issues. We all used the Fairtrade label on a broad range of products – but, as Fairtrade labelling increased in scale, these joint meetings became rarer and the place of those original pioneer, dedicated FTOs came under scrutiny. FLO had turned its attention toward mainstream players and supermarket own-label products and each EFTA member needed to respond in its own way and based on its own experiences within its own country. One of the senior members of staff at FLO once said to me that he lost sleep wondering what might become of organizations like Traidcraft and the rest of the EFTA members in the face of Fairtrade labelling becoming so mainstream. I never really believed him and had a sense that maybe he wished we didn't really exist because there were bigger fish to fry and because he had to deal with our regular challenge toward FLO to keep true to the founding principles of Fair Trade.

Each EFTA member would respond to the growing competition in their own countries from Fairtrade labelled products and, during the 2010s, some would remove the label from their products and would even regard the Fairtrade label as something that would tarnish their own-brand credentials. Not so for Traidcraft because of our continued good relationship with the Fairtrade Foundation and the fact that there was a huge overlap between Traidcraft supporters and those involved in their work.

The key EFTA working group that emerged during the 2000s was something called the EFTA Monitoring Group. With the growth of Fairtrade labelling – where third-party auditing was considered important – it became less and less acceptable for our products which did not carry a Fairtrade Mark to be under less scrutiny than those products that did. This would mean every handicraft product and every food product not covered by Fairtrade labelling. As described elsewhere in this book, many of us were already getting a bit more serious about this and had developed our own internal monitoring systems, but now it was time to centralize, to share resources and costs, and a new monitoring system was established. It was not third-party audited but many of us felt that it was as good as, if not better than, the systems used by FLO, and retained the personal touch and the partnership approach that were essential to the way we all operated as FTOs.

Chapter 15

MEMBERSHIP OF WFTO AND OTHER COLLABORATIONS

While Traidcraft was pivotal in the development of IFAT (International Federation of Alternative Trade), it settled into a membership role. Various members of staff participated in conferences through the years, both regional and global. I did not have much involvement in those early days of IFAT because it was fairly focused on handicrafts. Much of the membership from the global south consisted of handicraft producer organizations, whereas I was involved mostly with developing Traidcraft's food range and policy. In fact, it seemed that any FTO that had a food focus would find it quite difficult to be active within IFAT, but it was still considered that membership was important because this was the one place where all of the dedicated global Fair Trade players could come together as one. IFAT still retained its "alternative trade" principles and terminology well into the 1990s, despite "Fair Trade" having become the adopted global terminology. Finally, acknowledging the inevitable, IFAT changed its name and became the International Fair Trade Association. The acronym did not undergo any change and the organization was still known as IFAT until 2009 when it became the World Fair Trade Organization (WFTO). This change from "alternative" to "fair" was not without its detractors and, through the years, I confess that I occasionally found myself hankering after the old name and felt that it meant something different and bigger. For some of us, the word "alternative" was much more meaningful than "fair" and best described the whole approach to trading.

With the advent of the 2000s, the growth of Fairtrade labelling, and its participation in the FINE (FLO, IFAT, NEWS, EFTA) working group which led to more clarity on the definition of Fair Trade, IFAT decided that it needed to develop its own set of standards as to what properly defined a Fair Trade Organization. These standards, which then became known as "principles", were agreed in 2001 and became central to the way that Traidcraft organized its monitoring activities, both of its suppliers and itself. The principles have evolved over the years although remain largely the same as those early days. Considering their importance to Traidcraft and the fact that those of us working with our overseas producers began to live and breathe them, the 2018 principles are reproduced in full in Appendix 3, and the ten principles are listed here:

Ten Principles of Fair Trade[41]

1. Opportunities for Economically Disadvantaged Producers.

2. Transparency and Accountability.

3. Fair Trading Practices.

4. Fair Payment (fair prices, fair wages, and local living wages).

5. Ensuring No Child Labour, No Forced Labour.

6. No Discrimination, Gender Equity, Women's Economic Empowerment, Freedom of Association.

7. Good Working Conditions.

8. Capacity Building.

9. Promoting Fair Trade.

10. Respect for the Environment

---

41 WFTO, "Ten Principles of Fair Trade", reproduced with permission. See https://wfto.com/who-we-are

Not everything would be straightforward as a member of what I'll now refer to as WFTO. The application of these principles relied largely on self-assessment and neither Traidcraft, nor any of our fellow EFTA members would be able to take at face value that membership of WFTO was proof of a Fair Trade product. The EFTA centralized monitoring system developed during the 2000s would highlight some of the inadequacies of self-assessment. On more than one occasion, as our team visited some of our developing world suppliers (which would include WFTO members) to implement this monitoring system, we would identify issues which were potentially a threat to our reputation. There was a sense that WFTO were applying quantity over quality in its membership approach and this was something that worried many of us. There were other concerning issues within WFTO and the overall sense was that we could also use our membership fees more productively. This ultimately caused Traidcraft plc to withdraw its membership. Some would say that, as an act of solidarity, we should have remained but we chose instead to continue the membership through the Traidcraft Exchange which held membership in its own right as a charitable organization.

As WFTO entered the 2010s, it decided that a more robust monitoring system was required, one that had credibility and, while not being a system of certification as had been implemented by FLO, one which could be verified through external and independent auditing. So was born what is now the WFTO Guarantee System and it was time for Traidcraft plc to re-join the WFTO. I was to lead this process in 2017 as probably my final significant contribution to Traidcraft before I moved on. Ironically, this process shone a very bright light on how Traidcraft was implementing each of the ten Fair Trade principles and, for some of them, we had become a bit too complacent and needed to make improvements. Sometimes an organization like Traidcraft can regard itself more highly than it deserves and should practise more of what it preaches. On occasion we had been accused, with some justification, of arrogance – especially in the organization's most recent history.

Working with other brands

As well as membership of EFTA and WFTO, there was plenty of collaboration among other Fair Trade Organizations in the UK itself.

The Cafédirect coffee brand and the Divine chocolate brand had always featured in the Traidcraft range of products – although for these two, there were occasional tensions because they were effectively both collaborators and competitors. While we were one of the joint founders of Cafédirect, we were always going to continue to sell coffee and tea under the Traidcraft brand. After all, we had sold coffee products since the 1980s. Similarly, we had also been successfully selling Fair Trade chocolate before Divine even existed and would continue to do so. There was the occasional sense that, out of an act of solidarity, Traidcraft should drop its chocolate, coffee and tea and give those dedicated product brands clear space. Traidcraft, through the 1990s and beyond, always regarded itself as a kind of incubator for new brands, introducing them to the vast Traidcraft supporter base. However, this certainly was not at the expense of our own business, given that those brands would seek to become more aligned to supermarket selling – and we had no such plans. It was a bit different for other brands like Liberation Nuts, and it was a sheer joy to collaborate with the wonderful Zaytoun brand and bring their olive oil into the Traidcraft range. Their support of marginalized Palestinian producer communities played right into the "justice" theme of Traidcraft and, during the 2000s, was a great solution to our strategic intent of developing more edible oil products. Other collaborations, for example, with Tropical Wholefoods and Fullwell Mill were just as important and all of those key Fair Trade players in the UK would formally meet together regularly as the UK Fair Trade Leaders Forum to share and collaborate in all things relating to the world of Fair Trade in the UK and, occasionally, to work through some of those tensions. If it had a weakness, it was in determining who *were* the key Fair Trade players. Enthusiasm and participation tended toward those who used the Fairtrade Mark on their products and less on those who were involved solely in handicrafts.

During the 2010s, sales were declining gradually year on year. Attempts to stem this decline caused even greater degrees of collaboration through the listing of other Fair Trade brands, although we did try to become a little more discerning about which brands we would allow into the Traidcraft range. Online marketing messaging would use descriptions like "the best of Fair Trade" and the Traidcraft purchasing policy was adapted to give some rationale for decision-making and head off the possibility of Traidcraft ever selling something like a Kit Kat carrying a Fairtrade Mark. An extract from that policy read as follows:

- We will only buy the brands of organizations who share our values and who embrace Fair Trade as an integral part of their mission and objectives rather than mere compliance with a standard or certification to satisfy commercial objectives.

- There may be exceptional circumstances where we are unable to buy the brands of organizations described above. For example, where gaps emerge in Traidcraft Fair Trade product ranges because of supply chain problems or where there are temporary stock issues. In such circumstances, we will consider the selection of other Fair Trade brands.

- Recognizing that for some Southern Fair Trade Organizations or suppliers of Fair Trade products, marketing of their own brand is an important developmental step. Traidcraft will seek to promote such brands where appropriate and commercially viable.[42]

This latter category of Fair Trade brands was always something I was interested to give some focus to. Rather than Traidcraft being the incubator of newly developing Fair Trade brands based in the UK (as we were in the 1990s and beyond), maybe it was time to apply the same principle for those emerging brands in the global south. The concept of value addition or ensuring as much of the cost of a product could stay in the country of origin had always been a feature of Traidcraft's work and this was a good opportunity to put more of it into practice. Natural partnerships emerged with "Just Trading Scotland" who shared a similar principle, and "Proudly Made in Africa" which was an Irish development agency promoting and assisting African brands. We called the initiative "Producer Brands" and started to sell a whole range of products produced and packed within Africa but sadly, while

---

42 Traidcraft internal document, written by the author, 2012, also published on the Traidcraft website..

the principles were worthy, the execution was less so and the expected sales did not materialize.

A final word in this chapter goes to Rudi Dalvai, a leading advocate for Fair Trade in Europe for many years, and president of WFTO for much of that time:

> When I started to get involved in Fair Trade in 1987, Traidcraft was already a landmark for the Fair Trade movement in Europe and one of the "Fair Trade lighthouses" that indicated the right direction. It was the year in which EFTA and IFAT had been shaped and began their success story. Traidcraft played a leading role in this process and also played a leading role in forming the UK Fair Trade Leaders Forum and other UK Fair Trade Organizations. There are no doubts that Traidcraft is one of the Fair Trade pioneers and has significantly contributed to write Fair Trade history in the UK and at a global level.
>
> I was always impressed by the dedication of Traidcraft to support marginalized artisans and small farmer organizations in developing countries, and by their contribution to promote Fair Trade values at national and international level.
>
> The Fair Trade market is becoming more and more challenging for FTOs and great joint efforts are needed to be able to guarantee continuous work for artisans and small farmers. But luckily, there are still new opportunities for Fair Trade and for Fair Trade products which are there to be explored. WFTO will do its best to support its members to do so and to promote the identity of organizations which are fully dedicated to Fair Trade. I am sure that with continued working together we are able to continue to write the Fair Trade success story.[43]

---

43 From personal correspondence with the author, 2019.

PART FIVE

Innovation – A History
of Fair Trade "Firsts"

Chapter 16

A FAIR BREW

WDM (World Development Movement) tea, which was launched in the early 1980s, paved the way for a journey in tea which stretches almost the entire history of Traidcraft. Since I played a major part, I thought that it was worth writing about some of the details of that journey – the ups and downs, the experiences, and the "firsts" which can rightly be attributed to Traidcraft in the development of Fair Trade in tea.

I tried to remember how many tea factories I had visited over the years and stopped counting at thirty. I managed to cover virtually every significant tea growing region of the world including Sri Lanka, Darjeeling, Assam, South India, Kenya, Tanzania, Uganda, Malawi, and even Mauritius.

In the 1980s, those of us who visited the Waulugala tea estate in Sri Lanka enjoyed (although some would say "risked", based on the frequency of subsequent stomach ailments) the hospitality of the benevolent Dissanayake family who had set up the Sambodhi Trust which owned the estate. The trust was involved in a range of social development projects which included the construction of medical facilities and running care homes for orphaned children, mentally or physically disabled people, and the elderly.

The estate was quite small compared to a typical tea estate, producing small volumes and employing fewer workers. Half of the profits supported the work of the Sambodhi Trust, and the other half went directly to the workers on the estate, whether involved in plucking and collecting the tea leaf, or working in the processing factory. This was in the form of a lump sum annual bonus.

Wages for employees on tea estates in Sri Lanka were regulated by government and there were minimum requirements for working and living conditions which we found Waulugala to exceed. It was not quite the model established for Fairtrade in the world of tea later on, but it was not far off, and it met Traidcraft's requirement to source from origins which went beyond the minimums, in an industry where those minimums meant hardship and poverty.

Traidcraft's model for tea also included a 10% premium on the retail price which, in partnership with WDM, was used in a range of tea-related development projects, not just in Sri Lanka, but throughout the world. This model would apply until the standards for Fairtrade certified tea became established in the 1990s.

That first WDM tea was a reasonable quality, loose leaf, broken orange pekoe grade of tea produced by the so-called orthodox method, but it was inconsistent. There were occasional supply issues, and we didn't really understand the tea trade and its seasonal characteristics which meant that quality would be variable throughout the year. There was an added value element to the tea by having it packed in Sri Lanka, but this could not be the case when we came to add teabags to the range. That technology in Sri Lanka was at an early stage and it was very expensive, both to make and to ship. So began a close relationship with our local tea merchant and packer, Ringtons Ltd, based in Newcastle-upon-Tyne, which would last until the present day. Ringtons was a family business which had been around since the early 1900s and they were (and still are) very well known in the north east of England through their colourful vans delivering direct to the doorstep. They were an obvious outfit to get in touch with to help us out. They would later go on to be the largest importer of Fairtrade certified teas in the UK, but since Fairtrade didn't exist in those days, I suspect that Ringtons might have regarded that original activity as doing a bit of a favour for a fellow Tyneside business. They were willing to take delivery of the wooden tea chests that Traidcraft imported, pass the tea through their tea-bagging machines and refill those tea chests with teabags to be shipped over to Traidcraft which were then packed by hand into plastic bags ready for sale. And as a small sideline business, the tea chests proved to be popular since, in those days, they were useful when moving to a new home.

Through the 1980s and into the early 1990s, as sales grew, additional tea suppliers emerged, and new tea products were added to the range. One of our suppliers of craft products – Equitable Marketing Association, based in Kolkata (then known as Calcutta) in India – was doing some work with emerging worker cooperative tea estates in Tripura and Assam and we developed a project with them which would see another WDM branded product launched and with a similar added value model to the original WDM tea because it was packed in Kolkata.

Visiting some of these potential sources would take up much of my time in that era. On one occasion, I decided that I would visit the Woka tea estate, a worker cooperative estate in Assam. I recall the visit vividly since Assam had quite restricted access due to instability in the region. I managed to get my passport stamped with "permission to travel" and ventured alongside our key contact from Equitable Marketing Association into Assam. The memory is vivid because of the tight security, the constant need for all foreign nationals to report their movements, and consequently the time it took to travel relatively small distances due to sitting around in local police stations awaiting permission to move on to the next district. (And probably, unknown to me, my colleague passing on appropriate sums of money to move things along more quickly!) While the concept of a worker cooperative estate sounds good in theory, the visit resulted in us not progressing the relationship much further since the gap between theory and practice left a lot to be desired. I recall that it was with great relief that I left Assam!

While developing sugar sourcing in Mauritius, we came to understand that there was a tea industry there and that some of this tea was from an estate with a purportedly good reputation for worker care. We quickly verified this and linked up with our sugar packer in Mauritius – Craft Aid – and a third added value and packed-at-origin tea became part of the range. The tea estates we sourced from were named Bios Cheri and Dubreuil – but, in later years, the Mauritian tea industry would shrink to a fraction of the size as tea bushes were uprooted in favour of expanding sugar cane plantations.

During the 1980s, the Traidcraft purchasing policy was only just developing and allowed sourcing from "countries seeking justice for their rural poor through active development policies".[44] Tanzania was one of those countries, so a 100% Tanzanian tea was added to the range both in teabags and loose tea. This product was to be one of the longest standing products in our tea range and proved to be hugely popular with customers, despite Tanzania not really being recognized as a so-called "single origin" country, or renowned for "speciality tea". Sourcing from Tanzania this early would stand us in good stead in the future as we developed a relationship with the Kibena tea estate (owned by the Commonwealth Development Corporation) which would be an origin used throughout the Traidcraft and the Teadirect ranges for years to come.

The Nilgiri hills of Southern India is one of the largest tea-growing regions of India, although not as well-known as Assam or Darjeeling to the UK consumer. Three interesting sources were identified here. First, Tantea (the Tamil Nadu Tea Plantation Corporation) was set up by the Tamil Nadu state government to provide work for Tamil people repatriated from Sri Lanka; second, Incoserve (the Tamil Nadu Industrial Cooperative Factories Federation), which was a non-profit cooperative movement with many thousands of smallholder members who would have their teas processed in one of the fifteen Incoserve tea factories throughout the region; and third, there was the Priyadarshini tea estate run by the Mananthavady Tribal Plantation Cooperative.

Rather than buy from these producers separately we developed a relationship with a sympathetic tea broker based in Coonoor, who would source and blend these teas before shipping. It was here that I first observed in any great depth the science or art of tea tasting. Their most skilled tea taster could blindly detect the teas from any of the dozens of factories in the region and feed back to them on problems or improvements to be made in processing. It was also here that the challenges of putting together a tea range based solely on the ethical credentials of the origins were brought into focus. South Indian teas were, by and large, produced for the Indian market. Cheapness and questionable quality characterized the industry, given that virtually all tea would find its way into that Indian favourite, sweet chai. Tea bushes

---

44 Traidcraft internal document, early 1980s.

were stripped of their leaves as opposed to having the finest leaf plucked, especially for the Incoserve sources. These leaves would be processed in the local factory and all grades of the finished tea which normally would be regarded as "secondary" were promptly thrown back into the production process. This was most definitely a strategy of quantity over quality!

In my visits to Coonoor, I was made to work hard and on one short visit found myself having been committed to two speaking engagements – one in the local secondary school talking to pupils in the morning assembly about career development and one at the local Round Table meeting talking to the great and the good of the local tea industry about Fair Trade. A third speaking engagement emerged on that same visit when a mutual interest in Christian worship music cropped up in conversation with one of the owners of the brokerage and the fact that we both played in our local church music group. So I was promptly invited to that evening's band practice to talk and share about worship music!

We were importing from India, Mauritius, Sri Lanka, and Tanzania. All of these countries had one thing in common which was a coast on the Indian Ocean. What would become Traidcraft's largest single tea product became rebranded as Indian Ocean Tea Bags, a name which would last for years.

A range of single origin or speciality teas was added and it included another interesting origin from India, this time not really from any well-known tea growing region at all. The recently established Palampur Co-operative Tea Factory was based in the Kangra Valley region of Himachal Pradesh in the Himalayan foothills. Three hundred smallholder farmers who owned shares in the factory supplied their leaf – which was processed into teas similar to that of Darjeeling in taste and quality, but could not be called Darjeeling because it wasn't grown there. Despite the temptation, honesty was always the best policy, and Kangra tea was launched. Sadly, it proved short-lived because it just didn't sell, and no one could quite cope with a product which was marketed as "similar to Darjeeling".

Eventually, we would bite a bullet on Darjeeling tea and, as the Fairtrade certified tea origins started to develop in the early 1990s, we saw that many of the small Darjeeling estates were part of that. I confess that the producer selected was largely on the basis of who sounded the most impressive at one of the global trade shows in Germany, where most of these estates exhibited. The estate was Ambootia and I was very excited to finally visit Darjeeling and see the degree to which this region was unique in the world of tea, not only its geographical location and stunning scenery, but in the type of tea made, and the "crafted" nature of its manufacture. Ambootia was an organic estate in common with many in Darjeeling. In fact, it was also biodynamic, which is a kind of holistic approach to organic agriculture with not just ecological dimensions but also social and spiritual. It was great tea and quite expensive – but, sadly, yet another product that did not stand the test of time.

The greater appreciation of quality which emerged in the early 1990s caused several changes to Traidcraft tea ranges and we were very aware that much of the tea in the UK was sourced from Kenya. Not only that, but the infrastructure of the Kenyan tea industry included a large proportion of small farmer-owned tea factories producing tea regarded as excellent quality and substantially used in most UK mainstream teabag brands. We decided to explore the possibility of using Kenyan teas sourced from the Kenya Tea Development Authority (KTDA), who were responsible for marketing and selling on behalf of over 200,000 smallholder tea producers throughout Kenya.

I went to Kenya in 1995 when Fairtrade labelling on teas had been established across Europe and the first Fairtrade labelled tea had been launched by Clipper less than a year earlier. At that point, all of the tea origins being developed by Transfair International, the German-based labelling initiative, were private plantations.[45] For my part, in leading the sourcing activities in Traidcraft relating to tea, I was not particularly wedded to a strategy of merely switching all of Traidcraft's tea origins to private plantations. We still adopted the principle of favouring smallholder producer organizations or cooperatives – or, if estates, then ones with a social enterprise dimension to them. Also, the German market tended toward a different type of tea, so those early Fairtrade origins were dominated by Darjeeling or Sri Lankan estates and mostly organic. The other part of the backdrop was that Cafédirect had been launched successfully and would, at some stage, hopefully want to develop a tea product.

---

45 Transfair International would go on to join with other such organizations and become Fairtrade Labelling Organizations International a few years later.

That first visit to Kenya was another tea education. I was hosted by the KTDA, given a dedicated member of staff, a car, and a driver, and allocated almost a week to do what I wanted with them. I merely requested to be given a good overview of the smallholder tea sector and what followed was an extensive tour of Kenya visiting eleven of the (then) forty-four tea factories managed by the KTDA, both east and west of the Kenyan Rift Valley. At each of those factories, I met with farmers in the field and management in the factory, and was given a detailed tour. The concept of Fair Trade was unknown to anyone since this was "first contact" territory in every respect and in the eleven times I presented about Fair Trade, it was met with a high degree of scepticism and even disbelief.

I learned much about tea, about the differences between each factory and especially the quality differences in teas produced east and west of the Rift Valley. Also, about what it meant to be a real smallholder tea farmer as opposed to one who merely owned the land, worked elsewhere, and employed others to tend the so-called "tea garden". I also learned that it would be a challenge to source tea directly from a factory since the government controlled KTDA was the real decision-making body, held the power, and managed each of the factories. Despite the fact that, technically, the farmers owned each factory, their contribution to decision-making was not all that it could be. Apart from that, all teas were bought and sold through the Mombasa or London tea auction (the latter eventually closing in 1998). I also learned about the negative reputation of the KTDA in terms of alleged corruption and most of this negativity would emerge while talking to the farmers themselves.

I collected lots of information at each factory I visited and was given full access to KTDA statistics on all forty-four factories and their farmer members. Faced with the future prospect of choosing which of these KTDA factories to source from, I embarked on a bit of a trial selection process that would help determine who would benefit from Fair Trade the most. After all, one of the key propositions of Fair Trade was to work deliberately with the most marginalized producers or workers. Maybe there were some of these KTDA producers or regions that were more marginalized than others. I called it a socio-economic analysis since that was very much the buzzword of the time and developed several criteria which I applied to every factory based on the statistics and information I had obtained. The criteria included the following:

- Quality of tea as measured by average auction prices over several years. This would ensure that the finished product would be good and would break out of the historical ghetto of less-than-mainstream quality that had typified Fair Trade products in the past.

- Average smallholder land size and land occupied by tea bushes, which would give some indication of the level of farmer dependency on tea.

- Various geographical indicators like distance from urban centres, which would give some indication of access to utilities and healthcare, and some understanding of the likely dependency on tea as a crop and the likelihood of the landowner actually being a farmer.

This was a piece of desk research and it did highlight a particular region or tea zone which might be targeted as best deserving of the benefits of Fairtrade. We would come back to this piece of work in later years and explore it in a bit more detail. But even then, I had in my mind who that first Fairtrade certified factory would likely be.

As it turned out, Cafédirect did want to extend into tea and they would go on to call it Teadirect, launched in 1998. Of the four founders of Cafédirect, each of which held positions on the Board of Directors, Twin Trading and Traidcraft expressed an interest to help develop the next product. Was it to be a chocolate product or was it to be tea? We, of course, positioned ourselves as knowing a bit about tea and Twin Trading were starting to work in cocoa so they recommended a chocolate bar. This was on a very amiable and friendly competitive basis, but I suppose the logical outcome for a brand involved in hot beverages would be another hot beverage, so tea it was. Twin Trading would go on to be founders of the Day Chocolate Company which would ultimately become Divine chocolate. I suppose that had Cafédirect chosen the chocolate product instead of the tea, then things may have been very different in subsequent years, and Divine may not have ever existed.

Traidcraft was commissioned by Cafédirect to develop and manage Teadirect and the origins that Traidcraft had identified, explored, or developed would go on to be considered for inclusion in the blend. It was not a straightforward proposition since Cafédirect had given focus to smallholder farmers and to the directness of trade. Unlike coffee, this was not so simple for tea where directness of trade was not generally practised and there were brokers, agents, and auctions to navigate. In addition, a 100% smallholder blend would need a breakthrough in sourcing from Kenya merely to obtain the quality needed to bring a mainstream Fairtrade tea onto a supermarket shelf.

Fairly early on, it was decided that to work with the KTDA was just not going to happen. The KTDA took the position that they represented dozens of factories and that to single out one factory for Fairtrade certification was difficult. Apart from that, the reputation for alleged corruption in the Kenyan tea industry meant that it would be just too risky to work there. Further exploratory work was conducted, and we hired a couple of consultants to do this – Keith Stamp, who had previously worked at Traidcraft as Marketing Director, and Antony Ellman, an agronomist and socio-economist who would later consult for Traidcraft on numerous occasions. Additional sources were identified including smallholder-owned factories in Uganda with a similar organizational model to those in Kenya but without the baggage, but also without a great reputation for quality. There was a bullet to be bitten and it meant that teas from the plantation sector needed to be considered. The Kibena tea estate in the southern part of Tanzania, already in Traidcraft tea blends, was revisited as an option. It produced some of the best-quality East African teas on the market and the nature of their ownership was different to a typical private estate. In addition, there was huge enthusiasm and support from their ownership and management who were keen and willing to engage in the partnership.

Another estate was explored in northern Tanzania called Herkulu. It was quite small and not a typical estate, in that workers would live in the local community and not on the estate itself. The ownership, while private, had some experience of engaging with the Fair Trade movement since their organic estates in India had been some of the first recruits into the Fairtrade system some years earlier. Herkulu itself had been producing organically, supplying some of our counterparts in EFTA (European Fair Trade Association) but had reverted back to conventional production due to difficulties in selling enough organically certified tea.

In Uganda, the Igara Growers Tea Factory and the Kayonza Growers Tea Factory would provide the smallholder tea. The factories were managed by the European Union funded Agri-Industrial Management Agency Ltd as part of a Ugandan smallholder tea development programme and represented over 4,000 farmers.

So, the model for Teadirect was created. Traidcraft plc would import the tea on behalf of Cafédirect, also looking after quality for which we employed the services of a local, skilled tea taster. Traidcraft Exchange would develop and manage a so-called "Producer Support and Development Programme", (implemented by its Tanzanian-based partner AMKA) whose overall goal was "to improve the income, influence, security and participation of tea-growing producers and their communities through access to Fair Trade tea markets". A tea advisory panel was appointed to oversee all of this with staff from all participating organizations as well as external independent members.

This partnership continued for the next four years, sales of Teadirect grew, and by 2002 Traidcraft was importing several hundred tonnes of tea per year. More suppliers needed to be recruited and an additional smallholder origin in Tanzania, the Rungwe Smallholder Tea Growers Association, was added. Importantly, it was also decided to revisit the possibility of using Kenya teas. This was due to KTDA being restructured and privatized which opened up the possibility of direct engagement with factories and a removal of many of the risks identified some years earlier. Once again local consultants were engaged to do the detailed work. Building on that original work of 1995, one particular tea growing zone was targeted for further socio-economic research. Five factories were visited, and a recommendation made that Kiegoi Tea Factory and Michimukuru Tea Factory be considered.

On the next visit to Kenya, I visited these two factories alongside one of our consultants, Antony Ellman. I felt that I had known Kiegoi for years because, back in 1995, I had concluded that this would be the probable Kenyan source for Teadirect, so it was rather exciting to finally see it. Based in the Meru area of Kenya it had one other fascinating and perplexing characteristic. Another crop grown by tea farmers was the mildly narcotic khat plant, locally known as "miraa". The fresh leaves would be picked and sold to traders who would drive at breakneck speed to Nairobi for onward air shipment to the Middle East, risking their own lives and the lives of the numerous pedestrians along the road. After considering some of the issues around whether we could legitimately buy tea from a producer whose other crop was effectively a drug, it was decided to go ahead, given that the overlap was not enormous and that perhaps a better impact from growing tea might enable farmers to make the choice not to grow miraa.

Kiegoi was the first Fairtrade certified tea factory in Kenya and many other KTDA factories joined the system in later years, becoming the main blend component for many mainstream Fairtrade tea brands. Traidcraft's work in East African Fairtrade tea was pioneering and remains one of its important historical legacies in the development of Fairtrade teas.

Not everything was successful in the Teadirect and Traidcraft partnership. While there was good growth in sales of everyday teabags, an attempted entry into the speciality tea sector failed miserably. Traidcraft had already done some research into the fruit and herbal teas market and we had even got to an advanced stage in product development. Hibiscus from Kenya, sourced from the same region as Kiegoi, was used as a base for the tea, together with other herbs. Various dried fruit pieces and natural flavourings were added to create the range but, for various reasons, the project was parked. As Cafédirect was considering an extension to the Teadirect range, this project was revisited. Various alternatives were considered but eventually the decision was to go for something quite different and focus on the emerging green tea market.

For the first time since those early WDM tea days at the beginning of the 1980s, Traidcraft returned to Sri Lanka to work on tea. A new supplier was recommended by some of our counterparts in the European Fair Trade Association and I was able to visit the impressive Bio Foods, a smallholder farmer initiative not only working with tea but also in herbs and spices. The founder, Sarath Ranaweera, would become yet another source of inspiration to me. Eventually two products were developed and launched – a green tea mixed with cinnamon, and a green tea mixed with lemongrass. Given the subsequent growth in the green tea market, my feelings are that this was maybe a bit before its time. Sadly, it failed, and the relationship was short-lived.

Unrelated to this failure, the time came for Cafédirect and Traidcraft to go their separate ways and they took the decision to source and manage tea themselves and set up their own producer support activities. Later on, Traidcraft would sell its shareholding in Cafédirect severing any formal ties, but Cafédirect products would continue to be an important part of the product range of Traidcraft for years to come.

This meant that Traidcraft would revert to sourcing teas only for its own product ranges. It decided to do this through a deepening partnership with Ringtons, who had become a significant Fairtrade tea trader and favoured many of the East African teas pioneered by Traidcraft. The range comprised blends which were predominantly East African.

Traidcraft Exchange had renewed its programme work in East Africa in the mid-2000s and took a thematic approach, with a key focus on tea. Working with many of the KTDA factories and farmers in Kenya, it focused on product diversification, the strengthening of farmer organizations, and raising awareness about their rights and responsibilities in the tea sector. In India, Traidcraft Exchange programme work has impacted the lives of tens of thousands of smallholder farmers by bringing them together in a more formal community-based organizational structure, enabling them to harness collective power, strengthening their voice and providing economies of scale in buying and selling their produce. Similarly, in Bangladesh, the formation of local and national organizations for smallholder farmers has enabled them to gain formal recognition within the tea sector and their interests represented within the tea industry.

Meanwhile, the pioneering work in tea came to a natural end as mainstream Fairtrade tea became a sizeable part of the tea market, with supermarket brands converting to Fairtrade. Traidcraft sales of tea declined in the face of such competition and there was potentially very little to differentiate Traidcraft teas from any other Fairtrade teas. The only thing we could do was to continue the kind of positive discrimination approach, sourcing from the most disadvantaged and with occasional producer support activities based on needs identified or requested while travelling. Ultimately, Traidcraft teas moved to 100% smallholder teas and contained no estate teas at all.

Later on, we would use some of Ringtons' pioneering work in quality management, which would see their groundbreaking leaf-lock process applied to Traidcraft teas. This is a process which seals in the freshness of the tea from factory to consumer, creating some of the best quality Fairtrade teas on the market.

Quite some journey from that first WDM tea from Waulugala!

I finish this chapter reflecting on the broader influence Traidcraft had in the development of Fairtrade tea and I believe it went beyond merely developing tea ranges and introducing new suppliers. Phil Mumby was someone with a high profile in the tea industry over the years and many of us got to know him well. I'll let him relate his own Fair Trade journey in tea:

> I had been involved with Traidcraft since the mid-1980s, initially as a volunteer seller of Traidcraft products. At this time, I was early in my career in the tea industry with Typhoo and starting to travel to meet tea farmers. This brought some internal challenges. While I was committed to the Traidcraft principles of helping small producers, I was unhappy with much of the negative messaging used to promote the products, which I knew to be unfair generalizations based on "worst cases". There were some good things happening in the industry that could be supported. I stepped down from my volunteer role for other reasons but continued to stay connected with Traidcraft and attended annual conferences, even appearing on some panels as a corporate bod to provide a bit of contrast.
>
> The challenge to find a way of supporting good working practices in the mainstream tea industry became a focus for me and resulted in the Typhoo Quality Assurance Project (QAP), which we launched in 1990. This was built on a quality assurance platform, but included sections on employee wages, welfare, and safety. This was a pioneering idea at the time and

required some careful selling to the producers. Crucially, it was underpinned by two key principles: recognition of good practice already in place, and commitment from us to support this good practice with a long-term purchase commitment. I can trace this very clearly to Traidcraft's values.

We embarked on a programme of visiting every producer, and the project was ready to go public in mid-1992. Sometime around then we agreed to a meeting with Richard Adams (Traidcraft's founder), who was involved in the early stages of the development of the Fairtrade Mark and was doing a tour of the UK tea industry. I have very good memories of that meeting as we put the QAP on the table and rather interrupted Richard's script. There followed a year of working together with Traidcraft and other NGOs trying to make Fairtrade work with Typhoo, but it was too much of a stretch on both sides and we couldn't make it happen. The legacy from my side was some good working relationships with NGOs and also with trade unions that led to my involvement in the formation of the Ethical Trading Initiative in the late 1990s.

I continue to believe strongly that Fair Trade needs to be producer-focused, recognize and reward good practice, and that it should involve tea brands in commitment and cost. Unfortunately, most of what I see now are top-down corporate PR-driven models that leave the farmers invisible and powerless. Maybe this was inevitable once Fair Trade became more mainstream, but it is a long way away from the values that created Traidcraft and drove my own involvement over the years.[46]

---

46 From personal correspondence with the author, 2019.

Chapter 17

A COFFEE LEGACY THAT NEVER SEEMED TO BE FORGOTTEN

I bumped into one of the UK's leading management coaches several weeks after leaving Traidcraft – I knew him through attending one of his memorable training courses some years ago – and I told him I was writing this book. He always had a keen interest in Traidcraft and I mentioned that I didn't yet have a book title. His suggestion was "Traidcraft – great story, but the coffee's s**t" or something like that!

While Traidcraft is less well known for coffee pioneering work, maybe its historical legacy is more negative than positive, given the reputation of Campaign Coffee back in the early 1980s. Nevertheless, I think there are some really interesting stories to tell about Traidcraft and its coffee journey, especially for instant coffee.

Campaign Coffee was an instant coffee powder from what was then one of the few coffee "instantizing" plants in the world, located in Bukoba on the shores of Lake Victoria in Tanzania. The Tanganyika Instant Coffee Company (TANICA) was government-owned and sourced all of its coffee beans from local cooperatives of smallholder farmers, including the Kagera Cooperative Union (KCU) and the Karagwe District Cooperative Union (KDCU). All coffee trade in Tanzania was centrally controlled in those days and there was little scope for direct trade with those cooperatives. Several years later, this changed and KCU and KDCU would go on to be significant direct suppliers to the Fairtrade market in Europe and used in Traidcraft roast and ground products for many years to come. In 2005, KCU and KDCU obtained majority ownership of the Bukoba coffee plant and it still makes and supplies instant coffee, mostly for sale within Africa.

Traidcraft would buy coffee from TANICA for many years, with the Traidcraft Exchange providing support, including the provision of spare parts for the plant. Nicaraguan instant coffee, branded Encafé, followed a few years later as well as other brands like Café Primera (which it's very likely no one will remember at all, since it did not fare well in terms of sales).

When Cafédirect launched its instant coffee in the mid-1990s, all of the Traidcraft instant coffees with the exception of Campaign Coffee were discontinued and the focus was very much on the Cafédirect product. As with all instant coffees, it needed good volumes due to what is a highly industrialized process, subject to minimum volume productions. Campaign Coffee eventually became unsustainable and was discontinued. It was a powdered instant coffee in a sector which had evolved into granulated coffee, and where freeze-dried coffee (retaining more of the essential quality characteristics of the coffee beans) was emerging through an alternative industrial process.

And so Traidcraft instant coffee disappeared for a while and it was not until the mid-2000s that a decision was made to develop its own brand again. The decision was driven by a degree of uncertainty about Cafédirect's sustainability, uncertainty about Traidcraft's dependence on someone else's brand, and the fact that Traidcraft was no longer formally associated with Cafédirect having divested of its share ownership.

I was charged with the responsibility of developing these products. It was decided fairly early on that we would work with someone who knew about instant coffee intimately, where we could add the Fair Trade expertise to the partnership. So started a long and fruitful relationship with Complete Coffee in the UK, who were prominent in developing supermarket own-label instant coffee products. Complete Coffee had good access to instant coffee plants throughout the world and the first thing we established was that we would follow the principles established by those formative years of instant coffee of "adding value" to the coffee bean as reasonably close to coffee growers as was practical.

The first venture was in India. By then I had a reasonable grasp of the instant coffee industry and was aware of the different kinds of coffee beans. Instant coffee had historically been a major user of the cheaper, harsher, and more bitter tasting Robusta beans. The milder Arabica beans – more expensive and purportedly better quality – would be used more in roast and ground products. Campaign Coffee had been 100% Robusta, but things were changing and the concept of quality in instant coffee, especially freeze-dried coffee, had become clearer. I was introduced to a newly constructed coffee processing plant in the state of Andhra Pradesh and was aware that coffee was an important crop in that state and used by the factory. It also became clear that much of that coffee, which was Arabica, was grown by smallholder farmers from tribal communities in the Araku Valley, high up in the Eastern Ghats of India.

We initially hired a local consultant to check out the likelihood of those producers being Fairtrade certified (since by then a Fairtrade Mark was essential) and the report looked good. It was complex in that the farmer communities were part of an integrated development programme managed by the Naandi Foundation and so we needed to cultivate a relationship and work closely with them.[47] My first visit was an eye-opener in more senses than one. First, I had plenty of experience visiting Indian farmer groups and had occasionally visited coffee producers in other countries, but their formal description of being "marginalized" was apt and the low levels of development in the area were very visible. These coffee producers had been well and truly exploited by traders over the years and were exactly the sort of group we were trying to engage with at that time. And second, when visiting the coffee processing plant, I made the very big mistake of accepting an invitation to step into the freeze-drying chamber. It would only be for half a minute, therefore there was no need to don the Arctic clothing worn by the workers – so I thought – and I stuck with the short-sleeved shirt as required by the 32 degree outside temperature. Suffice to say that the transition to -40 degrees and a 70-degree swing in the temperature of the air I was breathing played havoc with my chest and I was to suffer for the rest of the trip!

---

47 Naandi means "new beginnings" in Sanskrit.

To cut a long and complex story short, a new farmer group was certified as Fairtrade in the next year and Traidcraft began to buy jars and tins of instant coffee from India. The group was formally called "The Small & Marginal Tribal Farmers Mutually Aided Cooperative Society Limited"; quite a mouthful and its acronym "SAMTFMACS" no easier to deal with so we referred to them as "MACS". Around the same time, we had developed a new relationship with a producer organization in Kerala called Fair Trade Alliance Kerala (FTAK) who supplied Robusta coffee, so the instant coffee we developed became a blend of FTAK and MACS coffee beans.

Yet another inspirational character in the world of Fair Trade entered my life in Tomy Mathew, who led FTAK – someone from whom I would learn much over the years. Looking back, the legacy of this instant coffee project was not so much in bringing a new Traidcraft instant coffee to the market, but in bringing a new producer into Fairtrade. MACS continued to sell its coffee as Fairtrade while the instant coffee we developed sadly did not stand the test of time. No matter how fantastic the story behind the product, this 100% Indian coffee struggled to sell and was hindered by not having some of the quality credentials, whether real or imagined, of Latin American coffees. And things were changing at Traidcraft in that sales had peaked and were about to decline and we still needed a better quality freeze-dried product.

A newly built instant coffee plant in Mexico was the next project and much credit goes to two of my colleagues – Chris Jewitt and Zenen Santana Delgado – who researched and built up this supply chain. In keeping with an approach developed years earlier, we thought that we should focus on producers who were in an earlier stage of their organizational development, were more disadvantaged, and who would benefit more from Fair Trade. We had supported our honey supplier CIPAC in Guatemala to be Fairtrade certified also in coffee and, while not in the same country, it was fairly close to the instant coffee plant just over the border in Mexico. What emerged was a great quality freeze-dried instant coffee, instantized, decaffeinated, and retail packed in Mexico and which was eventually launched in 2013. Suffice to say that when I visited this instant coffee plant some years later, I politely declined an invitation to step into the freeze-drying room!

This concept of adding value to a commodity by having it processed in or close to its origin always applied to our food product development thinking and was formalized as part of Traidcraft's purchasing policy in the early 2000s. An extract follows:

> Traidcraft will aim to maximize the value added in country of production by processing or packaging at or near to the source. Wherever possible this will be organized and controlled by the supplier… the maximization of sales, and benefits to suppliers resulting from that, should not be compromised by reducing the viability of a product through lower quality or higher costs.[48]

This principle was quite possible to implement for instant coffee and some other food products. But it was hard to do for everything and we found this to be the case for roast and ground coffee. Quality and shelf life were harder to maintain, and costs were high, but I imagine that with improvements in technology and logistics, it is probably more feasible now than it was in the past.

There was one very costly failure in 1995 as we collaborated with our partners in EFTA. The Forestal brand, which was processed and packed in Costa Rica, also included a premium for conservation projects. It was expensive and its vacuum packaging was occasionally compromised, so it was short-lived. Meanwhile, the Traidcraft roast and ground coffees were much more straightforward to manage and, since the 1980s, were always a collaborative process. Green beans were always bought through our partners in EFTA and then roasted and ground in Europe – first in the Netherlands, then Belgium, and finally in the UK.

As with tea, Traidcraft's coffees improved dramatically over the years, although that Campaign Coffee legacy was always hard to shake off, and maybe it tarnished the reputation of all Fairtrade coffees for a while. Despite that, we were all pretty proud of our coffees, not just the quality and taste but the significant producer impact that they made. There were few mainstream brands out there that could match that complete package.

---

48 Traidcraft internal document, written by the author, developed and implemented in 2002.

Chapter 18

SWEET JUSTICE: A SUGAR JOURNEY

"So, you're off on another holiday to Mauritius?" Maybe a fair question given its reputation as a major holiday destination, but I can faithfully report that during my seven visits to Mauritius, I can rarely recall stepping onto a beach, let alone entering the sea. In the early days, our hosts would assume that I wanted to be accommodated in a beach hotel but eventually I, and those I travelled with, would insist that we be accommodated locally to the work we would be doing. Although, to be fair, in Mauritius you're never far from the sea!

In the 1980s, Richard Adams had developed the supply chain that would see Traidcraft become a small importer of sugar from Mauritius. One of the original suppliers to Traidcraft (and to Tearcraft before that) was Craft Aid Services who supplied various craft products like pressed-flower cards, bookmarks, and decorative wall plaques. Richard had assisted Craft Aid in setting up a small hand packing unit, even supplying the weighing machine and heat sealer, which would provide meaningful employment to their workers, predominantly disabled people. Sugar would be their first food product, followed closely by tea. Sugar would prove to be the major product for Craft Aid for many years to come and an important retail product range for Traidcraft.

Mauritius is defined by its historical and colonial past. The so-called "Sugar Protocol" had been a feature of European Union trade policy with former colonies known as ACP countries (Africa, Caribbean, Pacific). This granted entry for cane sugar into the European Union at preferential rates based on allocated quotas. This was great for Mauritius since it effectively defined a minimum price for sugar which was much higher than the world market price.

In addition, the way that sugar was managed in Mauritius was regarded as beneficial to farmers; therefore it met Traidcraft's original food purchasing policy from the 1980s. The structure of this sugar agricultural industry was unique. It was state-controlled with pro-farmer objectives and with farmer representation at all decision-making levels.

The marketing and exporting of sugar products were undertaken by the Mauritius Sugar Syndicate (MSS). All sugar farmers (known in Mauritius as "planters") were members of the Syndicate whose ultimate responsibility was to represent their members equally and maximize their financial return. The member "planters" came in three categories – large, medium, and small. A large planter might be a plantation, and medium and small planters were defined according to the area of land they owned. More than 30,000 farmers were defined as "small" and many of these were organized into cooperative credit societies which managed all financial transactions.

Traidcraft managed to squeeze itself into a group of customers of MSS with some helpful support and assistance from one of their bigger UK customers; Billington's had invested much time and resource into developing some of the speciality sugars for which Mauritius is renowned. This was the beginning of more than thirty years of importing packed speciality sugars from Mauritius.

Fairtrade labelling

With the 1990s came the challenge of the proliferation of Fairtrade labelling with its clearer purchasing criteria and the need to source directly and transparently from identifiable farmer organizations. Partnership and collaboration characterized much of what was happening in those days. The European Fair Trade Association had been founded some years earlier and there were numerous projects undertaken jointly between fellow members. We began to collaborate with the Dutch member of EFTA. Mauritius had originally been a Dutch colony and it was the Dutch that first introduced sugar to the island. France and the UK subsequently held Mauritius as a colony, and not without conflict, but this Anglo-Dutch collaboration on sugar, which started in the 1990s, would last until the present day. Martin Boon from Fairtrade Original, myself and other colleagues from Traidcraft would regularly undertake joint visits and activities in Mauritius over the next several years.[49]

The complexities of the sugar industry and the number of stakeholders involved meant that things were not straightforward in implementing our desire for traceability. We had a good relationship with MSS and were introduced to all the players. One constraint was that MSS could not show any favouritism to any one part of their membership so we would need to find someone else to work directly with.

We discovered quite early on that physical traceability would be difficult. Making granulated sugar out of sugar cane is a highly industrialized process. A handful of sugar mills were scattered around the island, taking in the sugar cane and making a whole range of granulated sugar products according to customer demand. Buyers of anything Fairtrade might expect that the product they bought actually originated from the farmer's crop but this is occasionally just not possible where there is such a large industrial process. Surely better to ensure that the financial benefits are guaranteed to that farmer? This dilemma caused the standards for Fairtrade sugar to be exempt from any physical traceability rules. Some argue that you can't have Fairtrade products without physical traceability, although they tend to be from that contingent of Fairtrade supporters who believe that you can't have Fairtrade products unless they are also organically grown.

We were introduced to an organization who represented the very small sugar planters of Mauritius, the ones who were organized into cooperatives. In collaboration with them, we set up our own Fair Trade premium mechanism. By this time, Fairtrade International had developed cane sugar standards which included a financial premium of $60 per tonne, added to the buying price of the granulated sugar. This translated into around £50 per tonne at the time so that is what was agreed as our own premium contribution. There was no Fairtrade minimum price for sugar for ACP countries given the preferential rates they enjoyed for sales into the EU. We administered our own premium

---

49   Fairtrade Original is a Fair Trade Organization similar to Traidcraft and is based in the Netherlands.

fund for a while. One of the memorable activities set up with this premium fund was a seminar for small farmers to explore key issues they faced and to introduce them to the world of Fair Trade. Entitled "The Mauritius Sugar Industry and Co-operatives – Challenges and Opportunities", the seminar drew many small farmers and attracted much media attention.

By this time, both Fairtrade Original and Traidcraft decided that they would work collaboratively with Fairtrade International, with the objective of introducing Mauritius sugar as Fairtrade certified, since both organizations had started to use a Fairtrade Mark on their products. But first, it was important to identify whether or not particular product sectors were in need of Fair Trade. It was still maintained by both Fairtrade Original and Traidcraft that there should be some consideration of whether or not we were meeting our obligations and objectives of targeting the vulnerable or disadvantaged. Mauritius was a relatively prosperous country and we had met some relatively prosperous small farmers. It was important to question whether this was a place where Fair Trade could make a difference. With our accumulated, self-managed, Fair Trade premium, we decided to hire a consultant to do a survey of the small planter and worker sectors. The work was quite extensive and, fortunately, a lot cheaper than comparable market research in the UK. We concluded that we would press ahead with facilitating a process which would see Fairtrade International proceed with their certification activities.

Life is not always straightforward and, by this time, in the mid-2000s, Fairtrade International had become a very rigid – some would say bureaucratic – organization. More than twenty of the small cooperative credit societies had been lined up for certification and, in retrospect, not enough had been done to prepare them fully to meet the standards of Fairtrade International. The application failed, and a rethink was needed.

By this stage my colleague Monica Philbrick was leading much of the work from Traidcraft and enjoying the same frequency of travel to Mauritius and the same "not another holiday!" jibes from colleagues. Ultimately, a new application was prepared and a new organization, the Mauritius Fairtrade Cooperative Federation (MFCF), was established. It was sponsored by Fairtrade Original and Traidcraft, who would mentor and prepare each cooperative for certification. It was still not without setbacks and Fairtrade International would not recognise the MFCF as a second umbrella representative body that would be certified in its own right and represent its small cooperative members. Each cooperative needed to be certified individually. Five cooperatives were selected, and the application was successful. Mauritius sugar could now be Fairtrade labelled and, in 2009, Traidcraft became the first importer of Mauritius Fairtrade sugar into the UK.

In 2018, I visited Mauritius (probably for the last time) and the legacy of those early days is tangible. As the EU relaxed its sugar protocol and guaranteed pricing was gradually removed, Fairtrade became increasingly important to small farmers – although it needs to be said that many had to drop out of sugar cane cultivation. More and more mainstream buyers still look to Mauritius for their Fairtrade sugar, especially for use in chocolate, and more than $2 million of Fairtrade premiums which accumulated over the years has provided a rich source of benefit to a group of cooperatives which number more than thirty.

Sugar as an ingredient

Traidcraft had, for many years, only ever bought and sold sugar as a "ready for sale" retail range. The need to source sugar as an ingredient only cropped up when bakery ranges were being developed – initially cakes and flapjacks, but later on biscuits and cookies. By this time, Traidcraft had decided to use a Fairtrade Mark on food and beverage products and this was becoming available to products containing more than a single ingredient. A source of Fairtrade certified sugar was needed well before Mauritius sugar became certified. In any case, access to their bulk sugar had been denied. Traidcraft was a small player with larger companies dominating the sugar trade and there were all sorts of contracts and deals in place which constrained traders like Traidcraft. This would not be the first time that the power of big companies would come into play in our sugar dealings.

There were other Fairtrade sugar producers in places like the Philippines and Paraguay, but these were organic and expensive to use because they were not ACP countries and high tariffs were incurred. Yes, they would be important in some of the organic products that

Traidcraft had introduced, like chocolate bars and jam, but Traidcraft was looking to develop products which were not organic, and the cookies especially would be price sensitive.

African partners

Traidcraft Exchange had set up one of its overseas partners in Malawi in the late 1990s which comprised two organizations – Development Trading Ltd and Business Consult Africa. The Africa Programme Manager of Traidcraft Exchange, Murdoch Gatward, had temporarily relocated into Malawi to oversee this development and sugar was one of the commodities they were working with. Like Mauritius, Malawi was one of those ACP countries described earlier and therefore had preferential rates into the European Union. Sugar processing mills and plantations were in private hands but there had been various initiatives instigated by the Malawi government, in collaboration with those mills and plantations, to create grower schemes with small-scale farmers. Kasinthula Cane Growers Association (KCG) was one of these schemes and their journey into Fairtrade certification was facilitated by Business Consult Africa, and with Murdoch Gatward heavily involved. Murdoch had been hugely influential in setting up much of the Traidcraft Exchange development programme activity in Africa right through the 1990's and into the 2000's and, after leaving Traidcraft, went on to establish the Imani Development office in Scotland where that work would continue. He was certainly an inspiration to many of us.

My first visit to Malawi in 2003 was to establish links with KCG and with the processor. To finalize our first contract under Fairtrade conditions meant that Traidcraft would become the first buyer of Fairtrade certified sugar from the whole of Africa. It was not without complication and the traceability of sugar was exactly as we had found in Mauritius; in fact worse, given that the sugar provided to the local mill was a fraction of that provided by the large-scale plantation. But financial traceability was in place and at least KCG could earn a Fairtrade premium, which would contribute over the next several years to providing basic utilities and developments in local communities in a remote region of one of the poorest countries in the world.

Being first does not necessarily bring with it many commercial rewards, as Traidcraft would discover time and time again. We would eventually cease to buy sugar directly from Malawi. Once again, the power and scale of the large sugar traders played its part. Fairtrade sugar was very small-scale in those days and none of the large sugar traders were involved. There were aspirations for Traidcraft to sell this bulk sugar into the wholesale sector and, since no one else was doing it, there was some interest. However, any business will respond to customer demand and once Fairtrade sugar became established it was inevitable that the large sugar players became involved. Economies of scale meant that Traidcraft was unable to compete and it was even the case that buying directly was more expensive than buying from some of the large sugar traders. It wasn't a straightforward decision and there were factors beyond price involved, but in the end, it was decided to buy Malawi sugar from those larger sugar traders.

Challenges

Selling Fairtrade sugar became problematic as the 2010s arrived. The anti-sugar lobby had a good case and a lot of mainstream brands started to work on reducing the levels of sugar in their products or finding alternative sweeteners. Traidcraft began to be rightly challenged by its customers and supporters about the high number of "sweet" products in its range. We briefly toyed with the idea of developing a Fairtrade stevia product. Stevia was a natural sweetener and we were aware of small farmer organizations growing the crop. But the challenges caused by declining sales meant that this particular innovation needed to be put on hold, which we all found frustrating.

Also frustrating was the way that the physical traceability rules of Fairtrade International were being applied. I was very much an advocate of something called "mass balance", which measured the volume of sugar cane going into one end of a factory and linking it with the volume of granulated sugar coming out of the other end. As already indicated, there was financial traceability but not physical traceability, and farmers would benefit accordingly. But I wanted at least some degree of knowledge of the origins in the bulk sugar I was buying. I wanted to be informed of this by the large sugar traders who now dominated Fairtrade sales, and I didn't really want to buy sugar that might have physically originated from East Anglia through processed beet sugar. But there were no guarantees, and mass balance and physical traceability seemed to have reached a place which we at Traidcraft found to be unacceptable. Mass balance was accepted externally – but we were challenged by customers and supporters that someone like Traidcraft should be operating at a higher ethical level – especially if we told stories about producers and countries whose produce might not actually be inside the pack.

So we started to buy from another producer where we could at least say which country our sugar was from. We collaborated with some of the smaller sugar traders and successfully transitioned our sourcing to Swaziland. It was still an ACP origin, it still applied local-level mass balance, and it was an African country which could hopefully benefit from Fairtrade sales. The industry in Swaziland had a similar structure to that of Mauritius and, for a while, this became our new source for bulk sugars. But in the end, commercial challenges prevailed, and we needed to consolidate all purchases from a single origin. The restrictions on buying bulk sugars from Mauritius were removed and we eventually came full circle. We started out only buying from Mauritius and, more than thirty years later, ended up only buying from Mauritius.

In later years, as mentioned earlier, the European Union made a crucial decision to phase out the sugar protocol, impacting much of the sugar industry in ACP countries, especially the smallholder sector. In Mauritius, the sugar industry became a fraction of the size compared with when Traidcraft first worked there more than three decades earlier. Thousands of small farmers have given up their land to other activities and those that remained included members of some of those cooperatives who have benefited from being Fairtrade certified.

Fairtrade sugar sales are still significant although more recent models for single ingredient certification has caused more downs than ups, with some chocolate bar brands choosing not to use Fairtrade sugar, instead focusing only on Fairtrade cocoa. In its contribution to this, Traidcraft's sugar journey was complicated, but with many firsts, and its pioneering reputation was well founded.

Chapter 19

COCOA AND CHOCOLATE

Traidcraft is not really well known for its work in cocoa and chocolate; Divine chocolate is perhaps the best known Fair Trade brand. I was involved in some of Traidcraft's cocoa developments, especially in the 2000s, which would cause me to gain some understanding of the complex cocoa industry. It also led me to explore the country which is the biggest grower of cocoa in the world (yet also one of the poorest), Côte D'Ivoire.

Working with EFTA to create the first Fair Trade chocolate bar

When Traidcraft became a member of the European Fair Trade Association, it did so in order to join up with likeminded organizations who might want to work together to achieve practical goals that everyone shared. Working together to develop products that no one could develop on their own was one of those goals. The key first project was the development of a chocolate bar.

The Swiss member, OS3, was working with a cocoa producer in Bolivia called El Ceibo, and the German member, GEPA, was working with a sugar producer in the Philippines, Altertrade. Put cocoa and sugar together and you have the basis of a chocolate bar. Of course, it's not as straightforward as that, but a project was developed which would see sugar and cocoa beans imported centrally by an EFTA member, then OS3 would coordinate the development of a range of chocolate bars, which would hopefully work in all countries represented within EFTA. They would also coordinate a positive relationship with a Swiss-based chocolate factory who was flexible enough and small enough to make relatively small production runs. The rest of the EFTA members would commit to launch the single brand with multilingual packaging in their own countries.

So was born the Mascao brand, named after the muscovado sugar, and the cocoa beans that it contained. It was the first Fair Trade chocolate bar in Europe, if not the world. When Traidcraft launched it in 1991, it was the first Fair Trade chocolate bar in the UK. It must be remembered that the Fairtrade Mark did not exist at that time and others who make claims about being "first" do so only in relation to a Fairtrade labelled bar. When the Fairtrade label was first permitted on a chocolate bar, the sugar did not need to be Fairtrade. Mascao was always about both cocoa and sugar being Fair Trade.

Getting a Fair Trade sugar into a chocolate bar was a bit of an effort. There were no Fair Trade sources of a fine, refined, white, free-flowing, granulated sugar that would work well enough in chocolate manufacture. There was only muscovado sugar from Altertrade. That sugar was an unrefined whole sugar and quite moist. The great thing about that first Swiss chocolate manufacturer was that it was prepared to use this sugar, to dry it, and to adapt its processing. Consequently, the chocolate bar was a bit more expensive to make and it had a distinctive taste due to the type of sugar being used. A bit like Campaign Coffee, customers would either love or hate the product.

Traidcraft was a buyer and seller of this finished product but also heavily involved in the various EFTA working groups that developed strategy for both producers and product. Throughout the 1990s, I was invariably the Traidcraft-nominated person to be part of that working group. A visit to the chocolate factory in Switzerland in the early 1990s would be the first of many similar visits to a myriad of chocolate processors and manufacturers throughout the UK and Europe.

As the 1990s progressed, each EFTA member saw growth and became more familiar with the chocolate industry. It was never an advantage that Mascao was manufactured in Switzerland, apart from the country's reputation for producing good quality chocolate, as it was not a member of the European Union and tariffs into the EU prevailed. Several of the members chose to go their own way and have chocolate made in their own countries when volumes allowed. Why would EFTA's Belgian member, when they were able to, not have their chocolate made in Belgium? Everyone would eventually rebrand into something that worked better for them in their own country and the multilingual packaging would change accordingly. Traidcraft eventually went for Traidcraft branding so, while Mascao was no more, the chocolate remained the same. Quality improved, other sugars were introduced, and even the Altertrade muscovado sugar was worked on to tone down the distinctive taste.

I did pay close attention to the world of cocoa from that time onwards – who the key manufacturers and brands were, and especially those things that would impact cocoa farmers. For example, in the 1990s, there was huge controversy over the use of vegetable fat in chocolate. The European Union had for a long time banned the use of anything other than cocoa butter in chocolate, although countries like the UK were given dispensation when joining the EU. In the journey toward EU harmonization and a cocoa industry lobby to permit the use of vegetable oils as a substitution for cocoa butter, EFTA joined the lobby against, citing the fact that a lower demand for cocoa beans would force producer prices downward. This was just one of many examples in any commodity market where those who produce the raw material are invariably the victims of decisions made higher up the supply chain.

Getting involved with the big players

Traidcraft had no real reason to delve into these complications until it decided to enter the world of baked products at the end of the 1990s. A "bake stable" chocolate chip was needed to make a chocolate chip cookie. By that time, some of the EFTA members had diversified into other chocolate products and had started working with some of the large chocolate ingredient manufacturers. At that stage, the world of chocolate was dominated by the so-called "ABC" of cocoa, yet very few consumers might have heard of any of them. Archer Daniels Midland,, Barry Callebaut, and Cargill were the ABCs – three giant multinational commodity traders and processors who, between them, controlled more than 50% of the market. It would not be possible to develop a chocolate chip without working with someone like them so our collaboration this time was with the Belgian EFTA member Oxfam Fairtrade, who introduced me to the extremely large-scale manufacturing operation of Barry Callebaut based in Belgium. It turned out that it wasn't really too much of a problem to make a bespoke chocolate chip, as long as I accepted that the cocoa would not be fully physically traceable to a particular producer (which was allowed in Fairtrade International standards). The more significant issue was that I needed to commit to a very high volume in keeping with the scale of that manufacturing unit, given that no one else was asking them for a Fairtrade chocolate chip. The contract was duly signed, and I had committed to something like £50,000 worth of chocolate chips. As it turns out, this first contract would eventually pave the way for Barry Callebaut to adopt the recipe as one of their standard product lines.

In the 2000s, Traidcraft had a set of strategic objectives which included acting as a kind of catalyst organization which would influence the Fair Trade and ethical activities of the mainstream commercial world. This objective spanned both Traidcraft Exchange and Traidcraft plc and we very often worked together. When we were approached by Archer Daniels Midland (ADM), one of those very large cocoa multinationals, to discuss and review their own corporate social responsibility (CSR) programme in Côte D'Ivoire, it was too good an opportunity to turn down.

The Traidcraft organic and Fairtrade chocolate bar range manufactured in Switzerland was ticking over but there was a growing dependency on the Divine range, which was Fairtrade but not organic. The commercial landscape at that time was one of major sales growth for Traidcraft, and the strategy adopted was that Traidcraft would, rightly or wrongly, seek to be a kind of supermarket for Fair Trade products. This would mean carrying a range of branded and own-brand products. It was decided to explore the possibility of developing a Traidcraft range of non-organic chocolate bars. This would effectively "compete" with Divine and earn more profit margin by working directly with chocolate processors and manufacturers. We had already worked with ADM and had successfully developed a yoghurt flavoured coating for raisins which contained Fairtrade sugar, so the relationship was already there. It was decided to approach ADM for a bespoke ingredient chocolate (essentially a chocolate drop) which would be made at their factory on Merseyside. Traidcraft would use this ingredient in various products, including in moulding our own branded chocolate bars. This was relatively straightforward and chocolate bars were duly launched which were a little bit cheaper than Divine and which used a recipe which was benchmarked against Cadbury's Dairy Milk. Some would say Divine bars were nicer, others would say that Traidcraft bars were nicer. It's all a question of personal taste!

I was particularly keen at that time to explore the possibility of using cocoa beans sourced from Côte D'Ivoire, which up until then had not been represented very much in the Fairtrade certified world. The largest cocoa producing country, and the poorest, was surely a target for Fairtrade. Instead, more prosperous Latin American countries and stronger producer organizations dominated Fairtrade. I could understand why; the cooperative sector in Côte D'Ivoire was at a low level of development and child labour was rife, but I considered that these were both reasons to engage rather than to avoid.

ADM sourced much of their cocoa from Côte D'Ivoire and they were clearly quite proud of their CSR programme there. Maybe they wanted the endorsement of a reputable organization like Traidcraft. The head of their CSR programme flew in from Switzerland to meet with us on Merseyside. I was uncomfortable enough about this to invite Fiona Gooch from the Traidcraft Exchange Policy Unit to the meeting. She had focused much of her energy on private sector engagement and responsible purchasing, and had contributed to a study of the cocoa sector authored by leading NGOs.

While a CSR programme can look impressive on paper, and this one did, it's always interesting to be able to see things for ourselves. We were invited to Côte D'Ivoire to do just that. I always enjoyed these collaborations between Traidcraft plc and Traidcraft Exchange – the sometimes pragmatic practitioners of Fair Trade combined with those who could provide bigger picture thinking and context. This was 2009 and I would spend what would be one of my most insightful trips abroad hosted by ADM, visiting a range of small-scale cooperatives,

NGOs, and the vast industrial-scale cocoa collection centres and grinding plants of Côte D'Ivoire.

Here, a typical small cocoa farmer might be a member of a small cooperative, or they might operate as an individual farmer selling to one of the thousands of local traders, called *pisteurs*, for ready cash who then sell on to bigger traders, called *traitants*, who finally deliver into the collection centres. We carried with us chocolate bar samples; many of the people we met in local communities had never even seen a bar of chocolate, let alone tasted one. Ultimately, it was hard not to be impressed with what ADM were doing on the ground with the various small cooperatives and the benefits which farmers received, not least because there would be no *pisteur* or *traitant* involved in the supply chain. Some of these cooperatives were in preparation to be Fairtrade certified and maybe also Rainforest Alliance certified.

I was not ignorant of the dilemma facing Traidcraft. Many likeminded organizations would have been horrified that we would even consider "getting into bed" with a global multinational, operating an oasis of "goodness" in a much vaster cocoa sector. Accusations of "greenwashing" – a term widely being used to describe a company making unsubstantiated or misleading ethical or environmental claims – were always made against such organizations. Weren't these the very people holding the power, manipulating the market, and the culprits behind much of the poverty and child labour in cocoa? Village traditions meant that I left Côte D'Ivoire as honorary village chief and the proud recipient of the gift of a real live goat, but there was much to ponder.

Traidcraft had been given the opportunity to engage directly with one or more of the cooperatives to have traceable cocoa processed on its behalf and at volumes which were just about manageable at the time. I decided to undertake further analysis of the cooperatives with which ADM were working and maybe apply some social and economic indicators which would help to identify those in the greatest need of Fairtrade. This was also a bit of a test of ADM because it would cause them to put some effort into the project and disclose lots of information. As it turns out, they were as transparent as could have been hoped for and the information provided was extensive and detailed. A complete analysis was made against things like the following:

- access to primary healthcare
- access to utilities
- geographical remoteness
- regional poverty indicators
- prevalence of worst forms of child labour in the region
- access to educational facilities
- extent of dependency of farmers on cocoa as a means of livelihood
- average land holding
- gender profile of farmers
- gender balance in governance at cooperative level
- quality of cocoa and production capacity.

All very detailed, and some would say unnecessary, but at that time Traidcraft's approach to new supplier selection, when there were choices to be made, would consider such things. Two cooperatives were selected, and the next step would be to introduce ourselves personally to them through a second visit.

What happened next was conflict and civil war. Tensions leading up to the much-delayed presidential elections in 2010 had been building and the country erupted into violence as the results were disputed. Over the next two years, nothing was going to happen as far as this project was concerned.

I returned to Côte D'Ivoire in 2012 and tried to make progress. As well as another gift of a goat and being appointed as yet another honorary village chief, the relationship with the two cooperatives selected would develop, and we would appoint a consultant to work there on our behalf. But other things were changing. Traidcraft had entered a period of declining sales and the need for this new chocolate supply chain had diminished. ADM were considering their entire future in chocolate and cocoa, and would go on to sell their cocoa factories in Europe to another, even larger, multinational, and their cocoa grinding interests in Côte D'Ivoire to yet another. Sadly, the project had to be terminated.

Hindsight is a wonderful thing and I do partly regret all the time and effort spent on something that did not bear very much fruit for Traidcraft. However, that is the nature of such innovative activities and it certainly wasn't the first time that it had happened. The growth of Fairtrade from Côte D'Ivoire would continue apace and those CSR programmes of the big multinationals would go on to provide the bulk of certified Fairtrade cooperatives that would feed the Mars and Kit Kat brands and many others. By late 2018, there were more than 250 small cooperatives certified in Côte D'Ivoire and in the space of ten years it became the largest source of Fairtrade cocoa.

So, what then happened with Traidcraft and chocolate? These forays into the world of direct sourcing would come to an end. Divine would take on a higher profile in the Traidcraft offering. Other brands like the Meaningful Chocolate Company and their Real Easter Egg would be introduced, and any Traidcraft branded chocolate products would revert back to the model of the old Mascao brand and be sourced through those EFTA members who had been more successful than we had been in doing our own thing in chocolate.

Chapter 20

NOT SUCH A
DIRTY OIL

The 2000s were characterized by a high degree of innovation in the growth of new product sectors, new supply chains, and new commodities. Many of those developments were opportunistic, or were the result of others coming to Traidcraft with the ideas which we would then work on and implement.

Palm oil was different. I had my eye on palm oil as a potential Fair Trade commodity in the early 2000s. In various strategy meetings, edible oils often cropped up as being potentially the "next big Fair Trade sector". There were crops which were grown predominantly for their oil extraction, like sunflower or rape seed, but which did not originate in a developing country. Other oils like soya, sesame, coconut, or peanut were derivatives of a commodity grown for multi-use and not particularly large-scale. Olive oil was of some interest, although this would mostly need to be sourced from countries around the Mediterranean. By far the most interesting and potentially challenging oil was palm oil. In any analysis of global trade statistics, especially looking at developing countries, palm oil consistently cropped up as one of the largest scale, globally traded, agricultural commodities.

We were working very closely with Fairtrade Foundation at this time because they were also looking to innovate into other certified products. It was a solid partnership and played well to the Traidcraft strategy of the time as being a catalyst in the growth of Fair Trade.

Traidcraft Exchange was commissioned to carry out a study of palm oil and to provide a rationale for its inclusion as a Fairtrade certified commodity. The report was published in 2005 and an extract from the findings is as follows:

> On the face of it, the palm oil industry would seem to be an appropriate one for Fairtrade to facilitate an alternative route to market, with fair returns for small producers and some protection from the fluctuations in world prices. By definition, all palm oil is produced in developing countries and in some of the poorest rural areas. Indications are that the rapid and often ruthless growth of the industry has forced subsistence farmers from traditional lands, displaced communities and destroyed many of the natural food sources upon which they depended.[50]

There were plenty of caveats. Were consumers even aware of palm oil? It's very much easier to identify with Fairtrade coffee or tea than it is with Fairtrade palm oil. Palm oil is a hidden ingredient in so many consumer goods; it was estimated at that time that more than 50% of a typical supermarket grocery range might contain palm oil. At the same time the concept of "sustainable palm oil" was emerging and an organization called the "Roundtable for Sustainable Palm Oil" had been created comprising various traders and large-scale producers, together with environmentally focused development agencies.

While the proposition was considered by Fairtrade International, for the reasons mentioned above and a few more, it was ultimately not taken forward. This did not deter Traidcraft from continuing to champion the development of Fair Trade palm oil as formalized in its strategic plan for the period 2006/11:

> Palm oil will be a key product development. As well as applications as a food ingredient in snack bars, spreads, dressings etc, it would enable entry into non-food sectors such as soaps, detergents, and candles. Given rising concern

---

50 Traidcraft Market Access Centre, "Preliminary Paper on Palm Oil", November 2005.

about bad environmental practices in palm oil production, there could be real scope for a Fair Trade option with good environmental credentials.[51]

Traidcraft products consumed more than 50 tonnes of palm oil at that time, in things like biscuits, cakes, confectionery, and snack bars, so it was logical that a plan be put together concerning this commodity. We thought that if we demonstrated a successful project with Traidcraft products, using a Fair Trade palm oil, then maybe Fairtrade International would revisit their decision and eventually develop Fairtrade standards for palm oil. Sadly, this would prove not to be, since the focus for Fairtrade labelled products would be to grow existing categories rather than develop new ones.

The original product rationale paper authored by the Traidcraft Exchange focused attention on West Africa, and particularly Ghana. Various potential contacts had been identified already and there was a growing sense that we should be developing more African projects and new supply chains. In any case, the oil palm tree, from whose fruit the oil is extracted, is indigenous to this region of Africa. Production was predominantly by smallholder farmers who might grow other crops and there was much scope for Fair Trade to make a difference to them.

A chance meeting with a Ghanaian development organization working in rural Ghana led to an initial visit to get some sense of how easy it might be to develop a new Fair Trade supply chain. By this time, we had identified the expertise and knowledge of Fullwell Mill, a leading Fair Trade Organization in the UK which had merged with another FTO, Tropical Wholefoods, some years earlier. I had worked closely with their founder, Adam Brett, and we would go on to hire him as a consultant for this project. We travelled together to Ghana in 2010.

The first thing we learned was that we would not develop this project in conjunction with the development organization who hosted us. They were lovely people, but poorly resourced, and wholly unsuited to be a key partner in the project. The warning signs were there as soon as we left Dacca, and the early breakdown of a vehicle caused us to requisition another, more robust, vehicle in the nearby town, together with a willing driver who, for adequate recompense, would accompany us for the next few days. The situation was not as we would have liked

---

51   From an internal document: Traidcraft Strategic Plan 2006/11.

it and I had probably contravened much of Traidcraft's travel policy, but "needs must", and we all learned from the experience! However, it did introduce us to the Ghanaian palm oil industry especially in the remotest part of the country and we learned much more about that. As Adam Brett writes:

> West African palm oil producers suffer from extreme market failure. Visits by Fullwell Mill and Traidcraft staff to palm oil farms in Ghana revealed farmers unable to harvest their crop for lack of a market, struggling to maintain the trees and even to afford to pay labour to harvest the fruits. This situation is national and affects large numbers of farmers. It results in deteriorating palm orchards which pose a serious fire risk to local village communities as the rotting fruits are highly combustible. In the absence of an international market, or decent local processing industry, raw palm fruits are processed locally using the most basic technology. Local processing of the oil is disgraceful. Women and children work in dangerous, unhealthy conditions with smoky open fires that consume diminishing fuel wood resources and contribute to a wide range of respiratory illnesses. All work is done using hand-tools which extract less than 50% of the available oil from the palm fruits and nut/kernel. Injuries and accidents are common with women and children receiving serious burns from the poorly organized processing conditions.[52]

Through meeting various other development agencies, as well as visiting one of the large mono-crop plantations, our understanding of the situation deepened and we resolved to develop a new supply chain which would address some of these issues.

It was only later that we discovered that we were not the first to come to the conclusions we did. One of my regrets in Traidcraft's palm oil journey was that we had not yet connected with the wonderful North American organization, Dr Bronner's, who made and distributed soap products. They had resolved only a few years earlier to convert all of

---

52   An extract from a report that Adam Brett submitted to Traidcraft in 2010. Used with permission.

their raw materials to Fair Trade and, in 2008, a small-scale processing mill and farmer group had been developed, called Serendipalm which had started to supply palm oil for Dr Bronner's soap bars. The introductions were eventually made, and a project part-funded by the UK government's Department for International Development was conceived in a partnership between Fullwell Mill, Dr Bronner's, and Traidcraft. This would develop the productive capacity of Serendipalm, improve their efficiency, and create a new product range for Traidcraft with the brand name "Clean and Fair". The "clean" part of the brand name was intended to have a double meaning; it would do the job intended but it would also use "clean" palm oil.

It would not be until 2014 that the new product range was launched, and it would be one of the more complex product development projects undertaken at Traidcraft. Finding a manufacturer who would convert palm oil into a detergent and then formulate a range of cleaning products was one of the first tasks. This was not easy given that the desired range would consist of laundry liquid, washing up liquid, and a multi-surface cleaner which used palm oil as an ingredient. The only manufacturer who demonstrated a degree of interest in what we were doing, and who at least shared the vision, was an organization called Bio D who already produced their own brand of cleaning products. Ironically, one of the Bio D brand propositions was the avoidance of palm oil as an ingredient and here was Traidcraft coming to them with a proposal to use it.

Ultimately, the range also consisted of soap bars and liquid soap, in addition to those products originally planned. In order to highlight the Fair Trade palm oil from Serendipalm, we created a new logo which we called FairPalm and with the intention of offering this to other brands, who would hopefully follow our lead. Ultimately, this never led to any significant partnerships, although we were very pleased that the Co-op included the acceptability of FairPalm as part of their own palm oil policy. Our world view of palm oil would be expressed in the Traidcraft purchasing policy as:

- In a multi-cropping scenario the production of palm fruit is a positive activity for smallholder farmers in the developing world and especially if additional economic standards, unique to Fair Trade, can be applied.

- Palm can have positive agricultural attributes. It is the most highly yielding oil plant, more than five times compared for example to rape seed oil which is one reason for its lower cost but also uses less land in proportion to output.

- From a developmental perspective we support smallholder production of palm fruit, organically grown, and as an alternative to large scale, mono-crop agriculture.

- We choose to message palm oil positively which is counter to convention – our approach being to promote appropriate palm oil use and not to promote its boycott.[53]

This was one of Traidcraft's more radical pioneering developments. Biscuit and cookie ranges would eventually start to use Fair Trade palm oil or FairPalm, but the level of sales would ultimately prove to be disappointing.

"Palm Oil – It's great" was one of those initial marketing messages. But in the face of the anti-palm oil lobby who said "don't use it", perhaps it was a hard task to persuade consumers and other brands that there could be an alternative. For Traidcraft supporters who might have bought into this lobby or even heard it via other Fair Trade brands, a new message must have been confusing. I found it quite disheartening but rationalized it through my experiences in Ghana. I saw many farmers who cultivated both cocoa and oil palm trees on the same land and who could sell one of their crops as Fairtrade but not the other one. Trading in palm oil could even be complicated by events occurring thousands of miles away through the actions of large-scale multinationals in South East Asia, their unregulated mono-cropping activities, and resultant harmful impact on biodiversity.

---

53 Traidcraft internal document, written by the author, 2016.

PART SIX

Traidcraft and Supermarkets

Chapter 21

ENGAGING WITH
THE BIG PLAYERS

"Well intentioned paddlers in a pool of sharks" – that's what Philip Angier said as we considered the prospect of Traidcraft products being listed in supermarkets in the 1990s. It's true to say that for much of its history, Traidcraft has not really given much attention to selling its products in the mainstream supermarkets. With thousands of voluntary reps, later known as Fair Traders, together with an extensive supporter base buying through mail order, there was more than enough for our sales teams to get to grips with. When Cafédirect was co-founded by Traidcraft, Oxfam, Twin Trading, and Equal Exchange in the 1990s, it was to be the supermarket brand that none of us thought we could (or wanted to) carry off on our own.

But as the new millennium approached and supermarkets got a bit more interested in the world of ethical trade, things would change. Sainsbury's experimented with shelf space given over to a broad range of what they would refer to as "ethical" products. For a while, the Traidcraft Mauritius sugar and Traidcraft cookies would find themselves alongside organic products and "free from" products in a limited number of stores. Ultimately it was short-lived, but it was an interesting experience in terms of dipping our toes into mainstream supermarket selling.

With the arrival of a new marketing director things changed and it was then that Geobar was developed specifically as a supermarket product. It required dedicated resources to be given over to selling, marketing, and logistics, which worked alongside those same departments managing other sales channels. From its small beginnings, more than 10 million Geobars per year were being sold through a limited number of supermarkets.

Stuart Palmer was that new Marketing Director and tells the story in his own inimitable style:

> After several months of limping along and learning the business of food wholesale from my colleague Alistair Menzies, I knew something different was needed. The only way to get some bigger sales volumes, bigger volumes for producers and, I hoped, bigger profits for the organization was to look for bigger customers. That meant looking at the multiples. These large grocery chains were viewed with suspicion by the Fair Trade movement as it had grown from the alternative trade movement which sought to revolutionize the whole supply chain from producer to consumer. Selling into the multiples, who exerted such a dominant influence, meant "selling out" our principles, according to many in the movement. It was not a step I took casually.
>
> I took some deep breaths, packed up a single example of every food item I thought could possibly be of interest to any of the multiples, and just before Christmas 1998, I couriered the boxes off to every buyer I could identify. I prayed. This was my final gambit. If nothing worked here, then my work in Traidcraft plc was, pretty much, an unmitigated failure.
>
> Early in January 1999, I received a phone call. "I like the bar!" My mind started spinning... Which bar? I had packed up all manner of bits and bobs. "The one with the weird wrapper, the sticky one like a flapjack. I have been eating it on weekends away with the conservation trust volunteers I work with and I like it." So said the wonderful Waitrose buyer, John Stokes. Next, he explained, he would like it in time for Fairtrade Fortnight, the first two weeks of March. Then we got

to the volume question and John mentioned a very large number of bars, and my jaw dropped.

I spoke to Joe and we approached our local manufacturers, Fullwell Mill, who basically knocked up the bars in something only slightly larger than a domestic garage in Sunderland. When I mentioned the volume we needed to them, they confirmed that they couldn't make the bar in those numbers. "This is your recipe," I stated, "Why don't you find a subcontractor to make them for you?" They agreed. After much chasing, they found Halo Foods, based in deepest Wales.

Joe and I headed off to Halo Foods and, halfway through a long meeting, just after a factory tour, I thought I should check that they had received the recipe. No! One member of their team left the room, organized for it to be faxed down, and then returned looking somewhat embarrassed. "What's the matter?" I asked. "We can't make this! We cannot do baked products in this factory."

I was not a happy man, and neither was Joe. This was a long trip; we had waited several weeks to be given this contact to work with. What was to be done? "Can you do something similar with these ingredients?" we asked. Sure, we can start work on some sample recipes today!

The next week I was in London at a food fair. We arranged for samples to get couriered to London and the wonderful Jenny File, Marketing Manager at Traidcraft, taste tested them. Once her discerning palate was satisfied, we were good to go!

So, we had a new recipe but that was it. There was no name for it, no wrapper for it, and no box to hold them in! How to proceed? Another call to John Stokes at Waitrose followed. He introduced me to Darryl Ireland, a Geordie now based in east London, Shoreditch (before it became so achingly trendy), and suggested that he could help us with a packaging design. I went down to see him in his fantastic studio that he shared with his wife. The chemistry was there from day one. We needed a look that would sit well on Waitrose shelves and be appealing to their customers. The snack bar sector was just starting to grow, and we had a chance to be in on the ground floor. A rising market (tide) lifts all boats!

Not only did Darryl understand that we wanted a box that screamed "organic" and "natural", but he got that we needed a name. He kindly offered to test out a few and it was he that came up with the name "Geobar".

Cardboard boxes are quick to turn around, but printed film to wrap snack bars in takes longer. We made it onto the Waitrose shelves in time. Plain white wrap in a lovely Geobar box! We also had to convince the Fairtrade Foundation that it should put a Fairtrade Mark on a composite food product in a mainstream outlet. Thanks, in no small part to the wonderful relationship of trust that Joe Osman had with them, they eventually agreed we could put the mark on. We didn't manage to complete this by the first production run, but it was ready for the second and this meant we were launching the first composite Fairtrade marked food product in the UK. Yippee!

Finally, we had a vehicle for selling more sugar, dried fruit, and honey into the UK market in a way that did not mean finding yet more housewives who wanted to scratch cook sweet cakes! This meant we could help more producers lift their families out of poverty and have Fairtrade premium money that they could decide to spend for the first time.

The launch was successful. Initially they put the Geobar into some pilot stores. Within a year it was into all their stores – over a hundred of them. By the next Fairtrade Fortnight, another multiple had signed up and the ball was rolling. About this time, it was apparent that Twanna Doherty, a former Nike sales person, was an underappreciated asset in the marketing staff team. Time to let her rip on the Geobar. In year one, I was

> able to double turnover of the bar, but in year two,
> Twanna trebled it! Way to go, girl! Into all the major
> multiples and hustling up the volumes. Traidcraft was
> cooking on gas. But, with all these higher volumes came
> the challenge of managing all the logistics and staying in
> as a player with the "big boys", the multiples.[54]

Traidcraft was by no means an expert in the cereal bar market and we relied on our manufacturers to provide that expertise. We also had lots of other products to manage across the whole food and handicrafts sectors. To take Geobar onto the next level we needed to invest or to find a different business model. The brand licensing model had been born some time earlier which had seen Traidcraft canned pineapple and Fruit Passion enter the supermarkets. The model was quite simple. Our expertise was in developing and applying Fair Trade principles to supply chains – manufacturing and product expertise lay elsewhere. Developing partnerships which linked this expertise, and which would include a licence income to Traidcraft through the use of its brand would be regarded as the best route for achieving supermarket distribution. This became a key part of Traidcraft's strategy of the 2000s. The "win" would be greater volume of sales for producers but not for Traidcraft itself and the social accounts would report on volume of purchases from producers as an indicator of impact and success rather than sales revenue or profitability.

When the Geobar brand was licensed out to a manufacturing partner, sales dramatically increased and Geobar was listed in virtually every major supermarket in the UK. Income to Traidcraft would be useful through sizeable licence fees, but the greater volumes of ingredients consumed, especially honey and dried fruit, would dramatically increase our purchases from those producers. This resulted in different problems but ones which we were well able to respond to. New suppliers of honey and raisins were developed to meet this greater demand. We were even able to develop our own supply chain for Fairtrade crisped rice which was an essential ingredient in Geobar.

---

54   From personal correspondence with the author, 2019.

Marks & Spencer

One of the more fascinating forays into the world of mainstream retail for Traidcraft began in 2006 when we were approached by M&S who were developing their corporate social responsibility programme. They shared their overall plans with us – thry had many ethical components including the launch of clothing containing Fairtrade certified cotton (which they would be first to do). They were also interested to share their initiative in partnering with a large development charity delivering benefits to small-scale communities and enterprises in the developing world.

As well as clothing, the grocery requirements of M&S would be fulfilled by the introduction of a range of Fairtrade labelled products. At one stage, they explored the possibility of buying their rice and raisins from Traidcraft, which unfortunately did not amount to anything. They approached Traidcraft since there were no credible or reputable alternatives in the UK doing Fair Trade products in giftware, homeware, and the like.

The experience was complex and took a lot of staff time. Many of my colleagues were involved, including product development and quality management staff, as well as those of us looking after the Fair Trade credentials of supply chains and undertaking monitoring activities at source. The rewards were potentially enormous for some of our overseas producers. The original proposition was that we would introduce M&S to some of our suppliers and we would arrive at some sort of licence agreement to provide our services and expertise in Fair Trade, but that we would not be a supplier to M&S. As it turned out, that is exactly what M&S wanted us to be. After reviewing ranges and products, they homed in on handmade paper cards. Swajan in Bangladesh, who had been introduced to us through the Traidcraft Exchange Bangladesh programme, and Salay in the Philippines would be the two suppliers who would hopefully benefit from a big increase in orders.

It was not until the Spring of 2007 that these products were launched into M&S. This was after much design work, product development, and price negotiation. It was also after a couple of barriers had to be overcome. The first was that Tesco had fallen foul of issues of child labour which had been discovered in their garment factories in Bangladesh and we needed to demonstrate fully that this was not the case with the Swajan producers, some of who were from remote rural parts of Bangladesh. We managed to persuade M&S that these suppliers were very different to garment factories, so this barrier was overcome, but it did delay things for a while. The second was that a joint visit to both suppliers by me and one of our contacts at M&S was cancelled at the last minute. M&S had insisted that they should check out each supply chain personally and that I would be the person to accompany them. Sadly, issues in a part of the Philippines, which had a history of conflict, meant that M&S staff would not be covered by their insurance policy. In the end M&S decided to trust us and never did make those overseas visits.

Eventually, Fair Trade greetings cards found their way into the M&S larger stores. One interesting point is that all of these cards were Traidcraft branded and did not carry an M&S brand. At that point, M&S only sold products under their own brand and, to the best of our knowledge, Traidcraft became the first external brand to be listed.

Ultimately, the products had a short life cycle in M&S and there was an agreement lasting just two years. Swajan and Salay enjoyed those extra orders for a while but eventually the ranges were dropped because they did not deliver the volume or profitability required. Perhaps the execution could have been better. There was little in the way of coordinated marketing and messaging and the cards would merely be scattered around the greetings cards fixture.

Boots

It's a bit of a footnote to this chapter, but it's worth recounting that Traidcraft almost entered the world of optical accessories! Among the myriad of mainstream retailers trying to respond to the growth of Fair Trade were Boots, who were not renowned for selling grocery products so their access to Fairtrade certified products was fairly limited. It was Boots the Optician that approached us, perhaps after seeing what we had been doing with Co-op and M&S. Would we endorse as Fair Trade their supply chain of spectacle frames made in China? We had always harboured an ambition to see Fair Trade principles adopted in the manufacturing sector and beyond the small-scale social enterprise set-ups typified by our handicraft suppliers. It was worthy of meeting up and discussing the possibilities and I suppose that, had the factories been located somewhere other than China, then there might have been scope to make progress. In the end, there were too many hurdles to jump and the project came to a close, but I occasionally wonder how the concept of Fair Trade spectacles might have been received by the public!

Chapter 22

A NATURAL ALLY: THE CO-OP

By far the most significant brand licence relationship for Traidcraft was with the Co-op. Brad Hill was Co-op's Fair Trade Strategy Manager for many years and many of us got to know him very well over that time. Known as "Mr Fairtrade" to many, he was responsible for driving strategy which resulted in the Co-op being one of the largest retailers of Fair Trade products in the UK. It was not without opposition and occasional setbacks. The story starts in the 1990s, just as Traidcraft Exchange was becoming more involved in the wider ethical agenda. Brad tells his own story:

> During the 1990s, as customers were becoming more aware of ethics, the Co-op launched its "Responsible Retailing" campaign and, with the involvement of its own customer members, set about creating a whole new agenda. Co-op had already been doing some good things, but Responsible Retailing was transformational. Campaigning and action by Co-op addressed a whole range of ethical issues including the unregulated use of pesticides; animal cruelty; the reduction of sugar, salt and fat in products; the dishonest marketing of unhealthy products to children; and the unfair treatment of workers in supply chains. Today these are accepted norms, but back then Co-op was revolutionizing the food industry.

A Natural Ally: The Co-op

This is where Fair Trade came in. The Fairtrade Mark had launched in 1994 and Co-op was one of the first to list the first Fairtrade labelled product which was Maya Gold and then Clipper Tea. Cafédirect had been listed by Co-op in 1992, even before it carried the Fairtrade label. These products were listed but barely sold, but the Responsible Retailing strategy turned its attention to the subject of what we called "pillage", or how we in the west take from the world's poorest. Ideas around Co-op brand Fair Trade, and the fact that Co-op itself was born of Fair Trade values, began to form. In 2000, Co-op launched the UK's very first Fairtrade certified bananas through working with Agrofair (a dedicated Fair Trade Organization focusing on fresh produce), and had partnered with Divine to develop a co-branded chocolate bar, the very first supermarket own-brand Fairtrade labelled product in the world! This was being driven by just a handful of people within the Co-op, welcomed by members, but against the will of the wider business. The uphill battle to get Responsible Retail and Fair Trade accepted had begun and is why it was not until 2002 that Co-op began to create a presence in Fair Trade with a broader range, demonstrating commercial success to Co-op buyers.

Traidcraft was the first port of call for Co-op when developing products outside of the easily available "core" Fairtrade certified products like tea, coffee, chocolate, flowers, sugar, and bananas – and wine was the first such collaboration. It was Traidcraft that approached Co-op with the idea, having developed their Fair Trade wines. They had seen the Co-op's work with Agrofair and Divine and were aware of Co-op aspirations in Fair Trade. The product, a Chilean Carménère red wine, was presented as a finished product and the discussions really were around labelling and pricing in order to get the product listed. In some ways, it was awkward, as Co-op communications were focused on the Fairtrade Mark and using this "brand".

As it was in its infancy, it was possible at this stage for the message to be adapted. So, the bottle label carried the Traidcraft brand as the first venture into a kind of "surrogate Fairtrade Mark". The reverse label carried a convoluted message explaining that "this is Fair Trade without a Fairtrade Mark, since standards for wine do not exist, but that Traidcraft has replicated what those standards would have looked like if they did"! More importantly, the quality and price point, and the fact that we had a route to push our then reluctant buyers through an increasingly credible strategy, got the product on shelf. Co-op consumer members, many of them Traidcraft Fair Traders, embraced the product and sales were healthy from the off.

We then pushed Fairtrade Foundation to develop Fairtrade standards for wine grapes on the back of the launch. Taking advantage of Traidcraft's relationship with them and their involvement in standard setting, this was always expected. Once standards had been developed for wine in 2004, Co-op was ready to launch a wider range having created relationships through existing suppliers. The Carménère moved away from carrying the Traidcraft brand and became a Co-op brand carrying the Fairtrade Mark.

Traidcraft joined Agrofair and Divine as key strategic development partners. Although not formally labelled as such, it was through pioneer Fair Trade Organizations that Co-op was able to access and develop producer relationships and deliver its Fair Trade strategy.

Of all the products developed working with Traidcraft, charcoal is my stand-out achievement. It was a rollercoaster journey, but it was with immense pride and satisfaction that Co-op switched all of its charcoal to Fair Trade in 2017.

The product came about when our supplier, Rectella, began to ask questions of our buyer as to how the product could become Fairtrade labelled. Of course, this was passed to me and it became clear very quickly that Rectella was genuinely interested – from a sourcing, rather than commercial, perspective. They believed that their supplier in Namibia was already doing some good work with their workers and could become Fairtrade certified. We discussed standards and other requirements and I introduced Rectella to Traidcraft to understand if charcoal could be something that Traidcraft could endorse as Fair Trade.

And so the products launched in 2009. A visit to the producers in Namibia was planned for the Spring of 2014, but just as it was being finalized the buyer announced a de-list. This was due to the need for greater profit margin and a belief that price sensitivity meant we had to reduce the retail price. In all my time at Co-op I had never been so angry, and I was outraged that we could pull the plug to effectively remove some of our financial commitment to producers through additional premiums paid and redirect them into our own profits.

I continued to fight to get the product re-listed by explaining to senior colleagues that this could be seen as unethical buying practice. I was also able to raise the issue with some of my influential membership colleagues who then raised their collective concern. And so Fair Trade charcoal was reconsidered but rather than return to Rectella, an alternative and cheaper supplier was considered, potentially with Traidcraft being involved. But, of course, Traidcraft's charcoal relationship was with Rectella and its work in Namibia, so this proposal was never going to happen. If we were to have Fair Trade back, then it would be according to our original arrangement. The new Co-op buyer, thankfully short-lived within the business, showed no interest and was actively against the further discussion. When Rectella arranged a video from Namibia showing the impact of Fair Trade, which included a message of thanks from the children of the workers, I was aghast at the lack of compassion and empathy. I would not relent, driven in part by my own belief that we had sold out and left producers high and dry.

I was determined to find a way and probably stuck my neck out for Fair Trade charcoal more than for anything else in my career, believing in a strong moral duty to stand up for voiceless producers. At a Co-op Ethical conference, I was asked to find a speaker on Fair Trade and I invited someone from Traidcraft. Joe Osman's presentation would include a section on how we had worked together through the years and included a section on charcoal, highlighting the impact it had made in Namibia. But it also highlighted that this was no longer a live partnership. Not only was the audience full of suppliers but our own relatively new appointed Head of Commercial Trading was there. He was beginning to work out how we could do more on ethics now that we were recovering from some difficult commercial times. The newly appointed Head of Trading for non-food was also in attendance and I was introduced to him for the first time and able to continue the dialogue. Maybe he could be the one to bring Fair Trade charcoal back. And he did! The Co-op went back to sourcing three Fair Trade charcoal products from Rectella, completed a shift on all six lines the following year, and created a policy which wedded Co-op to Fair Trade charcoal into the future.

Visits to Namibia have helped the business see and understand the product and the people who produce it, and communications have improved with dedicated resources to actively share the story on social media. Rectella were rewarded with the Co-op Ethical supplier of the year award at the glitzy annual ceremony which was well deserved and helped to further raise profile. And in terms of the definition of Fair Trade, the Co-op now has a written policy which states that if Fairtrade standards are not in place for a product, then it is permissible to partner with a credible FTO

like Traidcraft to oversee standards development and
monitoring.[55]

Brad continued to champion Fair Trade in the Co-op and they firmly
embraced the concept into their organizational policy. Traidcraft's
partnership review model which included monitoring tools developed
jointly with our EFTA colleagues and based on the WFTO's ten Fair
Trade principles formed the basis of these product endorsements. For
the Co-op, Traidcraft had a robust system which was the equivalent
of Fairtrade and served as a third-party endorsement for Fair Trade
products not covered by Fairtrade International.

One of my colleagues, Alistair Leadbetter, had oversight of this
project from day one. It was his responsibility to ensure that Fair Trade
principles were adhered to, and to set up various projects which would
impact both the workers who sorted, assembled, and packed charcoal
ready for export, and also those who gathered wood and converted it
into charcoal. As with all products originating from wood, questions
were initially asked about how environmentally friendly this charcoal
was, but we were satisfied by the fact that the wood originated from
an invasive species of bush which was making land unproductive for
farming. A bit like clearing weeds and making good use of them.

But wine and charcoal weren't the only products that Traidcraft
and Co-op partnered up in. There were some quirky attempts like
Christmas crackers sourced from Traidcraft's handicraft partners. This
didn't last too long. But then coffins came along! Co-op Funeral Care
almost accidentally got interested in Fair Trade. The link between Co-
op Funeral Care and Co-op retail division was not exactly strong, so
this was quite a coup and eventually Fair Trade coffins became part
of the Co-op Funeral Care portfolio. It's not as high profile as other
Co-op products and not as easy to convey the Fair Trade message in
such products but it did introduce Oasis Transformation and their
Bangladesh-based manufacturer of bamboo coffins into the world of
Fair Trade and they would later go on to be members of WFTO.

Then there was rubber. In a similar way to the charcoal project, we
were introduced to one of the Co-op suppliers, this time of rubber
gloves. Ironically, after the initial introduction, the Co-op's interest

---

55 From personal correspondence with the author, 2019.

waned a little but, by then, we had completed all of the monitoring and evaluation work in Sri Lanka which I had undertaken myself. Traidcraft was interested in developing its own brand of kitchen and outdoor gloves. I suppose I took a bit of a purest view of what Fair Trade for rubber latex would look like when I visited Sri Lanka. I had been introduced to quite a few small-scale "farmers" who owned small plots of land which contained rubber trees but they were clearly not "real" farmers. Most were middle-class professionals working in Colombo but with a farm in the countryside to retreat to at weekends. It was also clear from the evaluation that there *were* dependent rubber farmers who tapped their own latex. We commissioned a piece of work to find out who and where they were, so we could be clear that Fair Trade would be appropriate. The work showed that we should target a specific region in the southern part of Sri Lanka. A supply chain was finalized, focusing on that region and on specific farmers, and we developed the products which worked relatively successfully at Traidcraft, but without the scale that was intended through the Co-op. Brad Hill takes up the story again:

> Eventually Co-op followed the wine model of 2001 and
> launched under its own brand with the Traidcraft brand as
> a "surrogate FT Mark". The product range was extended
> to include all Co-op rubber gloves, but it always struggled
> to capture the imagination, partly because rubber latex
> is part of a complex supply chain and partly because of
> the product itself. Rubber is not an expected Fair Trade
> product. Consequently, Fair Trade rubber gloves are a little
> under the radar in the Co-op, hardly promoted and sold as a
> functional item.[56]

The partnership with the Co-op has occasionally gone beyond the level of product development and some of their early overseas projects involved Traidcraft. As Co-op delivered a world first when it launched Fairtrade certified fresh blueberries, it encountered the complexities of managing fresh produce and needed more than one supplier to deal with seasonality. Starting off with South African blueberries in the early

---

56   From personal correspondence with the author, 2019.

part of the season, it would need to switch to Latin American sourcing later in the season. Apicoop in Chile was a long-standing partner of Traidcraft, supplying honey, and had taken a keen interest in the Geobar product in which their honey was being consumed. Being located in a region that also was good for growing blueberries and the fact that Traidcraft had a Geobar that also used dried blueberries, we partnered up with Apicoop to develop Fairtrade certified dried blueberries. A natural extension of this was for Apicoop to also partner up with Co-op to provide that second season fresh blueberry. Co-op decided to invest in a support project to provide Apicoop with a new packing machine and refrigerated transportation with Traidcraft overseeing the project and reporting on its impact.

This brings me to yet another hero partner – in Chino Henriquez, who managed Apicoop. Never was the word "partnership" so tangibly demonstrated than in that relationship. His keen interest in Geobar extended not just to frequent visits to Traidcraft and participating in our customer events, but to getting actively involved in selling the product. Traidcraft Marketing Director Larry Bush who succeeded Stuart Palmer recalls Chino accompanying him to meet supermarket buyers to great effect – including Tesco and Morrisons, with the latter actually leading to a listing. Larry commented: "Chino was certainly great with supermarket buyers and proved that they do (on the whole) have a heart!"[57]

Much to my amusement, when I visited Apicoop in Chile, I noticed that one of their tractors used in the blueberry fields bore the name "Big Joe". I wasn't sure whether to be flattered or not! Then when Traidcraft was going through its commercial difficulties in 2018, who should make such a practical offer of support, but Chino. The supplier to the buyer! He offered to ship forty tonnes of honey free of charge, and we would only pay for it if we managed to sell it!

It was not for the want of trying, but we could never get the Co-op to play into Traidcraft's innovative Fair Trade palm oil development. But who knows what might happen in the future? Hopefully the partnership between Co-op and Traidcraft will go from strength to strength, as the Co-op grows and extends its Fair Trade and ethical strategy.

---

57   From personal correspondence with the author, 2019.

PART SEVEN

Christian Roots and Mission

Chapter 23

A CHRISTIAN ORGANIZATION?

I was never really a great fan of the use of the word "Christian" as an adjective. It's fine in some contexts but I struggle when it's used in others. The Bible doesn't use the word "Christian" very often and only as a name given to those who declared themselves as "Christ-followers". In fact, I sometimes prefer to use that description of myself, given the disrepute that the word "Christian" seems to have fallen into! Is this a Christian book? It's a book written by a Christian, so if that makes it a Christian book, then so be it! Traidcraft was often called a "Christian organization", both by its supporters and by itself. I acknowledge why that might have been the case, but I have to confess my own discomfort. This chapter seeks to explore a little more the role that Traidcraft played as an organization founded by Christians, being supported by many churches through which its products have sold and money raised, and how the people that founded Traidcraft and those who followed sought to put their faith into practice.

Those of us who attend an Anglican church on a regular basis might be familiar with these words of confession:

> Most merciful God,
> Father of our Lord Jesus Christ,
> we confess that we have sinned
> in thought, word and deed.

> We have not loved you with our whole heart.
> We have not loved our neighbours as ourselves.
> In your mercy
> forgive what we have been,
> help us to amend what we are,
> and direct what we shall be;
> that we may act justly,
> love mercy,
> and walk humbly with you, our God.
> Amen.[58]

Or perhaps not so familiar given that many of us recite these words with little thought or concern for their implication, and I'm certainly guilty of that.

The latter words of the confession draw from Micah 6:8 which I have occasionally declared as my favourite verse in the Bible. "He has shown you, O mortal, what is good. And what does the LORD require of you? To act justly and to love mercy and to walk humbly with your God". They come in the middle of a prophetic word which was an indictment against Israel and its corrupt practices and injustice in many parts of society: bribery, greed, exploitation of the weak, rules which favoured the wealthy, stealing land from the weak, poor treatment of women and children. All themes which we could identify with today. While the prophet warns of judgement against such things he also talks about hope, restoration, and the coming of Jesus.

Much of the Old Testament reflects the character of God. Psalm 146:7–9 says:

> He upholds the cause of the oppressed
> and gives food to the hungry.
> The LORD sets prisoners free,
> The LORD gives sight to the blind,
> The LORD lifts up those who are bowed down,
> The LORD loves the righteous.
> The LORD watches over the foreigner
> and sustains the fatherless and the widow,
> but he frustrates the ways of the wicked.

---

58 Archbishop's Council, *Common Worship: Services and Prayers for the Church of England*, 2000.

Then when Jesus starts his own work, he declares in Luke 4:18-19 – in what is sometimes called his "manifesto" – by using the words of the prophet Isaiah.

> "The Spirit of the Lord is on me,
> because he has anointed me
> to proclaim good news to the poor.
> He has sent me to proclaim freedom for the prisoners
> and recovery of sight for the blind,
> to set the oppressed free,
> to proclaim the year of the Lord's favour".

And as Jesus says in Matthew 5:17, "Do not think that I have come to abolish the Law or the Prophets; I have not come to abolish them but to fulfil them", prompting many of us who declare ourselves as Christians to reflect on what these things mean outside of our sometimes cosy church buildings.

There are some quite radical parts of the Old Testament where God lays out the way things ought to be. A just society would have integrated ways of addressing the needs of poor people. In fact, if they were practised correctly – and unfortunately, they weren't, as the prophets pointed out on numerous occasions – then any issues of poverty and slavery might be addressed. Every seventh year would signal the cancellation of debt and the freedom from slavery. Then after the seventh of these periods, that year would be known as the year of "Jubilee" where all lands would be returned to their original owners. It was a kind of resetting of society. Then there were the rules for tithing and gleaning. One-tenth of a person's annual income would be given, not just to the upkeep of the temple, but to the poor and weak in society. Landowners would not be allowed to gather all of their crops. Instead, a portion would be left for the poor and landless to gather themselves. This, of course, entailed those people helping themselves rather than receiving a charitable hand-out. Occasional criticism of today's Christianity might be in its application of a rules-based faith, but perhaps rules applied appropriately might have their place.

Traidcraft's founders were ultimately driven by a desire to put their Christian faith into practical action, informed by their understanding of these radical yet scriptural principles. They were able to express this in one of those original statements of objectives:

> Traidcraft aims to expand and establish more just trading systems which will express the principles of love and justice fundamental to the Christian faith. Practical service and a partnership for change will characterize the organisation, which puts people before profit.[59]

In developing its first purchasing policy, the Christian principles underpinning it were much considered at trustee level. I look back at some of the documents produced with a degree of incredulity, and reproduce some of them below. However, it must be remembered that Traidcraft's birth was not an easy one as it emerged from Tearcraft, which would continue almost as a competitor. That such theological depth was needed in developing a purchasing policy and principles demonstrates the kind of thinking happening at the time, although I'm left feeling that maybe there were a few too many theologians involved with Traidcraft's birth!

> Traidcraft has the view that the aims of trading should embrace the provision of physical and spiritual necessities in accord with the total message of the Christian gospel. The company sees its particular area of activity as part of the global commitment of Christians to bring about peace, reconciliation, justice and wholeness in the world. This will be worked out through the development and marketing of Third World products and associated educational work. Traidcraft wishes to deal with groups which share this viewpoint but also recognises the Christian principle of love for neighbour and will assist those in need who do not have a declared Christian basis. When dealing with groups not sharing a Christian viewpoint the company would trust to the activity of the Christian church worldwide, the action of the Holy Spirit and its own practical example of love in action to assist in creating fullness of life.[60]

---

59 Traidcraft internal document, July 1986. See Appendix 1 for full version.
60 Traidcraft internal document, 1979.

Apart from its trading objectives, what would a business that applied Christian principles look like practically? Initially, virtually all staff were practising Christians from a relatively narrow range of denominations and traditions. The culture was "inclusive" with a high degree of participation in decision-making and group discussion about mission and objectives, trying to make sense of this thing we were doing. We would occasionally even close the business for a day and meet somewhere to reflect and discuss things. By the time I joined Traidcraft in 1981 (having worked at Tearcraft from 1976 to 1981), prayer and worship featured quite prominently with weekly, non-compulsory, gatherings of staff. Important meetings tended to open with prayer. Before that, in the very early days, when survival was not entirely guaranteed, prayer would particularly be put to good effect. One of the founders of Traidcraft, Brian Hutchins, would later write in a newsletter to shareholders:

> In July 1979, Traidcraft came into existence with a sales
> budget of £120,000 for its first year. We were thrilled when
> we received fifteen orders in one day, even though some
> were from our friends just to encourage us… there were
> times in those early months when I didn't think Traidcraft
> would survive. I remember anguishing over a donation
> from a close friend of mine who could ill afford it, because
> I thought we would have to wind up the company. There
> were times when we urgently needed finance to pay for
> goods that we had ordered, and miraculously, just in time,
> the hand of God intervened and provided what was
> required, sometimes from the most unexpected sources.[61]

Jean Whitehead, a staff member right at the start of Traidcraft writes:

> That first Christmas season in 1979 was very quiet with
> few orders arriving for the products which had been
> arriving to stock the warehouse shelves, but we were not
> downhearted. There was an air of confidence that we were
> on the edge of something that would grow. Slowly, more
> staff joined the team and I seemed to move office every

---

61 Brian Hutchins, Traidcraft shareholder newsletter, "Nostalgic Memories", 1993.

six months to accommodate them. As the 1980 Christmas season came along, so did the orders and we worked long hours to process, pack and despatch orders to the reps and individuals. We felt WE WERE OFF!

Along with the work, came a family spirit with wonderful camaraderie, social events and a feeling of being valued no matter what job was done. And we could also finally afford heating in the offices and I no longer had to wear my sheepskin coat, scarf and hat to keep at bay the cold winters in the north!

As Christians, we worked together for the greater good of the organization and that meant good timekeeping, good working practices, going the extra mile without expecting to be paid for it, being patient with each other, and bearing with one another in times of difference of opinion. There was a very happy atmosphere. There was a strong emphasis on this shared faith and personal experience. I can't remember much about praying together about the work in those first months. I do remember sitting in the office with Brian Hutchins and he asked me if I thought Traidcraft would survive and grow. I said it would, and that for me was born of faith and not natural optimism. The day we received a cheque for a large amount of cash from a donor unknown to us was recognized as a gift from God at a time when funds were very low. Looking back now, it seems we believed that there was an underlying assurance that the Lord was guiding us through unknown territory.[62]

A ten-point "basis of faith for the Traidcraft Trust" was developed and senior staff, trustees, and directors were all obliged to sign their affirmation of that statement. This practice would continue for the whole of Traidcraft's history – although, eventually, the basis of faith was replaced by the less restrictive Apostles' Creed, and only trustees and directors would need to declare their affirmation. This practice was

---

62 From personal correspondence with the author, 2019.

not without some degree of controversy over the years and particularly in relation to staff representation at director level and to career development. As the balance shifted between staff who were practising Christians and those who were not, so there would be an underlying tension when it came to the election of staff directors. In later years, for numerous competent members of staff, promotion to a senior management role would not be possible because of this Christian requirement and, sadly, those people would be lost to Traidcraft as they pursued more senior and responsible roles elsewhere.

The "inclusive" culture would be a double-edged sword. Traidcraft was not without its disciplinary procedures and, on more than one occasion, dismissal of staff was enforced. This would tend to be for gross misconduct rather than linked to everyday work performance. It's fair to say that for much of its history, Traidcraft practised high levels of tolerance for under-performance. However, the vast majority of staff over the years, in acknowledging the mission and objectives of Traidcraft, worked hard and would go the extra mile. Working beyond contractual obligations was commonplace. In fact, on occasion, staff would need to have it pointed out that they were working too many hours! On other occasions, some members of staff certainly took advantage of this culture and, in some of the darker days of the 1990s, this developed into something which I can only describe, with the benefit of hindsight, as institutional bullying. I take no pride in some of the things that happened during that time. Fortunately, they were short-lived.

There were other examples of applying Christian principles to running a business and one of the most important, related to salary differentials, would again prove to be a double-edged sword. There was much to be said then, as now, about global inequality and the difference between rich and poor. There are plenty of statistics around about how global wealth is divided and the fact is that it's worse now than when Traidcraft started. Right from day one, it was decided that the difference between the highest paid worker would be no more than 2.75 times that of the lowest paid worker. The principle would be that the lowest paid would earn a little more than the average for equivalent local work and the highest paid would, of course, earn far less than they could for equivalent local work. This was a principle that would continue throughout Traidcraft's history, although the differential would gradually widen in order to attract the right calibre of staff, perhaps for roles requiring a professional qualification. But, for much of the time, many members of staff were recruited having taken a large pay cut and, for most, it was a conscious vocational choice, whether or not driven by their Christian faith.

As the numbers of staff that Traidcraft employed grew, so the balance changed between those of faith and those without. There were few jobs where employing a practising Christian was a requirement and, indeed, it would have been discriminatory to apply that thinking during recruitment. Eventually, only those who were legal directors and a few selected other jobs were deemed be roles which formally required the job holder to be a practising Christian. Traidcraft did still attract Christians to come to work for it and, for much of the first half of its history Christians comprised probably the majority of staff. But times changed, multi-site working evolved, which included overseas offices, and Christian staff would eventually become the minority. Those acts of prayer and worship would still continue in a smaller way, but more informally and eventually outside of working hours. Personally, I think I was always conscious of the danger of an "us and them" scenario emerging and, while regularly challenged, I chose not to attend those corporate acts of worship and prayer.

Those of us, Christians or otherwise, who travelled abroad to visit producers or were well networked into the commercial world in the UK would choose their own way of communicating about and representing Traidcraft. For me, I always found it important whether in formal presentations or general conversations when describing the work of Traidcraft to producers or suppliers to be very explicit about the origin and heritage of the organization being rooted in the Christian faith. It was something to be proud of and not something to hide and would often result in an interesting conversation. I know that many of my colleagues felt the same way.

I was always conscious that I had started my working life at Tearcraft and then Traidcraft and that my personal vocation emerged as part of that early journey as a Christian. I was also born in the north east of England and I had no idea what it was like to come from the so-called "real world" of commerce, make a vocational change, uprooting to move to Gateshead, and taking a pay cut. I asked my friend Andy Redfern, International Director of Traidcraft from 1999 to 2004 and who would go on to co-found Ethical Superstore, to tell his story. Andy writes:

> When I arrived at Traidcraft in July 1996, a finance team member looked at my recently unpacked bookshelf and books commenting, "Why do you have so many books written by the trustees and management members of Traidcraft?" His tone suggested that perhaps I was sucking up "t'management" and shouldn't be trusted.
>
> I was surprised by his response as I was someone who had travelled with Traidcraft as a supporter since 1983 when I first met Graham Young. I met him at a Christian youth conference when he appeared on stage with a dressed shop window dummy to promote his book *Letters to Auntie Flo*.[63] This book, about the struggles of a young evangelical Christian bloke trying to get his ethical choices right, struck a chord with me and other books like *Radical Discipleship* (by Chris Sugden who was another early trustee of Traidcraft) were formative in my personal radical-edged, Christian belief.[64]
>
> I ran my own "Traidcraft" shop in Colchester during the early 1990s, borrowing money from key supporters in my local church. This was a practical and radical outworking of faith in action. Nearly all our staff and volunteers were Christians who prayed and laboured the shop business through some turbulent times. Joining Traidcraft was vocational for me. This was about calling, commitment, and sacrifice (having taken a 70% reduction in salary to get under the 2.7 times salary cap!). And yet the Traidcraft I joined was imperfect, flawed and, on occasions, a tough place to put faith into action.
>
> I attended the weekly staff Christian worship sessions for all eight years of my time at Traidcraft. It

---

63 Graham Young, *Letters to Auntie Flo*, London: Harper Collins, 1983.
64 Chris Sugden, *Radical Discipleship*, Basingstoke: Marshalls, 1981.

was poorly attended with many Christians not attending as it did not scratch where they were itching. Things began to change. I remember a board member saying to me in 1999 as we struggled over the new legal documents for the organization, "If I'm lying on the operating table about to go under, I want to see the best surgeon with the scalpel rather than a Christian surgeon". The context was changing. Traidcraft seemed to become "embarrassed" by its Christian identity and so it was played down and even hidden in its communication. Around this time a new supporter of Traidcraft Exchange who happened to be Jewish, wrote an angry letter as they had sent financial support for several months only to find we were Christian organization. He wasn't angry we were a Christian – he was angry that we had hidden it.

Traidcraft was created out of the belief, inspiration, and perspiration of radical, committed Christians. It was their Christianity in action that drove them and inspired them. Knowing how and why something was created is fundamental to its identity and its veracity. Professor Rao, an Indian academic in small business development, spoke at a Traidcraft conference in 2000 and likened Traidcraft to a turtle on a post – you know it didn't get there by itself, you know someone put it there, and you know it was put there for a reason. Traidcraft was founded on the Christian principles of love and justice – that is, context provides meaning and helps people know what you do.

In 2000, I travelled with Nick Kightley from Traidcraft Exchange to Pakistan to conduct some research into whether a small business development service in Lahore or Islamabad would be beneficial to the local ethical business community. We worked with a local team of academics and researchers who were all Muslims. Several times during the trip they would ask to be excused while they prayed in the corner of the room. After one such interval, I asked the lead academic,

> "Why are you working with us? Surely, as we are a
> Christian-based organization, this must be difficult?"
> He looked at me: "We understand you. We know why
> you care. It makes sense that Jesus' example of helping
> the poor inspires you. Others we do not understand.
> We struggle with Oxfam and don't understand why
> they do what they do." I was humbled by his faith and
> by his insight that being true to Traidcraft's founding
> principles opened more doors than it closed.[65]

Stuart Palmer, Traidcraft's Marketing Director from 1998 to 2004,
writes about his own experience of his "calling" as a Christian:

> I joined Traidcraft in the autumn of 1998. At Easter that
> year, I was in Leeds with my wife Zoë, staying with friends.
> We got up late and bought the Sunday paper. A tiny advert
> for an "International Marketing Advisor" role at Traidcraft
> Exchange caught my eye. "If we ever want to live and work
> in a developing country this could be an ideal next step," I
> proffered to Zoë. "The only downsides are that it pays less
> than half my current wage, it is nearly 300 miles away where
> we don't know a soul and you are expecting our first baby."
> "I think God wants you to take that role," she says without
> hesitation!
>
> I applied and got offered the job. I resigned from
> my role in London and I was working my notice when
> I got a phone call one day... "Hello, this is Traidcraft
> calling. You are very "salesy" aren't you? Well, that's
> what we think. Would you consider doing a different
> role for us please? One with less travel that might suit
> your situation, what with your wife expecting a baby,
> and one that would pay a slightly higher wage?" So, that
> was how I ended up being taken on for an unadvertised
> job in a sector I had never worked in by a charity I had
> never heard of before.
>
> On a Friday I handed back the keys to my company
> car. On the following Monday I mounted my newly

---

65   From personal correspondence with the author, 2019.

> built delivery bike and zoomed down the hill from
> Beacon Lough, high above Low Fell in Gateshead, into
> the Team Valley and Traidcraft.[66]

In preparation for writing this book I leafed through every single catalogue that Traidcraft produced since 1979 and was struck by the huge amount of content given over to understanding what we were doing through the lens of its Christian founding principles. I suppose it was understandable, given that trading and education work were interlinked, and that the vast majority of sales came through the voluntary reps. All of the statistics would show then – and right up to the present day – that a very high proportion of these important supporters and re-sellers were practising Christians, who operated through their church, putting their faith into action. Right through Traidcraft's history this has continued and some of those staff roles mentioned earlier, which had a requirement that the job holder be a practising Christian, were designed to meet the requirements of those Fair Traders. The Christian content of publications would move away from catalogues to more dedicated resources, setting the work of a Fair Trader in the context of their own Christian service. Over the years, a myriad of materials would be published to serve those needs and included materials that could be used in a church worship setting.

I think that it's fair to say that, for a few years leading up to its fortieth birthday, the explicitly Christian identity and messaging of Traidcraft has somewhat eroded. The Fairtrade Foundation did a good job in promoting itself to the wider church and developed the concept of Fairtrade churches and Fairtrade diocese in addition to Fairtrade towns, cities, and even countries. They develop and supply resources and materials by way of support to those entities in the way that Traidcraft did in its most prosperous days, and they have effectively picked up a dropped baton. Traidcraft could no longer claim to be the "go to" organization for all things linking Fair Trade and Christianity. In any case, the most recent communications and websites linked to Traidcraft plc and Traidcraft Exchange give a lower profile to the Christian heritage of Traidcraft. Perhaps that's the way of all such organizations. But irrespective of this, Traidcraft's role in mobilizing

---

66 From personal correspondence with the author, 2019.

the church to effect change in the UK is undeniable. As Larry Bush, Traidcraft Marketing Director 2006/16 wrote:

> Who would have thought a tiny, north-east-based alternative trading company with a bunch of church-based stalwart customers and activists could spark such a massive change? It's David and Goliath stuff. I think this is one of the most significant "real world" achievements of churches over the past few decades.[67]

While writing this chapter, I was reminded of a blog I wrote in 2016 as part of a series linked to our "Justice Matters" campaign and it seems fitting to end this chapter by reproducing it:

> In my desk drawer I have a copy of the very first Traidcraft catalogue from 1979 – maybe a collector's item now? The opening two introductory paragraphs were as follows:
>
> "Traidcraft is a company founded and run by people trying to put into practice some of the implications of their own Christian faith. We feel that there is every opportunity to demonstrate God's desire for love and justice in the world through responsible and fair trading.
>
> Traidcraft is supported by, and accountable to, people of all denominations who believe that redressing economic injustice in the world is part of their responsibilities."
>
> Thirty-seven years on it's always useful to be reminded of our founding principles and it's all too easy to reduce "Fair Trade" into something which is about "doing some good to someone", or helping a "poor person", or building a school or providing medical care – all good things in themselves but tending toward the language of charity. Arguably injustice is kind of "hard-wired" into traditional global trading systems and Traidcraft set out to create an alternative. How well we have done that is open to debate but the fact is that the gulf between rich and poor is as wide as ever and so we continue with that mission.

---

67 From personal correspondence with the author, 2019.

A Christian Organization?

In the world of commodities, I've seen a lot – tea, coffee, cocoa, sugar, rubber, palm oil, nuts, fruit, honey, you name it! Whatever the commodity it usually starts with a very hard working farmer, conscientious and knowledgeable in the main, but very often burdened by the uncontrollable, like market price fluctuations, the power of traders, geographical circumstances or remoteness causing problems in accessing markets.

I've seen examples of the "dishonest scales" that the book of Proverbs in the Bible talks about, the lure and necessity for ready cash in hand rather than a better price by waiting or planning, the urgency to trade or face throwing away a perishable crop that needs to be processed quickly, or rejected because it doesn't quite meet the stringent standards of the buyer, or maybe having to sell for less than it cost to grow. All of these things can happen wherever crops are farmed but when you're a smallholder farmer in some remote region of Africa or Asia the consequences are amplified.

That's the downside, but I've also seen the upside. Farmers who, through organizing, can even out the power imbalance in supply chains. Farmers who through knowledge and understanding of markets can use their crop as the equivalent of currency. Farmers who invest in technology or equipment that adds value to their crop. Farmers who can earn a guaranteed income through the economically "disruptive" model of Fair Trade.

The world of Fair Trade is unrecognisable compared to those early days. Certifications systems like "Fairtrade" are great but the extent to which you can "certify" things which are fundamentally about addressing injustice in trade is an interesting point of debate. Here at Traidcraft we aspire to "act justly" rather than merely complying with a set of standards. I hope we're around for the next 37 years to continue that important work.[68]

---

68   Traidcraft website blog post, written by the author, 2016.

Chapter 24

A CHRISTIAN RESPONSE TO POVERTY

As Traidcraft entered the 2000s and Paul Chandler became CEO, there was a noticeable shift in the way that Traidcraft messaged its Christian principles. This is best represented by an extract from one of the vision documents produced at that time which described what it called "Traidcraft's Christian identity":

> **Traidcraft is a Christian response to poverty**
>
> - We draw our inspiration from the life and teachings of Jesus. We were founded and continue to be led by people with an active Christian faith.
>
> - We work with people of all faiths and none who share our vision and our commitment to the fight against poverty, but have a particular focus on mobilizing the support and prayer of the UK Christian community.
>
> - We commend the Christian faith through practical action and service to others, rather than through evangelism. Our Christian basis enables us to work effectively with other faith-based organizations and communities around the world.

- We believe every person is made in the image of God and has a right to flourish and fulfil their God-given potential, both individually and in community with others.

- We understand poverty to be complex, and not limited to material shortage alone. Promoting well-being, dignity, participation, and relationships are key parts of our practice, and reflect our Christian perspectives.

- We recognise the importance of caring for the world that God has created and promoting good environmental practices.[69]

This chapter is based on the reflections Paul Chandler made to the author in May 2019.

Paul believed that it should come as no surprise to anyone who investigates the development of the Fair Trade movement that Traidcraft was established as a Christian organization. Not only are the principles and values that underpin Fair Trade entirely consonant with those of a Christian worldview, but it was principally within church-based organizations that the practices of Fair Trade first evolved. Paul's analysis of the origins of Fair Trade would back this up.

The earliest known example of Fair Trade goes back to Edna Byler, an American Mennonite, who began to work with producer communities in Puerto Rico in the 1940s and 1950s, importing their textiles and crafts as a way of building solidarity between relatively affluent church-going Americans and those suffering poverty in nearby countries. This early initiative developed into Ten Thousand Villages, a chain of Fair Trade craft shops backed by the Mennonite Church.

In Europe, it was Dutch Catholics who led the way, with one Paul Maejs providing particular inspiration. Again, they initially focused on importing crafts, often from projects linked to Catholic missionaries in places like Haiti and the Philippines, setting up craft shops through an organization called SOS Wereldhandel (now Fairtrade Original), and gaining support from Christian agencies such as Misereor and Bread for the World, which allowed their work to spread to Germany,

---

69 Traidcraft, reproduced from Strategic Planning document, December 2005..

Switzerland, and Austria, again gaining the backing of church institutions as shareholders and donors.

And in the UK, although Oxfam preceded it by some years, Traidcraft grew out of the work of Tearcraft, which had been founded as an arm of the evangelical mission and relief agency, Tearfund. Within a few years, Traidcraft became one of the most significant forces within the growing British Fair Trade movement, thanks to the enthusiasm of its supporter base firmly rooted within the Christian community.

There are a number of theological strands that Paul believes have underpinned the positive reaction of Christians to Fair Trade approaches.

At its most basic there is the simple response of compassion toward those living in poverty and need: a calling rooted in a clear biblical mandate across the Old and New Testaments to reflect God's heart for the poor. Texts such as the teaching about the sheep and goats in Matthew 25 (seeing Jesus in the hungry, thirsty, naked, and imprisoned), and Jesus' description of his own ministry as "bringing good news to the poor" – combined with warnings such as those in James 5 about the moral consequences of exploiting labourers – have all resonated with Christians and encouraged them to support Traidcraft and other Christian initiatives seeking to fight poverty.

This concern for the poor became even stronger when combined with the growth of liberation theology in Latin America, with its themes of justice, solidarity, and empowerment underlining the need to promote the right of all people to be treated with dignity. Given that the early American and Dutch Fair Trade initiatives started in this region, it is unsurprising that this theological outlook was influential. Small-scale cooperative producer groups mirrored, in many ways, the development of base communities within rural churches. In addition, the liberation theology worldview created a more radical, campaigning approach, focused as much on issues of justice as simply responding to perceived need.

And Fair Trade has also drawn much inspiration over the years from the principles and traditions of Catholic Social Teaching. Over the last hundred years, papal encyclicals have argued prophetically that markets must be subordinate to the common good and the promotion of human well-being, that creation should be safeguarded, excessive disparities of wealth challenged, and relationships and human dignity promoted over a mere fixation on transactional wealth creation. Pope Benedict's encyclical, *Caritas in Veritate*, reads in parts almost like a manifesto for social enterprises and Fair Trade, as it throws down the gauntlet to neo-liberal free market approaches![70]

These strands of Christian teaching and belief have all supported and sustained the growth of support for Fair Trade within churches. The evolving relationship between the development of Fair Trade and Christian thinking is a subject Paul explored in greater depth in a lecture given at St Mary-le-Bow church in 2012 as a contribution to their JustShare initiative.[71]

But even if Fair Trade and Christianity have been so closely linked, what was the particular nature of Traidcraft's Christian motivation and how did it affect the way Traidcraft worked and developed in practice? In what ways did espousing its Christian identity make it distinctive from non-religious Fair Trade Organizations?

The split from Tearcraft/Tearfund in 1979 highlighted how Traidcraft's approach differed from the traditional evangelical approach to mission, but also underlined the importance of faith to Traidcraft's founders and their concern to protect Traidcraft's Christian identity. Tearfund's mission purposes meant it wanted Tearcraft to focus on trading with Christian producer groups, or at the very least with producers linked to church projects with an explicitly evangelistic intent. Traidcraft's founders, however, found this constraining and wished to work with producers of all faith backgrounds and without a hidden agenda of conversion. It was a broader and inclusive approach, working with and for people of all faiths and none, but was nonetheless unapologetic and explicit about Traidcraft's Christian motivation to serve those in need.

In Paul's time at Traidcraft, he found that this Christian basis, far from creating obstacles to co-operation with Muslims, Hindus and Buddhist groups (as some assumed it would), in practice actually helped to build strong relationships. This was because producers and partners who had a faith of their own found they could relate better

---

70   Pope Benedict XVI, Encyclical Letter, *Caritas in Veritate*, Rome, 29 June 2009.

71   Paul Chandler, "Fairtrade and Christian Attitudes to the Market", JustShare Christian Social and Political Thought Lecture, St Mary-le-Bow, 29 February 2012. Available at: https://youtu.be/5cAkXMGRxuk

to the Christian worldview than they could understand or warm to a neutral or secular mindset. Paul particularly remembers an afternoon discussing the religious basis for business ethics with a Muslim trading partner in Malawi. This led to his taking Traidcraft's social accounts to a conference of Muslim businesses as a challenge to put the Koran into practice more explicitly in the same way that Traidcraft was trying to root its behaviour in the Bible. Paul reflects that this open approach also enabled the organization, when it began, to set up overseas offices as part of Traidcraft Exchange's work and to happily recruit Hindus, Muslims, and Buddhists as members of staff. Although Tearcraft's approach to choosing partners did develop over time to enable partnership with a wider range of producer groups, attempts in Paul's time to re-merge Tearcraft and Traidcraft ultimately foundered on Tearfund's Board fearing that Traidcraft's broader churchmanship would make it an unacceptable partner to many of their more conservative evangelical supporters, emphasizing the continuing significance of this difference of approach.

Paul believed that the commitment of Traidcraft's founders to being inclusive in mission was not, in their view, to diminish the Christian nature of the organization in any way. It was simply reflecting a wider understanding of what it meant to express Christian love and compassion in practice. Far from downgrading the organization's faith commitment, governance structures were created to underpin and safeguard its Christian identity. The Traidcraft Foundation was created with a brief to defend and develop the Christian mission of the organization, and a basis of faith was written to which Board members and senior staff were expected to subscribe. This was initially framed in very evangelical language, reflecting Traidcraft's origins. Then in 2002, soon after Paul arrived, he felt it important to replace this specific wording – which an observant Catholic would have found hard to sign up to, for example – with a requirement that Board members should subscribe to the Apostles' Creed as a more generally acceptable statement of faith across the denominations. Paul reflects that this did not please everyone – Quakers and Mennonites disliked signing up to any credal statement at all, and from the start there were non-Christians of goodwill who did support Traidcraft's work despite its Christian basis and rather wished this was not part of the package.

However, surveys undertaken in the 2000s indicated that over 90% of shareholders and Fair Traders were motivated to support Traidcraft and Fair Trade by their own Christian faith and found Traidcraft's religious adherence an important factor in their choice of organization to support. Paul was always particularly pleased by one of the straplines in the marketing campaign for Traidcraft's share issue in 2003: "invest in Traidcraft and make yourself a prophet" which seemed to him to underline the Christian motivation of investors and Fair Traders to change the world rather than to make a profit through investing in or trading in products.[72]

Paul reflects that this rootedness in the church community formed a strong foundation to Traidcraft's work. Church supporters proved loyal and generous – the ideal supporter base for any organization – and through churches Traidcraft was also able to make good inroads into raising awareness of Fair Trade in schools, using the large network of church schools as a starting point. The Fairtrade churches initiative proved hugely successful in encouraging churches to make a formal commitment to supporting Fair Trade, especially in the period around the Make Poverty History campaign in 2005, although Jubilee 2000 had already had a major impact in raising concern for poverty issues in churches – even if, frustratingly, many churches still seemed to serve Nescafé after services rather than Fairtrade alternatives! Interestingly, the momentum to sign up to supporting Fair Trade often seemed to be driven by lay members of churches, with clergy support being much more variable, perhaps reflecting a wider range of priorities or perhaps a greater discomfort with dealing with issues of money, trade, and business. Nonetheless, official church bodies became increasingly keen to pass motions making public declarations of support for trade justice and Fair Trade, particularly in the era of Make Poverty History, and this was very helpful to campaigning work through Traidcraft Exchange.

Traidcraft's appeal was cross-denominational and, as far as it could be established, it seemed to reflect the relative proportions of mainline church affiliation in the UK more or less. However, within each denomination, Traidcraft failed to connect so readily with more conservative evangelical churches – perhaps because they were more

---

72 Traidcraft share issue material, 2003.

focused on seeing evangelism as the primary calling for mission work and were reticent about Traidcraft's decision to focus on social action. Traidcraft also faced some resistance within churches to running stalls on the grounds of their wanting to discourage Sunday trading – although the frequency of opposition on those grounds was much diminished by the time Paul joined the organization; perhaps the resistance to Sunday shop opening being viewed as a lost cause by then.

Paul asserts that Traidcraft's Christian identity was not just about the motivation of its leadership and supporters. As one might expect, it also influenced the way it went about its core work. One dimension of this, something that Paul was always conscious about, was the importance of seeking to reflect Christian principles in the way that it treated its members of staff. It was important to seek to understand their needs as people and treat them fairly and well, and this was part of the organization's Christian witness; even if, perhaps inevitably, it did not always manage to live up to its own standards. While the economics of the business meant that salaries were rather lower than one might ideally have wanted to pay, Traidcraft introduced a culture of flexi-time designed to underpin work/life balance, and reflecting a belief that however important Traidcraft's mission was, its staff had much to contribute to their home lives and local communities as well as to Fair Trade.

Paul reflects further that when unpopular decisions had to be taken (including disciplinary action and redundancies), there would be accusations by some staff that the organization "was not being very Christian", but of course "being Christian" should not be confused with always being "nice". Paul was keen always to try to act with fairness and consistency, showing compassion but also a readiness to be tough when necessary, and not to tolerate poor behaviour or low standards. Occasionally, Paul's belief is that Traidcraft was able to be prophetic as an employer, such as supporting an initiative to provide work to prisoners approaching release, allowing them to re-familiarize themselves with the workplace, get a reference, and build up some savings before re-entering the outside world; all factors shown to reduce rates of re-offending.

Paul believed that Traidcraft's Christian calling also placed a premium on acting with integrity and transparency. The organization could not claim to have been anything other than far from perfect, and sometimes there would inevitably need to be compromises made with a purist interpretation of its Fair Trade principles. However, calling itself a Christian organization meant that there was a high premium on trying to keep to "the straight and narrow". Paul always found it helpful that by encouraging transparency in its social accounts then Traidcraft could point out its shortcomings and failures as well as trumpeting successes.

Paul also found Traidcraft's faith basis a particular encouragement to be brave and to stand up for what it preached in relation to challenging supermarket practices. When the Office for Fair Trading (OFT) called for evidence of supermarket bad practices, every supplier in the country went silent, fearing the consequences of publicly declaring their dissatisfaction with practices about which they readily complained in private. As Chief Executive, Paul too was very nervous about agreeing to the request of Traidcraft's Policy team to submit a dossier of instances where supermarkets had breached their own codes of practice toward Traidcraft as a supplier, weighing this up against the possible loss of business should, for example, the Geobar product lines, widely available in supermarkets, be de-listed. In the end, however, Paul convinced himself that Traidcraft's Christian principles demanded that it act with integrity and Traidcraft was one of only a handful of companies that was prepared to send in evidence of frequent abuses of good practice. What was submitted was sufficient to convince the OFT to require Asda and Tesco to release millions of their emails, which ended up demonstrating systematic breaches of the Grocery Code and ultimately led to the establishment of a Grocery Code Adjudicator. Had Traidcraft not been an avowedly Christian organization, Paul doubts whether he would have decided to present that evidence – and yet the creation of an Adjudicator has been a major step forward in providing access to just treatment for weaker participants in UK supply chains.

Paul reflects more generally that being a specifically Christian response to poverty was an encouragement to an approach to business that was more about being a catalyst for change than about pursuing its growth, profitability, and market share. Traidcraft was one of the main supporters among UK Fair Trade pioneer organizations of initiatives to mainstream Fair Trade and allow commercial organizations to use the Fairtrade Mark on products that had been appropriately sourced. Traidcraft did not do this blindly. There was an explicit consciousness that encouraging Tesco, Sainsbury's, Nestlé, and Cadbury's into "Traidcraft's territory" (and sharing knowledge and sometimes even its suppliers with them) meant that putting Traidcraft out of business was a real risk. These much stronger competitors would be able to achieve economies of scale that Traidcraft could never match – and they would therefore be able to undercut Traidcraft prices in the market. But the Board was clear that if Traidcraft was to maximize the positive impact of Fair Trade on as many producers as possible, it would need to engage with the big players, even if this might mean its own ultimate demise. Certainly, Paul consciously saw this as a self-sacrificial act based on Traidcraft's Christian calling – being prepared to lay down its corporate life for the greater good and to help change the world (even though Paul hoped that Traidcraft would remain around to protect high standards and push for further change to business practices). Paul doubts that had he been Chief Executive of a purely commercial business he would have been allowed to do this.

A further dimension of putting Christian faith into practice emerged in the second half of Paul's time as Chief Executive. This was when he led the initiative to become more systematic in measuring impact on producers – particularly in relation to the development projects of Traidcraft Exchange. Encouraged by challenges from the Traidcraft Foundation, the organization came to recognize that it was not good enough to use financial benefits alone as a proxy for achieving its stated mission commitment to "help people and communities to flourish". True human flourishing needed an appreciation of wider dimensions of well-being – dignity, community, quality of relationships, the capacity to be generous, and the capacity to look after one's environment – which were not adequately captured by measuring sales and income alone. So Traidcraft began a collaboration with a team from Bath University to see if a cost-effective way could be developed of measuring qualitative as well as quantitative aspects of flourishing in ways that could help the organization learn whether different styles of intervention were more or less effective in this regard. Challenging the exclusive dominance of value for money and profit in the thinking of decision-makers and consumers seemed to Paul to be an important Christian message for this generation, and one that is becoming increasingly important as part of the challenge to today's culture of seeking ever more growth that the planet simply cannot sustain.

Paul reflects further that there were more negative dimensions to Traidcraft's Christian identity as well. Non-Christian staff could understandably feel frustrated by the "glass ceiling" of Traidcraft's constitutional requirement that certain senior roles had to be held by those with a Christian faith. Although care would be taken to make that faith basis explicit in recruitment materials, so new staff could not claim to have been misled about the nature of Traidcraft as a mission organization, it did require some sensitivity to ensure they did not feel second-class citizens, and this also meant that prayer was not a common part of staff meetings so as not to make those not of the Christian faith feel uncomfortable or excluded. Some staff were also very challenging about this Christian basis focusing us unduly on serving a church market that was in numerical decline. They did not perhaps recognize the greater levels of loyalty and readiness to provide financial support in the Christian community that actually (in Paul's view, at least) underpinned all of Traidcraft's work and gave it a distinctive and sustainable competitive advantage that it would never have in the mainstream marketplace. Paul's view was that the Christian marketplace should never be the sole focus of Traidcraft's work, but it provided a secure base from which it could reach out to influence other sectors.

To Paul, Traidcraft's Christian identity was never just an accident of history or an incidental aspect of the work. It was the essence of what enabled Traidcraft to make a unique contribution to the development and application of Fair Trade in the UK. By mobilizing the Christian community, Traidcraft was able to create a sufficient market to enable Fair Trade Organizations to learn how to do their work, and then to generate an amazing body of campaigners who got Fairtrade products into supermarkets and placed trade justice onto the agenda of corporate board rooms. The faith basis of Traidcraft affected its approach to Fair Trade, the way in which it acted as an employer, and its readiness to adopt strategies that might at the end of the day put it out of business. Paul's view was that Traidcraft's Christian faith sustained it through difficult times and inspired it in good times. Undoubtedly, the organization would often fail to fully live up to its ideals – such is the predicament of all Christians in a fallen world. But the aspirations and motivation of the organization, and of the majority of Traidcraft supporters, were clearly informed and indeed driven by the belief that in fighting for justice and promoting solidarity with and opportunities for those living in poverty, Traidcraft was contributing to God's work in the world.

PART EIGHT

Traidcraft's Most Recent History

Chapter 25

NOT SUCH A
FLOURISHING BUSINESS

In 2010, Traidcradt initiated a new strategic plan called "From Fair to Flourishing", but those years after the departure of Paul Chandler (who left in 2013) were difficult ones – commercially, culturally, and missionally for Traidcraft plc – although for Traidcraft Exchange, things would be a little rosier. Profitability would be a challenge and the financial year 2010/11 would be the last to turn in a profit throughout the whole of the 2010s. Even that was largely the result of cashing in shares of Cafédirect and severing formal ties to the organization that we had co-founded nearly twenty years earlier. Turnover would continue to decline and, by 2018, it was nearly 40% lower than its peak. Whatever new initiatives that were tried could not reverse the trend. Traidcraft plc was a bit like a super tanker, ploughing on in the same direction; turning it would be a long and complicated process.

Of course, it's also complicated to turn the super tanker without a captain on the bridge and replacing Paul Chandler would be a long, arduous, and frustrating process. There seemed to be enough candidates but few who were considered suitable or who would accept the position. For almost five years, a combination of interim appointment, promotion from within, and the parachuting in of non-executive board members filled the gap – but these short-term fixes would not be able to replace the need for stable, long-term leadership. Those of us in the senior management team entered into defensive mode, "holding the fort", but unable to effectively turn the super tanker until a new captain took the helm.

Losses for Traidcraft plc were certainly not unknown historically but annual losses over a protracted period were something quite new and certainly not sustainable. The balance sheet of Traidcraft plc was relatively healthy at the start of the 2010s and would continue to be so for several years but, as anyone familiar with business practice will be all too aware, regular losses will lead to an unhealthy balance sheet and lack of cash to run the business. The situation was not helped by liabilities relating to a pension scheme instigated at the birth of Traidcraft which linked future staff pensions to their final salary. While this pension scheme had closed in 2001, Traidcraft was still liable for keeping the pension scheme fully funded by regular top-ups which would eat into cash reserves. Traidcraft plc would need to get back to profitability or face the consequences.

Those early volunteer representatives, our Fair Traders, had been the bedrock of Traidcraft – not just in their activist role, but in their support for the wider work of Traidcraft, which included fundraising for the Traidcraft Exchange. I was never directly involved with Fair Traders, but I was always slightly overwhelmed by their commitment and passion as I attended AGMs and occasional Traidcraft roadshows (the annual events where we would go out to meet and introduce new product ranges to them). Our volunteers had been responsible in great part for the growth and success of Traidcraft over the years and had played a pivotal role in the wider growth of Fair Trade in the UK. Their role as re-sellers of Traidcraft products had always contributed the bulk of sales turnover but those sales had begun to decline. From a peak in 2008, sales would decline by nearly 50% over the next ten years. Buying Fair Trade products through Fair Traders at the back of the church every Sunday, or through setting up their stalls at a myriad of small events, wasn't the only way to do it. Mainstreamed Fairtrade products and the host of other Fair Trade brands available would take their toll on Traidcraft sales. Perhaps some Fair Traders thought that they no longer needed to operate in the same way. Maybe some of them thought that because Fair Trade was pretty much established in the mainstream, then they would regard their role differently. Some would coin the phrase "the job's done" to describe this. Admittedly, some of the Fair Traders who had been early supporters of Traidcraft and had journeyed alongside us were, like all of us, getting older. Finding a younger generation to replace them wouldn't be easy, nor would any reinvention of that sales channel or switching to other kinds of selling.

Margaret Vaughan took on the role of acting CEO, then CEO, for a short while after Paul Chandler had left. She writes of her time at Traidcraft:

> It's hard for me to imagine a world without Traidcraft – its mission and activities have been so intertwined with my life from an early age – but, as the years went by in the period from about 2010 onwards, a world without Traidcraft started to feel a real possibility.
>
> The various changes impacting Traidcraft have been captured in previous chapters; the light-hearted comments that we had sometimes made as a leadership team such as "wouldn't it be great if Traidcraft was put out of business because Fairtrade and/or Fair Trade was the accepted norm?" started to have a serious and threatening meaning. The skills and competencies required to lead an organization when the external environment changes substantially are well documented in management journals. Did Traidcraft's leadership team over the years have these skills and competencies to navigate the choppy waters?
>
> I was privileged to serve on the staff team at a senior level, and then to lead the organization both as acting CEO and then as CEO. I knew that the organization was in significant peril, the commercial realities of Traidcraft plc being, in essence, a food retailer in the UK, were biting hard. There was no escaping this and only rapid decisive actions would reverse the commercial fortunes. Hindsight, of course, is a marvellous thing. It is easy to blame those who come before for not having set the compass on the right course when there was time to allow the organization to change course smoothly. And it is easy to look on those

who come afterwards as being overzealous and knee jerking in their reactions.

My reflections on these difficult years are that there were points where bolder commercial decisions could have been made. Did we grasp all the opportunities that technology, combined with the physical assets (warehouse space), could have provided? Did we resist becoming a "Fair Trade supermarket" and holding multiple brands for too long? Could we have been more collaborative across the UK Fair Trade movement of like-minded organizations? And what of our relationships with producers, who themselves in many cases were seeing major changes in their own home markets? Did we grapple with the opportunities that these might hold for both Traidcraft and the producer groups we had worked with for so long? Did our mission and focus on justice in trade mean that we lost some of our connectivity to churches in the UK as they grappled with poverty in their own communities – establishing foodbanks, campaigning for a living wage? The list of questions to ask as I look back could go on, and the answers to them will vary from respondent to respondent. However, I wonder if the importance is not the questions (or the answers for that matter) but more what we do together looking forward, continuing to strive for justice. Justice in trade, justice for our fragile world and its climate, justice for those who find themselves powerless. Traidcraft, the organization, will change (it has to) but what it represents, a community of people passionate about making a difference to the lives of others, will remain.[73]

---

73 From personal correspondence with the author, 2019.

Chapter 26

ONE TRAIDCRAFT?

The integration of Traidcraft plc (the business) and Traidcraft Exchange (the charity) had been a key objective of the new strategy, but it was time to put this into practice more tangibly. Personally, I had yearned for a return to those times of the 1990s when there was a huge amount of working together across business and charity. But, for the previous decade, there was little overlap and the strategic intent of each had diverged. Would this new strategy reverse the trend? Those of us working with suppliers in Traidcraft plc as part of the Supplier Support team joined together with key staff from the Policy Unit and those who managed the overseas programme work to discuss and make plans. Key staff from the overseas offices would also come to the UK to join in these debates and they were extremely positive, enjoyable, and productive.

One of the key points of agreement was that "we were at our best when we worked together" and that we should seek to develop projects and activities that involved all of us, while also continuing to pursue our separate priorities. We also re-emphasized our common objective that would take us back to our roots. Here was an organization comprising an exemplar innovative business putting the principles of Fair Trade into practice, albeit on a small scale, a cutting edge Policy Unit which had a history of campaigning success and influencing government and corporate practice, and an overseas development programme with larger-scale projects which would impact the lives of the poor and marginalized on a larger scale. Working together more practically would surely be the way forward.

One Traidcraft?

For a while, it might have looked from the outside that there was just "one Traidcraft". Social accounts had evolved new terminology and were now called Impact Reports. In the published material – whether impact reports or the so-called "annual development review" – the branding was solely "Traidcraft" and reference to each of the legal entities covered only on the inside pages. Employee contracts stipulated whether or not they worked for the business or the charity but there was now a significant number of staff who held shared contracts. Personally, and despite the fact that I had a contract that said I worked for Traidcraft plc, I quite liked the idea that I could say that I worked for Traidcraft only, and any presentation I made about Traidcraft externally would reflect this.

One practical outcome of working together, and in common with other development agencies, was the creation of our own so-called "theory of change", which covered the whole organization. This was a formal statement defining the change we wanted to see in the world and our collective contribution to how that might be achieved. This would replace the trade/support/influence model of the 2000s. The common goal would be formally expressed as "trade is just and enables people to move out of poverty in a sustainable way" and each of us played our own role toward that goal.

Despite the problems of growth and commercial challenges in Traidcraft plc, we still tried to be innovative in product and supply chain development. We had started to sell some products made from bamboo, including a very popular range of socks from a UK supplier. They ticked the "ethical" box in terms of rationale for selling them, since bamboo fibre was purportedly a good sustainable raw material, but they were certainly not Fair Trade products and neither would that UK supplier claim that they were. We embarked on a new project which would scope out the potential for Fair Trade bamboo from China, where those socks were made, and had high hopes that the next new Fair Trade commodity might be bamboo, with a high degree of potential product applications from clothing to household products.

Then there was Fairtrade rice. At the beginning of this project Geobar was still a strong product which contained a lot of Fairtrade rice and we thought it might be hugely innovative to target Myanmar, formerly Burma, which had just emerged from a period of oppression and conflict and could be a potential new region for Fair Trade to move into. A project was developed which had good support from the Fairtrade Foundation which would see rice producers organized and become Fairtrade certified. Traidcraft plc would be the first importer of Fairtrade rice out of Myanmar in 2016.

The experience of developing the first Fairtrade juice brand in the UK in the early 2000s did not have a great ending. The brand Fruit Passion was no more – however, I still had ambitions to do it again, but better! To fill a gap in our product range we had introduced the Calypso brand, but it did not fill many of us with any real satisfaction that we were selling such a product and it did not really comply with the Traidcraft purchasing policy. It carried a Fairtrade Mark but was not really any different to selling a Cadbury's or Mars Fairtrade labelled chocolate, which I don't imagine the majority of our supporters would countenance, or at least I hope wouldn't! So, we started a juice project which would demonstrate the best of all of the parts of Traidcraft working together. There would be a need for fundraising, project development, and project management. Ultimately a project was dreamed up with a specifically Traidcraft plc objective. This new product would turn into a much larger project managed out of our programme office in East Africa but with a focus on Senegal. Initially the scoping of the project had been undertaken by Fullwell Mill and with seed funding from the Fairtrade Foundation, so it was truly a collaborative activity.

By that time, I had started to write blogs and one which I had written on my visit to this juice project in Senegal in its early days still manages to convey the practicalities of different parts of Traidcraft working together:

> I'm writing this in Dakar, Senegal at the end of a short
> visit to a new project and in a new country for Traidcraft's
> work. It's the classic Traidcraft model of development –
> engaging with farmers, working with them to organise,
> delivering training activities to increase skills, protection and
> preservation of the natural environment, and enabling their
> produce to reach markets at fairer prices and terms.
>
> There's a bit of a difference in that crucial to this
> project are Senegalese traders and manufacturers, social

enterprises themselves and wanting to trade fairly in securing their raw materials. I'm here with a consultant to the project looking at some of the technical issues around these products and we hope at some stage to develop products for sale in the UK.

We're working in the Casamance region in the south of the country, a place which ought to be more prosperous than it is, but which has been blighted by a military conflict that goes back decades. It's a conflict that has been pretty much forgotten by the rest of the world. We're in a period of calm but the underlying tensions are not forgotten. There are good reasons to work here – natural resources, great people with great potential, and plenty of opportunity for development.

The project focuses on forest fruits, with baobab probably the best known – so technically the communities we are working with are not "farmers" but "collectors" of fruit which grow naturally in remote forest areas – a key source of income.

We visited three of the five communities we are working with – each with their own unique character – accompanied by one of our partner traders who has never engaged at this level before. We talk with farmers about their current situation – trading with the so-called "bana banas" who come with ready cash but at uncertain prices – and we aim to develop a new supply chain which is much better than this. We hear about how the fruit is collected and the challenges of managing quality for perishable products, but we also see lots of enthusiasm for the project, lots of expectations for an improved income and a better life. We talk to local dignitaries – they are vital "enablers" and we need them to be fully aware of what's going on and have their support.

We hear the mayor of one of the communities tell us that he hopes that this project will help in the process of bringing peace to the region. The link between poverty and conflict is well documented and Fair Trade can contribute by enabling farmers to focus on social and economic structures which are just, to put aside differences, and to seek common well-being. The road toward peace in Colombia is said to have been aided in part by the development of such structures but to hear it from a key figure in a rural African community tarnished by conflict is an enormous encouragement.

The project lasts four years. There will be challenges and setbacks as we continue the journey – but it's a great start.

And we have a spare few hours before the flight home so time for a visit to the Island of Gorée, located a mile off the coast of Dakar. It seems fitting somehow to end the week at this preserved world heritage site which, over five centuries, was purported to be the largest slave trading centre on the African coast. There's some dispute as to the number of slaves who passed through this island, and the tour guide's estimation of the number of slaves who died here even before they managed to embark seems unreal. But it's not about numbers, it's about the fact that here is a symbol of one of the greatest acts of exploitation and injustice in world history and it's a poignant experience.

Exploitation and injustice still exist on our planet – it's what Traidcraft seeks to address in its work. Let's hope that this project will have huge economic impact in a region of Senegal where it's much needed.[74]

As well as these significant cross-organizational projects, Traidcraft Exchange was making its own mark in the world. Programme activity in East Africa, India, and Bangladesh grew. At any one time, there might be more than a dozen projects on the go across these regions. There was a sense from some of us that a small number of these projects were veering away from what Traidcraft was all about and perhaps driven by what funding streams were available, and this refocus on trade justice was timely. Traidcraft Exchange projects were at their best when they

---

74 Joe Osman, "Forest Fruits: New Supply Chains in Senegal", Traidcraft website blog post, 18 November 2016.

worked directly with small farmers and producers, organizing them into groups, training them to be more astute in business, and enabling them to have greater power and a louder voice in marketing their produce. It wasn't "Fair Trade" as a consumer might understand it, but it was certainly addressing issues of injustice in supply chains. Product sectors in which projects were developed still included familiar names like jute, cotton, tea, and honey, but they also covered domestic trade, horticultural and fresh produce, and even chickens.

The Policy Unit contributed some incredibly impactful work way beyond the world of Fair Trade but again still applying the underlying principle of dealing with injustice in supply chains. The Grocery Code Adjudicator (GCA) had been established in 2013, a kind of watchdog scrutinizing the actions of supermarkets that were negatively wielding power that comes from scale and treating their suppliers unjustly. This theme would continue throughout the decade as the GCA would eventually be given more power to impose fines on supermarkets for proven indiscretions. Then the later Justice Matters campaign would start to scrutinize and challenge the power of large businesses having overseas interests, seeking to bring their entire supply chain under UK law.

Chapter 27

AVERTING DISASTER AND A NEW HOPE?

In Traidcraft plc, losses had been higher than anticipated and belts needed to be tightened. Several key members of staff moved on in 2016 and their roles and responsibilities were redistributed rather than replaced. I found myself overseeing stock and warehouse management for a while as a throwback to my early days in Traidcraft. It wasn't ideal and tensions would emerge. These tensions would not just be among staff but also at director level. The relationship between executive directors (those employed with management responsibilities) and non-executive directors (independent or external directors without day-to-day management responsibilities) had always been cordial and positive. Indeed, in the 2000s a structure had emerged for a while where a non-executive director would "pal up" with an executive director, almost acting as a mentor. Similarly, the relationship between chief executive and chair of the board of directors would usually be important, even pivotal, to organizational success. Sadly, the relationship between executives and non-executives would deteriorate professionally and we badly needed a change.

All of the good cross-organizational working would suffer and the 2010 strategic plan From Fair to Flourishing, while not being torn up, would be largely ignored. Interim leadership would bring in new short-term plans under such titles as "the million pound challenge", focusing on short-term sales and cost cutting initiatives, which was partly successful. Then there was "project simplify" – focusing on new information technology and the web store – which would be less successful. Non-executives would try their best to offer their expertise and spend more time in day-to-day activities, although these would generally be ineffective or unhelpful. These were not great times and we badly needed stability through long-term leadership.

I had known Robin Roth for some time – first through his role in Germany working for Fairtrade International, and then as he jointly headed up the Fair Trade Organization GEPA, also in Germany. We admired the way that GEPA had expanded during his time there. They were now turning over more than 80 million euros and having the kind of impact abroad that we aspired to. GEPA was very different to Traidcraft in that it was only a business and did not have a charitable organization linked to it. More than one of us also aspired to see Robin come to Traidcraft to do the same thing as he had done at GEPA and had occasionally asked him whether he was up for a new challenge. So, while those of us who were executive directors were excluded from the recruitment process, which we found a little unusual in an organization such as Traidcraft, it was with great excitement that we discovered that he was to be Traidcraft's new Chief Executive in 2016.

What happened in the next two years was certainly unexpected and would nearly see the demise of Traidcraft plc. I knew that turning the super tanker would be a hard task but I hadn't anticipated near capsize. These two years would probably be the most challenging and certainly the least enjoyable of my time at Traidcraft – cumulative losses would exceed the cumulative losses of the previous five years. Sales turnover continued to decline but at a higher rate than in any of the previous eight years and this certainly wasn't helped by a disastrous new webstore launch which hindered many customers placing their orders online, majorly affecting customer confidence.

As well as the business difficulties there was a definite shift of Traidcraft's profile in the wider Fair Trade movement. From a Traidcraft plc perspective we took on a rather isolationist position and disengaged from a lot of the networking activities which had long been part of our culture and had resulted in Traidcraft's stature and reputation being second to none in the world of Fair Trade. Indeed, many of our contemporaries couldn't really understand what was happening or why, and that stature and reputation would certainly be tarnished.

The relationship between Traidcraft Exchange and Traidcraft plc also changed. The "one Traidcraft" approach mentioned earlier had its strengths but one of its weaknesses was the complex organizational structure that resulted. Selling to and fundraising from the same supporter base was, for some, to the detriment of establishing a focused sales culture for the business and one of the reasons for the slow decline in sales. Others disagreed, but in this new era came complete separation, not just for jobs and contracts of employment but also physically, with virtually everyone finding themselves in a new office location. I had not anticipated that the separation would go any further, but what then happened was a complete divergence between the two organizations – strategically, structurally, physically, and culturally. It signalled a reversal of that decision reached at the end of the 1990s and separate leadership would then emerge for each organization. Some would say this was correct and that the problems of Traidcraft plc should not be allowed to affect the good things that were continuing in Traidcraft Exchange. But I could not help but bring to mind those words that had been agreed some years earlier: "we were at our best when we worked together".

Some of those management structures which enshrined principles of transparency and accountability also changed. Communications reduced and staff directors and executive directors were removed, although I chose to step down before it was enforced. To be fair, the role of the elected staff director had always been a bit of a problem, given the need for that person to be a practising Christian, but it was certainly sad that an adequate alternative was not established. For me, this was the beginning of the end of my time at Traidcraft and made my final departure easier to deal with.

When the announcement was made in 2018 that Traidcraft plc would cease trading, it came as a shock to many, but as inevitable to others. Robin's appointment was, perhaps, just too late and time had run out. For some, there was a feeling that perhaps Traidcraft plc had run its course and, without some of the activities and characteristics that made it unique, there was little point to it. All staff were put at risk of redundancy and it was time to share the difficult news with suppliers, supporters, and customers.

The shock waves were literally global. The small group of folks communicating with our producers bore the brunt of the emotional feedback and, especially for those who had been supplying us with handicrafts for many years, it was hard to hear. For many, the relationship went beyond mere supplier and customer. Traidcraft's influence had been enormous and, for some, it felt like losing a close family member. Beyond the initial emotion, the commercial realities cut in. For some of those suppliers who would see no more orders from Traidcraft, not only jobs would be threatened but their very survival. In terms of impact, it's hard to replace orders which create work, but a charitable appeal by the Traidcraft Exchange to raise money in support of the suppliers who were most affected would at least mitigate some of that impact. And then a project which would aim to matchmake and to seek new importing contacts for some of those suppliers would also help.

Here are extracts from three of the many responses received from producers which reflect the nature of that partnership that we had developed over the years:

From Moon Sharma of Tara Projects:

> It is difficult to believe that the letter received is a hard reality and we are heading for the end of our Fair Trade relations, which began decades ago! It is very shocking and full of sadness. I still remember the visit of Richard Adams and the beginning of our cooperation... none of us could imagine that the changing times will bring us to this sad end. We never expected to receive such terrible news. Nobody wants to believe it, yet we know this is the reality. While faced with very difficult times, we will always be grateful to Traidcraft for their continuous support provided over the last four decades. It has played a tremendous role in our lives and of thousands of producers. With the support and solidarity we have received from Traidcraft, we will continue to fight for the rights of the producers and the excluded in our society. Though these are very difficult times for all of us, we are committed to our Fair Trade values and actions.[75]

---

75 From email to Traidcraft, 2018.

From Bertha Gity Baroi of CORR–The Jute Works, Traidcraft's very first supplier:

> It seems like a thunderbolt hit us! And it just seems like yesterday that the Traidcraft team knocked on our door for our crafts, on credit, to start the new market. Forty long-long years of walking side by side. On this quest we believe we never looked at each other as buyer and producer but rather companions with a goal to make the world a little better. Looking back to our past, we can see the leaf covered hut of some of our artisans now turned to a nice brick built house. Many, many of such works we did together. Without you that couldn't have been possible. We know we have "miles to go" but we need friends-partners in solidarity to walk that long road. We have to share the message now with the artisans and are we ready for their reaction? A lot of emotion, a lot of stories are braided with the crafts they made for Traidcraft.[76]

From Chino Henriquez of Apicoop in Chile, supplier of honey:

> It is with disbelief and astonishment to say the least! I have read several times the letter announcing the shut-down of operations by the end of the year trying to find between lines if there's any hidden message of hope in what seems a nightmare. I must admit that actually this is one of the saddest chapters I've have had to witness in my 30 years linked to Fairtrade and although I had the feeling that Traidcraft was facing tough times, definitely at this level wasn't in my radar… I feel that after so many years working with Traidcraft, inevitably you become part of the family, for good and bad times… I rather focus thinking on the impact this decision will bring for the network of producers that have supplied Traidcraft for so many years, the long-term Fair Traders that have devoted an important part of their lifetime to promote our products , the workers of the company who have played a key role bridging producers

---

76 From email to Traidcraft, 2018.

and, consumers and how our message of "fighting poverty through trade or going the extra mile" will survive in coming years. Unfortunately, for the time being, there's not much in which we as long-term partners can contribute, aside from having especially all our friends at Gateshead in our hearts and thoughts in these uncertain and bitter times. If it helps in any way, throughout the world there's uncountable numbers of producers whose lives have truly changed for better as a result of your devoted work, and believe me, there's no letter that can undo the relationship built up among us over these years.[77]

Following this, a small number of championing staff, backed up by external consultants, put together a business plan which proposed to keep the business going. The Board agreed with the proposal and the decision was met with a high degree of celebration from many of its customers and Fair Trader supporter base. For others, it was a bittersweet reaction since the new and reset business would be forced through lack of finance to pre-finance, to cease the sourcing of craft products directly, and would not have any meaningful commercial and direct relationships with any of its overseas suppliers nor import their products. The new and smaller team who conceived the model for this reset business were forced into those hard decisions. It meant that Traidcraft plc could continue into its fortieth year – and hopefully beyond – but whether it can regain its reputation, uniqueness, and importance within the Fair Trade movement remains to be seen.

The team at Traidcraft plc writes:[78]

Traidcraft has come full circle. Forty years of remarkable achievements and a long, long list of notable successes came to a stop late last year when we were informed that there was no way forward.

We were angry that the story should be ending without a proper resolution. Have we really "put the principles of Fair Trade into commercial practice"? If we had, then we hadn't done it successfully enough

---

77 From email to Traidcraft, 2018.
78 From personal correspondence with the author, 2019.

because we had run out of money. That didn't feel like success.

Forty years ago, Traidcraft was founded by a small team. We felt strongly that it would take a team to make Traidcraft 2, as we began to call it, a reality. Four of us sat down and badgered the CEO, Robin, to give us the chance at resurrecting the company, and to present our business plan to the Board. He did, and the Board provided us with an external business expert to help formulate the plan, firm up the numbers, and stress-test the cash flow projections.

So, while the company was beginning to "close down" and as more and more staff left the organization, we began the resistance movement to keep us going. We knew that with the extraordinary outpouring of support from Fair Traders, churches, business partners, and individuals there was an appetite and an energy to support the mission. We were aware that finance was being put in place on a temporary basis from a dedicated shareholder just so that we could ride out the worst of our cash flow problems, and we knew that thousands of people were going out of their way to sell just a bit more than normal to keep us going. We received hundreds of letters of support, and not a few telling us to "stop being wimps and to get on with it."

It was clear to us all that Traidcraft 2 needed a cultural revolution. The way we had settled into the path of least resistance meant that we had lost our appetite and our edge to be radical. We knew we needed a different management style too, since reducing the company to just twelve people meant a lot of responsibility being shouldered by just a few relatively "young" shoulders. There was no room for middle managers, or even, dare we say it, a boss. So, as nearly 1,000 years of Traidcraft experience left the building in December of 2018 and January 2019, including Joe Osman, we agreed to write the rules all over again. No holy cows, no secret deals in the background, just the twelve of us and a mission that was not, by any stretch of the imagination, complete.

We were inspired by a book *Be More Pirate: Or How to Take on the World and Win* by Sam Conniff Allende which seemed to capture the real heart of what Traidcraft had once been and which it needed to find again.[79] In terms of our management style, we began experimenting with "holacracy" – a challenging, but liberating process of self-organization.

And our mission for the future? We wish to throw nothing away from our original call to fight trade injustice, but we also see that the world has changed dramatically, and our approach needs to reflect this:

1. The world economy is five times larger than in 1970.

2. The concentration levels of carbon dioxide, methane, and nitrous oxide in the atmosphere are unprecedented in at least 800,000 years.

3. Natural global warming in the past occurred at the rate of 0.5° to 1.0°C per 1,000 years. Through human activities the global temperature has increased by 1.0°C in the last 200 years, and the trend is accelerating.

4. About two-thirds of the carbon dioxide emission quota consistent with a 2°C temperature rise limit has already been consumed (in other words, it's already in the atmosphere or oceans).

5. The current global pledges by individual nations will still allow a global temperature rise of approximately 3.2°C by 2100.

6. At current trends, however, the global average temperature will rise by 4.8°C by 2100.

Figures are figures and statistics can be boring, but a rise of 1.5°C will bring with it significant dislocation in our world: marginal land will become unproductive and farmers

---

79   Sam Conniff Allende, *Be More Pirate: Or How to Take on the World and Win*, London: Penguin, 2018.

will continue to migrate to the megacities of the South or the richer countries of the North; fish stocks will decline substantially as the oceans (which have already absorbed 30% of the CO_2 emissions) lose oxygen. At 2°C, the Arctic ice sheets will melt irreversibly.

And, of course, the poor will suffer first. If our mission is to fight injustice through trade, then we need to take this theme more seriously than any before.

When Greta Thunberg, the 16-year-old climate activist from Sweden, spoke to the European Parliament on 16 April 2019, she said that she wanted us to act as though our house was on fire. Every time she used this phrase, politicians tried to convince her that it was a bad idea to spread panic. She said she would agree if the panic were unfounded – except that it wasn't. If your house is on fire, you need to panic at least a little bit to stop it from burning.[80]

Traidcraft has a strong history of building up small communities of farmers, making them resilient and able to withstand the shocks of a bad harvest or a lack of access to market. Our mission is urgent. We need to wake up and panic because we want to be part of a movement that stops the house from burning to the ground. This involves supporting farmers who produce organically, invest in biodiversity, reforest their communities, educate their children, and build solid communities. More than ever, our way of doing trade is the antidote to conventional, slash/burn, extract, pollute, and move on farming practices. And if we have to adopt more radical methods of communicating this, then so be it. You have been warned!

---

80 Greta Thunberg, *No One Is Too Small to Make a Difference*, London: Penguin, 2019.

Chapter 28

REFLECTIONS ON A FORTY-YEAR JOURNEY

I've been on many a training course over my time at Traidcraft and have found most of them beneficial. One of the most interesting was one that covered organizational change management and I was fascinated by one model which I would often speak about to my colleagues, trying to make sense of Traidcraft and how its people might deal with change. I'm not sure who developed the theory, but the so-called "Wild West theory of organizational change" basically categorizes people as one of four types, all based on nineteenth-century USA history.

- "Trailblazers" describe people who venture into the unknown. They discover new territories, tend to be lone players, and love taking risks. They don't dwell in one place for too long and they look for the next new thing and then move on.

- "Pioneers" are those who follow those trails and draw the maps of the newly discovered territories. They still take risks but do so with a degree of knowledge obtained from those who went before. They can't do this entirely on their own so are more of a team player.

- "Settlers" populate the maps created by the pioneers and create the conditions for growth and prosperity but needing structure and rules to do so. They tend to be less creative and not prone to taking risks.

- "Outlaws" are the negative people populating most organizations, who might previously have been any of the previous three categories but hide behind rocks, occasionally taking aim and firing, or who ambush their colleagues.

Every organization needs the characteristics of a trailblazer, pioneer, or settler. They probably don't need outlaws, but every organization has the potential for people to turn into outlaws.

I used this theory in an analysis of Traidcraft which has ably demonstrated its trailblazing characteristics throughout its early years, which then developed into pioneering characteristics for almost all of its history. The thing that Traidcraft was less good at was the role of a settler. There were several other organizations and dedicated Fair Trade brands that developed after Traidcraft which were much better at being settlers. In the world of Fair Trade, they were not trailblazers and many of them were not even pioneers, since Traidcraft and a small number of its contemporaries had drawn the map. More often than not, it is the settler that manages to reap the rewards. In the resetting of Traidcraft plc as it continues into its fifth decade, then perhaps it needs to take on more of the settler characteristics to get on with running a sustainable business.

There is a museum in Newcastle-upon-Tyne called the Discovery Museum and one of its exhibitions tells the story of Tyneside through the ages. I was walking through the period covering the twentieth century and was drawn to a photograph of a group of people among a montage illustrating notable business and industrial development. I was drawn to it because I recognized Richard Adams, Traidcraft's founder, and then also recognized myself standing as part of the group. The photograph was taken during the Tearcraft days and no one really knows how it got there. As Richard would say when I asked him about it sometime afterwards, "At least we can say that posterity ranks Tearcraft alongside Swan Hunter, Parsons, and Vickers"! As I recounted the tale to my colleagues in Traidcraft, apart from having to deal with the realization that I was now a museum exhibit, there was some sense of pride that those humble beginnings were the start of something that became much bigger, although I was more than aware that those other north-eastern industrial giants no longer exist! The influence and impact that Traidcraft has had on the world of Fair Trade and ethical business is hard to quantify, but it's undeniably significant. Whatever the future holds, the legacy remains.

As well as my own reflections, it seems also fitting to include the reflections of others, so here are a few.

Andy Biggs, Non-Executive Director from 2013 and then interim CEO of Traidcraft from 2015, writes:

> If we review the history of many organizations, we see an ebb and flow of success. Looking back at the period when I was involved, first as a non-executive and then in interim leadership, seems to mirror the ancient words from the book of Ecclesiastes 3:1–9, which says:
>
> *There is a time for everything,*
> *And a season for every activity under the heavens:*
> *A time to be born and a time to die,*
> *A time to plant and a time to uproot,*
> *A time to kill and a time to heal,*
> *A time to tear down and a time to build,*
> *A time to weep and a time to laugh,*
> *A time to mourn and a time to dance,*
> *A time to scatter stones and a time to gather them,*
> *A time to embrace and a time to refrain from embracing,*
> *A time to search and a time to give up,*
> *A time to keep and a time to throw away,*
> *A time to tear and a time to mend,*
> *A time to be silent and a time to speak,*
> *A time to love and a time to hate,*
> *A time for war and a time for peace.*
>
> No organization has an inviolable right to exist, and Traidcraft is certainly no exception. After making public

declaration some years earlier that Traidcraft would like to see Fair Trade as mainstream success and by encouraging its supporters to buy Fairtrade products in supermarkets it deliberately acknowledged its own mortality and prepared itself for a time when its mission would be complete, and it would no longer be needed.

Very few organizations have this kind of boldness. There has been a strong cultural understanding that Traidcraft was birthed to be an exemplar of how a company should trade, treat, and remunerate its employees, and coordinate itself with charitable projects where direct trade was not the most appropriate way of building sustainable justice for the poor and marginalised.

Traidcraft embedded many good principles into its practice and governance. It drafted its governance documents carefully with checks and balances through the supervision of a charitable Foundation to ensure adherence to the underlying Christian ethos and missional focus on benefit to the poor. It set in place policies and procedures to mirror the kind of corporate governance required of large listed companies.

In and of itself this is all commendable but it contained the DNA that would ultimately lead to the struggles experienced from mid-2000 onwards. In a post-credit-crunch world, the rapidly changing retail landscape in the UK meant that the "party plan" model (used by Fair Traders and which was the bedrock of Traidcraft's historical growth) was unsustainable as a business model in the face of aggressive supermarket behaviour and the availability of online shopping.

In summary, the trading model and governance structures were designed for an era which had passed, even if its mission was as vital and relevant as it had been for forty years. Traidcraft the trading entity was too slow, too bureaucratic, and arguably too distracted by worthy charitable endeavour to recognize that it was out of step with the realities of the UK consumer goods market.

Its more recent failings have simply been that it has not (yet) managed to re-invent itself for a retail environment which exists currently. Ethical and environmental issues are increasingly part of consumer consciousness, but commercial opportunities are being exploited by agile organisations with innovative, start-up mentalities with a keen-edged focus on singular product concepts and testing consumer demand and developing brands with meaning that resonate with consumers' values.

Traidcraft as a brand is in essence a charity brand – and quite rightly so, given the impact and scope of its charitable mission. However, that makes it very difficult for its trading operation to command a price premium or sell its products at scale. Its organization, infrastructure, and methods have been too cumbersome and arguably the biggest issue is that it has had lacked focus on understanding and exploiting whatever market opportunities do exist.

The initiatives that I started like "the million pound challenge" succeeded in the goal of providing some short-term relief from the loss-making trends – but, without a fundamental reworking and rebirth of the Traidcraft trading model, the enterprise has been consigned to wait for its eventual demise. Ultimately, the adverse exchange rate movements that followed the 2016 Brexit referendum unwound all this good work and plunged the trading company back into a loss-making crisis and made this a very difficult time for all who worked there, including my permanent successor as CEO.

Traidcraft should not beat itself up too much about this, since it has fought hard and survived when many household-name retailers have gone out of business in the period since 2014. As a proud resident of the north east of England, it is only too aware of the heritage of coal, steel, and shipbuilding that once were the bedrocks of the local economy but are now consigned to museum displays and cultural legacies.

The only solution for such an enterprise which, unlike human bodies, can be reborn here and now on earth, is to reinvent itself. It must run with an innovative start-up ethos – with singular and clear purpose – to meet and adapt to market opportunity and customer demands, without losing the connection to its founding principles of enabling trade justice and empowerment of vulnerable people who are suffering due to poverty.

It faces many obstacles, not the least of which is the historical legacy of a generous pension scheme which makes receiving new investment extremely difficult and risky. Nevertheless, it still has many assets, perhaps the biggest of which is the supporter movement who have been the faithful buyers, givers, advocates of Fair Trade and trade justice for several decades. Their legacy is not dead.

I wish it well and pray for its success.[81]

Harriet Lamb was Executive Director of the Fairtrade Foundation from 2001/12 and writes:

I love Traidcraft because they connect social movements at the two ends of the global supply chain. They connect men, women, and young people in this country who care so much about building greater fairness in trade that they will stand at the back of the church or at cold market stalls to sell Traidcraft goodies to all those who hunt them out because they want to use their consumer power for a purpose. And then there are the smallholder farmers organized in coops and the workers in developing countries selling us their tea or coffee, rice or raisins, dates or olive oil, and working hard to meet the conditions of Fairtrade including caring for the environment.

Traidcraft connects these two sides of movements of fairness in trade – and then takes the learning to lobby for the bigger policy changes that we need from government in the UK, EU, and globally.

---

81 From personal correspondence with the author, 2019.

I have met many farmers and workers selling to Traidcraft. I travelled in India with Joe Osman, meeting rice farmers who had organized in their village to sell on Fairtrade terms, and cotton farmers who told us about the terrible low prices they got on the open market and how they were struggling to grow anything on their dry, dry lands. Indeed, many were using the Fairtrade premium to bring badly needed irrigation to their fields. Many were trying to go organic but found themselves surrounded by farmers spraying their crops repeatedly and using GMO seeds which risked contaminating neighbouring smallholder plots. There are always challenges and it is never easy to mix social and environmental principles with the market – but Traidcraft has always been ready to wrestle with the problems, to discuss and debate, and find solutions in a spirit of openness. They have also been ready to share their learning, serving on Fairtrade International's Standards Committee for example, or feeding into multiple consultations on how we can get Fairtrade right.

Traidcraft's retail network also provides vital outlets for other dedicated Fairtrade companies such as Divine chocolate, Zaytoun, Cafédirect, or Tropical Wholefoods to sell their goods to the public. Their outlets are a fantastic way for people to learn about Fairtrade and talk with others about what it all means.

I have long admired Traidcraft's long-term, big vision. When we were building up the wider sales of Fairtrade marked products, it could have been seen as a threat to an early pioneer like Traidcraft. But they always embraced the challenge, welcomed companies coming to Fairtrade, and pushed themselves to distinguish in other ways – for example, when they had a smash hit with Geobars, when they were very early to introduce energy bars into supermarkets, or when they introduced new Fair Trade products such as rubber or charcoal. So I raise my cup of Fairtrade coffee to Traidcraft, their strong principles married with strong pragmatism, and I for one will always hunt down those lovely Traidcraft stalls.[82]

Safia Minney was the founder of People Tree and a pioneer in the development of Fair Trade and sustainable fashion. She writes:

Traidcraft was a wonderful "home" from which I learnt about Fair Trade and developed People Tree. I was twenty-five and it was 1990, I think. I would come to selection meetings and we would talk about design changes for products for the Japanese market where I set up and sold Fair Trade products. I was a campaigner for social justice and environmental issues and felt that Fair Trade had the power to change the system. I think it did in many ways – as I have described in my book *Slave to Fashion*.[83] Thanks to Fair Trade we have a powerful citizens movement, businesses are becoming more ethical, and we have the Sustainable Development Goals and the Modern Slavery Act. The problem is it's not enough. We need to change the system as it is perpetuating global heating, social and environmental injustice. I would ask everyone to join Extinction Rebellion, as I did, while doing their bit to support a transition economy where Fair Trade plays an important part.

That's one thing I loved about Traidcraft – that campaigning was always part of the DNA for change. We know that buying a Fair Trade dress and recycling isn't going to save our world and protect the future of humanity and other species. So I hope you'll stop eating meat and flying if you do – or at least massively cut it down. We all need to do our bit!

The climate crisis was there thirty years ago when I was a Traidcraft rep. Today there is no denying it. School kids and people throughout the world are suffering and we need to do everything we possibly can

---

82 From personal correspondence with the author, 2019.
83 Safia Minney, *Slave to Fashion*, Oxford: New Internationalist, 2017.

to reduce our CO_2 emissions, and to use the influence that we have to get others to do the same.

Read the book *This is Not a Drill: An Extinction Rebellion Handbook*.[84] Buy twenty copies and give them to your friends. I used to do this with Traidcraft Christmas hampers and crafts. Follow me on Twitter and Instagram.[85] Listen to my new podcasts, "The Ethical Agenda Podcast" – it's a fun way of learning about new things. Stop buying stuff unless it's Fair Trade and sustainably produced.

And please, let's be kind to ourselves. Let's realize that we are all products of our time, that sometimes we need a re-boot, that we can reinvent and reimagine, and that through the fear of climate collapse comes the opportunity to build the society that we all dreamt of.

Love you Traidcraft and thank you for the memories![86]

Michael Northcott, Professor of Ethics at Edinburgh University and former Trustee of Traidcraft, writes:

I served for ten years as a trustee of Traidcraft and, in that time, I came to know well its work in pioneering fairly traded commodity supply chains. Creating, researching, and guaranteeing fairly traded commodity supply chains from farm field through manufacturing, packaging, and sales of new products is a dauntingly complicated process and no one knows this better than Joe and the team at Traidcraft. Their exceptional knowledge of smallholder farmers and commodity supply opportunities in a number of developing countries and their ability to get into the field, to network, and to research and generate a fully transparent and socially just supply chain from field to factory, is really extraordinary – and it is the kernel of Fair Trade. The process can

---

84 Extinction Rebellion, *This is Not a Drill: An Extinction Rebellion Handbook*, London: Penguin, 2019.

85 @SafiaMinney and https://www.instagram.com/safia_minney/

86 From personal correspondence with the author, 2019.

take up to six years and requires tremendous reserves of optimism, patience, and fortitude – as is clearly displayed in this engaging and readable book. Their unique and multi-decadal experience in this pioneering work has given them an amazing fund of stories, and an unequalled knowledge of the hidden realities of global commodity-sourcing and international trade. With what they know, they could be running Britain's efforts to negotiate just and sustainable international trade agreements after Brexit! But, of course, the history of Fair Trade in which they played a central role shows just how hard it is to persuade governments and corporations to create genuinely ecologically and socially transparent supply chains.[87]

Mike Gidney succeeded Harriet Lamb as Executive Director of Fairtrade Foundation having led Traidcraft's policy work before that. He writes:

One of the most inspiring and distinctive characteristics of Fair Trade is that it is truly a movement. Yes, it's a brilliantly simple idea – trade where people and planet matter more than profit – but its unprecedented success in recent years has been thanks to people. Fair Trade has thrived thanks to the passion, dedication, and commitment of individuals, communities, and families coming together around shared concepts of justice and respect. Nowhere was that more clearly felt than in Traidcraft. I joined the staff team in 2001 as Policy Director, with a brief to take the experience of Traidcraft's fair trading to policymakers and companies in a world which was rapidly coming to terms with concepts of "Corporate Social Responsibility". From day one, everyone on the Traidcraft team was welcoming, inquisitive, and endlessly challenging and energetic – it was the most inspiring place to learn about Fair Trade and how to widen its scope.

Joe Osman and the team were central to this. They had the challenging job of bringing Traidcraft's products to market, which meant creating Fair Trade supply

---

87 From personal correspondence with the author, 2019.

chains from scratch, turning exploitative trade on its head. I remember their almost daily challenges: how to tackle a change in EU policy that would make it possible to import African honey; how to help producers build more resilient organizations so they could withstand the enormous challenges of selling to multinational buyers. Throughout, I remember Joe was ever calm, ever optimistic, always convinced about the importance of what Fair Trade was trying to achieve. I don't think I ever saw him concede defeat. That dedication saw more new Fair Trade products available in the UK than ever before. Through this, the team at Traidcraft also became a mine of information, developing very close personal relationships with producers across the world and full of practical advice on how to "do Fair Trade" properly. In this way, Traidcraft stood for what Fair Trade is all about – individuals responding to the scandal of poverty, using all the skills and energy they could muster to build an alternative model of trade, but putting people first at every stage.

Traidcraft in those days was a fascinating place to work; very much a family feeling, a small, dedicated group of people modelling, challenging, and championing what it meant to be running a Fair Trade business. It taught me a great deal of how good business should be run. Fair Trade was not a sideline, not managed by a PR or sustainability team, but was shot through Traidcraft's governance, through the social accounts of Traidcraft plc. There was meaningful consultation, people were valued, there was real honesty, transparency, and a commitment to ethics. These were values not widely shared by big companies at the time.

And Traidcraft was the most incredible foundry of new ideas. Many of their innovations remain and are part of the landscape of the British economy: Traidcraft was the first company to publish audited social accounts (extraordinarily valuable as a model for others to follow). It helped establish Shared Interest, still providing vital finance to small-scale entrepreneurs in the global south, where mainstream finance still fears to tread. The Fairtrade Foundation was established in 1992 by deed of trust signed by Traidcraft's Directors; they also co-founded the Ethical Trading Initiative, which has done much to forge collaboration between companies, unions, and NGOs to improve labour standards. None of these was easy to establish, all of them have been vital in making trade fairer.

Joe led Traidcraft's innovations closer to home too. Under his watch, Traidcraft developed the first Fair Trade wine supply chains, later taken up by the Co-op and now a growing significant market share. Alongside a wealth of food products, there was also rubber from Sri Lanka and charcoal from Namibia. In 2019, as we celebrated twenty-five years of the Fairtrade Mark in the UK, there are now 5,000 certified products available, from coffee and bananas to cosmetics and gold. It is inconceivable that the Fair Trade sector in the UK would be as established as it is without Traidcraft's entrepreneurship and risk-taking.

If Fair Trade didn't exist, we would need to invent it. Despite the huge gains we have made, and the impact on farmers and business attitudes, enormous injustice remains. Price volatility continues to wreak havoc on the lives of smallholders – in 2019, the global coffee price fell to below $1 per pound – well below the costs of production. Under Fairtrade, farmers earn between $1.40 and $1.60. It's not just the increased income that matters, but also the predictability which is so important in giving farmers confidence to invest in their farms and next year's harvest. By contrast, "mainstream" trade makes smallholders much more vulnerable. At the same time, we all need farmers to make further investments in their farms to adapt to and help mitigate climate change. How can they afford to do this if they cannot earn a fair price?

Price volatility, climate change, and rising global inequality: a triple whammy for producers in developing countries. With these ever-present threats and the uncertainties of Britain's trading future, Fair Trade is needed now more than ever. Happily, the sector is booming, sustained by the talent and experience of those early pioneers. The concept of corporate accountability is here to stay; social media has made this the age of scrutiny and poor corporate practice is being called out daily. Certainly there are huge challenges ahead, for producers and consumers alike, but Joe and those other champions of the Fair Trade movement are living proof that a small group of individuals really can change the world.[88]

---

88   From personal correspondence with the author, 2019.

Epilogue
A PERSONAL REFLECTION BY RICHARD ADAMS

(Founder of Traidcraft)

Inevitably my perspective stretches a little further back than most. The 1960s was the major decade of decolonization, and newly independent countries soon realized that trade on fair terms would be vital to their futures. It's a battle that has yet to be won. Twelve years before Traidcraft was founded the core ideas of what should be involved in trade justice were coming together in my mind as I started the final year of a sociology degree at Durham University. They weren't new but the context of a rapidly changing world was. Principally they drew on the cooperative movement and the emerging influence of liberation theology. But how to practically interpret what an "option for the poor" should involve in the UK's energetically growing consumer society?

Radical change was clearly needed (as always!) but maybe not along the lines of the Cultural Revolution, already in full swing in China and proving to be a disaster. Partnership seemed a more productive route, first between my own agricultural imports company, Agrofax, and Tearfund, resulting in Tearcraft, Traidcraft's predecessor. It was in Tearcraft that many of the principles carried forward in Traidcraft evolved. The importance of a close, direct, and mutually supportive relationship with producers, a close rapport with all the other organizations seeking to develop alternative trade – Oxfam, Project Hand, and One Village in particular – and not least a strong partnership with the growing number of reps who gave their time, money, garages, and spare bedrooms to stocking and distributing an exotic range of products.

Organizations, particularly ones that are successful and growing, don't take long to establish their identity and so Joe already found a distinctive business when he joined us in 1976. As far as I'm concerned, his comment that he found it a delight to go to work each day hit the spot. I always felt that work, whenever possible, should be enjoyable and worthwhile and having the opportunity to shape such an environment while still in my twenties was immensely satisfying. Although by that time I'd worked in both the private and public sectors and had the opportunity to see, through two of my jobs, how a wide range of companies operated, I hadn't discovered a good model. So Traidcraft not only practised D-I-Y but also D-I-D – Do it Differently. One feature of this approach was openness – to new ideas, to collaboration, and to experimentation. One of the distinctive things that Traidcraft offered was a total commitment to helping producer groups around the world improve their products and get into wider markets, not only for export but in their own countries. Traidcraft had no option but to be a middleman between supplier and final customer, but we were determined to do things that few others did, such as design and technical help, market experience courses for key staff from producers, and seeking grants on their behalf from our partner agencies like Christian Aid and CAFOD. Unlike most businesses, we didn't demand exclusivity agreements.

I left Traidcraft in 1988 at the time when the green consumer movement was beginning to take off. This was very much part of my vision of ethical, sustainable consumerism which had been developing though Traidcraft's promotion and, indeed, production of environmentally friendly products. A few months earlier, I hadn't been able to persuade the board that Traidcraft could be a leader in this field – "stick to the knitting" was the response. As the growing environmental effects of our lifestyles became clearer it seemed obvious that trade justice also needed to take into account our impact on the planet. I'm still uncertain whether this was a missed opportunity or would have been a bridge too far. In 1988 we were producing and servicing the sales catalogues of several other "justice" organizations and this gave us a unique perspective on the growing ethical consumer market. Thirty years on, awareness of the need for sustainability in every aspect of our lives is much higher but the market is saturated with products and it seems unlikely that Traidcraft has the depth or capacity to carve out a distinctive role in this area now.

One of the tensions that Traidcraft lived with – maybe it still does – were the very different perceptions of what it was trying to do and what lay at its heart. As this book shows, Traidcraft has meant many things to many people over the last forty years. For producers, it was more straightforward as it offered an outlet for products, access to markets, and above all a friendly face in an increasingly competitive world. For customers, it was different. It could be seen as a radical voice challenging one of the fundamental ideas of capitalism – self-interest. For other customers, it was an opportunity to enable the poor to stand on their own two feet. Using this tension to motivate and inspire a wide range of people was undoubtedly one of Traidcraft's successes. Similarly, the Christian ethos that inspired Traidcraft was most dynamic within the company when it was inclusive and universalist. There were very few faith-based organizations that could appeal to every major strand of the Christian church and, at the same time, draw support from people of all faiths and none.

One of our themes was how to use the market to change the market, to offer people an opportunity to make a more direct link between their own lives and those of others in oppressive economic circumstances around the world. The "Trade not Aid" concept had emerged from the setting up of the United Nations Conference on Trade and Development in 1964, which aimed to give an effective economic voice to the global south. The Traidcraft name was itself a reflection on this with economic justice rather than poverty relief being the main message. I now chair the Fair Trade Advocacy Office in Brussels, the voice of what is now a global and influential drive for trade justice and, from this perspective, it's possible to confirm that Traidcraft played a leading role in shaping this movement to improve the livelihoods of marginalized producers and workers in the South.

"Love and justice in the world through responsible and fair trading."[89] This was how the first handwritten Traidcraft catalogue summed up the fundamental idea that motivated many who worked for the business or who would go on to buy some of the one hundred or so handicraft products illustrated. The next paragraph drove home the message. We were "redressing economic injustice in the world" as part of our Christian responsibilities. We were doing it in partnership with our customers and in particular, with all the producing groups supplying our product range, each of which we knew well, dealt with directly and relied on in a mutually supportive relationship. We saw ourselves as radically "alternative", challenging unthinking consumerism, big business, corporate greed, political insensitivity, and corruption.

So what might the future hold for Traidcraft? How much of the substantial legacy of the past can be carried forward? The business that evolved from a greengrocer's shop in north London has certainly had a formative role in what became known as the international Fair Trade movement from the mid-1990s onwards. At a national level, Traidcraft became an accepted partner of the major churches, of campaigning groups and of government in delivering aspects of the international development programme. At a local level, Traidcraft has, over the years, provided many hundreds of jobs on Tyneside and been the progenitor of several flourishing businesses. It has achieved recognition in many ways, my favourite being the period when Traidcraft was frequently mentioned in the scripts of *The Archers* on BBC Radio 4. But the recent past has been one of decline, uncertainty, and false starts. In this sort of situation what is the way forward?

Taking a path which builds on its strengths is the obvious route and those strengths remain based in partnership – with other organizations, with the thousands of dedicated Fair Traders and customers and, above all, with the people Traidcraft is trying to serve – the producers. Internally, Traidcraft has become a very different organization from what it was in the past, though this is perhaps not yet fully apparent to

---

89 Traidcraft catalogue, 1979.

those on the outside. With such a radical change of staff in the present organization, the institutional memory can no longer be said to be held within the company but lies elsewhere, with producers, customers, and the international Fair Trade movement. It remains an open question as to whether their voice will be heard.

Appendix 1

TRAIDCRAFT'S OBJECTIVES[90]

These were some of Traidcraft's early organizational objectives, developed in 1986, as explained in chapter 3.

Traidcraft, following an extended discussion and consultation period with staff, shareholders, customers, and representatives of partner production groups, sets down the following objectives as defining the main purposes of Traidcraft plc as it works in collaboration with the Traidcraft Exchange. These objectives should not be regarded as a mould within which all future developments take place but rather as a framework enabling a steady and purposeful growth. A regular review every two years by the Trustees of the Traidcraft Exchange and Directors of the company in consultation with those groups mentioned above will seek to ensure that Traidcraft tests its experience acquired in practical action for justice in trade against these objectives in a continuing process. These objectives should be read in conjunction with the Basis of Faith of the Traidcraft Exchange and the current purchasing criteria policy statements for food and craft products.

Traidcraft aims to expand and establish more just trading systems which will express the principles of love and justice fundamental to

---

90 Traidcraft internal document, July 1986.

the Christian faith. Practical service and a partnership for change will characterise the organisation, which puts people before profit.

Just Trade = Fairer Systems

Traidcraft will aim to contribute to the development of a distinctive trading system that:

I. Will be a system based on service, equity, and justice drawing its driving force from these values applied in love. It will be distinctive in its overall effect, though not necessarily in every individual application, from a system based on profit maximization or personal gain.

II. Will regard the existence of gross material inequities between peoples, where some are without the basic means to enjoy health, security, and opportunity for personal fulfilment and development, as a condition to be remedied through the economic system and not perpetuated by it.

III. Will regard all personal decisions, processes, and structures as stemming from the ethical and practical framework for love in action to be found in the life of Jesus Christ. It will announce good news for the poor, proclaim release for prisoners, recovery of sight for the blind, and freedom for the broken victims. It will feed the hungry, give drink to the thirsty, house the stranger, clothe the naked, support the ill, and visit the prisoner.

IV. Will not exploit customers by depending on their goodwill to excuse poor service or misleading them so that they give support which would not be forthcoming if they had the full facts.

By making the development of fairer trading systems an objective, we recognise the inequity of present systems. Many of these systems are entrenched in national and international laws and conventions as well as the result of personal selfishness and greed. We recognise that changing some systems will mean changing those laws and conventions where national or political self-interest have been put before the good of all and the rights and interests of the poor.

Traidcraft will regularly consider, in discussion with its staff, directors, shareholders, representatives, producers, and supporters, the extent and nature of political lobbying and campaigning in support of its practical trade campaigns and long-term objectives.

Just Trade = Developing People's Potential

Traidcraft recognises that all people are made in the image of God. We will seek, in our work with producers, our own staff and supporters, and with our customers, to enhance the creative liberating potential of each individual as well as their community. In particular:

I. Producers – many of the workers in craft groups have great expertise which is often not reflected in the crafts Traidcraft buys. We should aim not only to develop the group's "mass production" potential but also craftsmanship and individual talents.

    It is important that producers Traidcraft works with are allowed and enabled to achieve their own, differing, growth rates without pressure resulting from Traidcraft's growth putting at risk their viability, integrity, or social concerns and care for their workers.

    Traidcraft plc and Traidcraft Exchange will provide development support services to producers who request practical help in achieving their growth potential, in diversification and quality as well as production volume.

    To ensure that this objective is achieved Traidcraft will be methodical in applying the producer criteria to suppliers and will seek to obtain regular, objective evaluations of the benefits to artisans.

II. Staff – greater attention and investment will need to be made in training to allow staff to undertake existing work more effectively and to cope with the increasing demands likely through future development. Attention needs to be given to broadening experience through job exchanges internally and with similar organisations. Overseas experience is particularly useful and participation in study tours and overseas work placements or exchanges should be encouraged. Staff understanding of development issues and their role as Christians in the development process must also be expanded.

III. Customers – developing their potential will involve improving and increasing our educational work. It should be aimed, in a different way, at reps, mail order customers, shop customers, and the general public and should aim to achieve the following:

a. To enable people to be so aware of trading issues that they will buy from "just sources" and be prepared to pay more.

b. To educate people about the third world including those who appear uninterested.

c. To help people understand the consequences of materialism and to put their lifestyle into global perspective.

d. To help people understand that the Kingdom of God and its values are relevant and practical.

e. To help in educating the electorate toward voting for governments that are concerned for love and justice.

f. To challenge complacency in churches and replace it with a determination to make a stand for issues of love and justice.

g. To provide press releases and material for media coverage of issues.

h. Unions – to provide information to enable them to be more internationally aware and prepared to take informed action across national boundaries.

i. To enable reps and other supporters to influence their own communities.

j. To encourage the adoption of our policies as the standard for all trading companies.

We should recognise that to achieve a. and b. in particular will require Traidcraft to operate an efficient service to customers so that they have a positive experience of just trading.

Just Trade = More and Better Jobs

Traidcraft will seek to create, through its development of the market for products from developing countries, the opportunities for more jobs and better jobs. These criteria apply to all work, both in the rich and poor nations. It is recognised that the wide variety in standards and opportunities will need to be assessed locally with an approach in which realism is tempered by love and justice.

By "better jobs" we mean jobs that provide:

I. Fair wages.

II. Recognition of each person's worth and the need for the job each person does.

III. A good match to each person's skills and capabilities and ones which will encourage personal development.

IV. Adequate facilities and equipment to do the job to the standard required.

V. Adequate safety precautions.

VI. Opportunity and encouragement to participate in decisions, to associate in free trade unions where appropriate, and to share in the responsibilities and benefits of ownership.

VII. A caring and friendly atmosphere and pleasant work environment, wherever possible.

VIII. Recognition of work load and the flexibility to cope with this.

IX. Opportunities to take advantage of the skills gained or pay received or saved to go on to other forms of training or employment or self-employment.

Some jobs may be regarded as tedious or unpleasant by all. Where possible these should be shared, rotated or consideration given to mechanisation. Where mechanisation will lead to replacement of jobs, as well as increased efficiency, it should lead to improved job satisfaction for the remaining workers, and workers should only be replaced by equipment if other work is available for them. Great care will need to be taken to ensure that any equipment or technology introduced is "appropriate".

Recognition needs to be given to the unpaid jobs done by our 1,000 or more voluntary reps and care taken to ensure that, where appropriate, these comply with the above objectives.

Just Trade = Fairer Relationships within Traidcraft

Traidcraft will seek to establish an inclusive community of purpose and relationships free of personal or departmental interest, acknowledging the Christian precept of love by putting the interests of others before our own. To this end:

I. There should be an open style of management which will encourage the consultation and participation of staff and, where possible, producers and reps in the decision-making processes of the company.

II. All staff should be helped to identify their abilities through an effective and fair job appraisal system and helped through appropriate training to develop their potential.

III. The Traidcraft Exchange should be responsible for the maintenance of the overall policy of the company and should be well informed about its activities.

Just Trade = Efficient and Practical Structures

To support the processes which will achieve these objectives the company will establish and refine operating structures appropriate to the fundamental strategy of the business. They will concentrate resources and efforts and ensure the harmonious development of human capital and physical resources. A key element in assessing the efficiency and effectiveness of the business will be the achievement of determined profit levels, currently a target of 2% of sales retained after tax.

Appendix 2

TRAIDCRAFT WEBSITE BLOG POST, 2015[91]

This was an example of Traidcraft stating its position in the light of changing approaches to certified Fairtrade standards – see also chapters 13 and 19.

The announcement in October that Mars UK would be the first UK Company to commit to Fairtrade's new "cocoa sourcing programme" came almost two years after this new initiative was announced. We've been tracking this development and, now that it's happened, we thought it would be useful to give some reflections from a Traidcraft perspective on something that will significantly increase the volumes of Fairtrade cocoa beans traded globally – something which has to be good!

Back in early 2014 we issued our own press release and comment via our website. At that stage we were cautiously optimistic but raised some concerns. We spent time at Traidcraft roadshows and beyond outlining these concerns to supporters but now, as we approach the end of 2015, were they valid?

We were concerned that producers of smaller commodities might be disadvantaged by these changes: we think that this concern still exists. Fairtrade Sourcing Programmes (FSPs) were always about a single commodity. Now that cocoa has launched there will be no requirement to use other ingredients as Fairtrade. Back then we were concerned

---

91 Traidcraft website blog post, written by the author in 2015.

about nuts and dried fruit producers but, as we know, the single biggest ingredient in a Mars bar is sugar which does not need to be Fairtrade certified.

We were concerned that smaller producer organisations might not get the benefits of this extra volume of Fairtrade. Maybe big brands would only want to work with the larger producers who could deliver bigger volumes. Mars sources much of its cocoa from the Ivory Coast, the largest cocoa producer in the world and where there are large numbers of small farmers and small-scale cooperatives. We have some experience in this country so it's good news to see the growth of newly Fairtrade certified cooperatives – more than fifty the last time we looked – and many of them quite small-scale. So lots of benefits going to lots of producer organisations across a broad region.

We were concerned that the Fairtrade Mark would lose consumer trust. We wondered back then how the Fairtrade Mark would look visually, how similar it would be to the recognised and trusted mark, and whether consumers would be confused over the message. Well, Mars Bars do use the FSP label, which is different, in the small print on the back of the pack so that's at least one level of confusion removed. But we wonder whether there will still be confusion. We know that consumers will still refer to the product as a Fairtrade Mars Bar, but actually it isn't! None of the official press releases use that form of words. Mars themselves used the words "Fairtrade certified cocoa Mars Bar". To call a retail product "Fairtrade" it needs to have all ingredients that can be Fairtrade included (and importantly sugar!) and it needs the recognised Fairtrade Mark on front of pack. There is a difference but will consumers spot that?

We were concerned that big brands that had already committed to the Fairtrade Mark would move away from it. Of course, this FSP initiative is a cheaper way to do Fairtrade. No expensive ingredients apart from the cocoa. Will the Malteser brand remove its Fairtrade Mark and use the FSP Mark? We hope not but will continue to watch this closely.

On that 2014 press release we also laid out in bold type these words: **Fair Trade has always been about justice!**

This has always driven Traidcraft's work for the last 35 years. Would Mars use the same words – probably not! Mars launched their sustainability programme some years ago. Its focus has been to increase productivity and crop yields and thus output and farmer earnings. This has been with a backdrop of increased global demand for cocoa and reducing supply so something needed to be done and it's great that farmers benefit – we wouldn't criticize this and some of Traidcraft's development programmes apply similar principles. But FSP is another way to offer such brands a certification platform that meets their sustainability goals. It's convenient that the Fairtrade cocoa minimum guaranteed price falls below the global market price and has done so for some time and that producers are encouraged to target the Fairtrade additional premium on quality and productivity activities. Therefore, FSP is an ideal "sustainability" certification initiative for Mars.

But Traidcraft and other dedicated Fairtrade brands available through Traidcraft like Divine, Cafédirect, Liberation, or Zaytoun believe that Fair Trade is more than just a certification system. It's an alternative model of trade which applies fairness and justice to farmers and workers. We hope that consumers will continue to choose such dedicated brands.

Appendix 3

WFTO: TEN PRINCIPLES OF FAIR TRADE[92]

WFTO prescribes ten principles that Fair Trade Organizations must follow in their day-to-day work and carries out monitoring to ensure these principles are upheld.

Principle One: Creating Opportunities for Economically Disadvantaged Producers

Poverty reduction through trade forms a key part of the organization's aims. The organization supports marginalized small producers, whether these are independent family businesses, or grouped in associations or cooperatives. It seeks to enable them to move from income insecurity and poverty to economic self-sufficiency and ownership. The organization has a plan of action to carry this out.

Principle Two: Transparency and Accountability

The organization is transparent in its management and commercial relations. It is accountable to all its stakeholders and respects the sensitivity and confidentiality of commercial information supplied.

---

92 World Fair Trade Organization, "10 Principles of Fair Trade", December 2017, reproduced with permission.

The organization finds appropriate, participatory ways to involve employees, members, and producers in its decision-making processes. It ensures that relevant information is provided to all its trading partners. The communication channels are good and open at all levels of the supply chain.

Principle Three: Fair Trading Practices

The organization trades with concern for the social, economic, and environmental well-being of marginalized small producers and does not maximize profit at their expense. It is responsible and professional in meeting its commitments in a timely manner. Suppliers respect contracts and deliver products on time and to the desired quality and specifications.

Fair Trade buyers, recognizing the financial disadvantages faced by producers and suppliers of FT products, ensure orders are paid on receipt of documents or as mutually agreed. For handicraft FT products, an interest free pre-payment of at least 50% is made on request. For food FT products, pre-payment of at least 50% at a reasonable interest is made if requested. Interest rates that the suppliers pay must not be higher than the buyers, cost of borrowing from third parties. Charging interest is not required.

Where southern Fair Trade suppliers receive a pre-payment from buyers, they ensure that this payment is passed on to the producers or farmers who make or grow their Fair Trade products.

Buyers consult with suppliers before cancelling or rejecting orders. Where orders are cancelled through no fault of producers or suppliers, adequate compensation is guaranteed for work already done. Suppliers and producers consult with buyers if there is a problem with delivery, and ensure compensation is provided when delivered quantities and qualities do not match those invoiced.

The organization maintains long-term relationships based on solidarity, trust, and mutual respect that contribute to the promotion and growth of Fair Trade. It maintains effective communication with its trading partners. Parties involved in a trading relationship seek to increase the volume of the trade between them and the value and diversity of their product offer as a means of growing Fair Trade for the producers in order to increase their incomes. The organization works cooperatively with the other Fair Trade Organizations in the country and avoids unfair competition. It avoids duplicating the designs of patterns of other organizations without permission.

Fair Trade recognises, promotes, and protects the cultural identity and traditional skills of small producers as reflected in their craft designs, food products and other related services.

Principle Four: Fair Payment

A fair payment is one that has been mutually negotiated and agreed by all through on-going dialogue and participation, which provides fair pay to the producers and can also be sustained by the market, taking into account the principle of equal pay for equal work by women and men. The aim is always the payment of a Local Living Wage. Fair Payment is made up of Fair Prices, Fair Wages and Local Living Wages.

Fair Prices

A Fair Price is freely negotiated through dialogue between the buyer and the seller and is based on transparent price setting. It includes a fair wage and a fair profit. Fair Prices represent an equitable share of the final price to each player in the supply chain.

Fair Wages

A Fair Wage is an equitable, freely negotiated, and mutually agreed wage, and presumes the payment of at least a Local Living Wage.

Local Living Wage

A Local Living Wage is remuneration received for a standard working week (no more than 48 hours) by a Worker in a particular place, sufficient to afford a decent standard of living for the Worker and her or his family. Elements of a decent standard of living include food, water, housing, education, healthcare, transport, clothing, and other essential needs, including provision for unexpected events.

Principle Five: Ensuring No Child Labour and Forced Labour

The organization adheres to the UN Convention on the Rights of the Child, and national/local law on the employment of children. The organization ensures that there is no forced labour in its workforce and/or members or homeworkers.

Organizations who buy Fair Trade products from producer groups either directly or through intermediaries ensure that no forced labour is used in production and the producer complies with the UN Convention on the Rights of the Child, and national/local law on the employment of children. Any involvement of children in the production of Fair Trade products (including learning a traditional art or craft) is always disclosed and monitored and does not adversely affect the children's well-being, security, educational requirements, and need for play.

Principle Six: Commitment to Non-Discrimination, Gender Equity and Women's Economic Empowerment, and Freedom of Association

The organization does not discriminate in hiring, remuneration, access to training, promotion, termination or retirement based on race, caste, national origin, religion, disability, gender, sexual orientation, union membership, political affiliation, HIV/AIDS status or age.

The organization has a clear policy and plan to promote gender equality that ensures that women as well as men have the ability to gain access to the resources that they need to be productive and also the ability to influence the wider policy, regulatory, and institutional environment that shapes their livelihoods and lives. Organizational constitutions and by-laws allow for and enable women to become active members of the organization in their own right (where it is a membership-based organization), and to take up leadership positions in the governance structure regardless of women's status in relation to ownership of assets such as land and property. Where women are employed within the organization, even where it is an informal employment situation, they receive equal pay for equal work. The organization recognizes women's full employment rights and is committed to ensuring that women receive their full statutory employment benefits. The organization takes into account the special health and safety needs of pregnant women and breast-feeding mothers.

The organization respects the right of all employees to form and join trade unions of their choice and to bargain collectively. Where the right to join trade unions and bargain collectively are restricted by law and/or political environment, the organization will enable means of independent and free association and bargaining for employees. The organization ensures that representatives of employees are not subject to discrimination in the workplace.

Principle Seven: Ensuring Good Working Conditions

The organization provides a safe and healthy working environment for employees and/or members. It complies, at a minimum, with national and local laws and ILO (International Labour Organization) conventions on health and safety.

Working hours and conditions for employees and / or members (and any homeworkers) comply with conditions established by national and local laws and ILO conventions.

Fair Trade Organizations are aware of the health and safety conditions in the producer groups they buy from. They seek, on an ongoing basis, to raise awareness of health and safety issues and improve health and safety practices in producer groups.

Principle Eight: Providing Capacity Building

The organization seeks to increase positive developmental impacts for small, marginalized producers through Fair Trade.

The organization develops the skills and capabilities of its own employees or members. Organizations working directly with small producers develop specific activities to help these producers improve their management skills, production capabilities, and access to markets – local/regional/international/Fair Trade/mainstream – as appropriate. Organizations which buy Fair Trade products through Fair Trade intermediaries in the South assist these organizations to develop their capacity to support the marginalized producer groups that they work with.

Principle Nine: Promoting Fair Trade

The organization raises awareness of the aims of Fair Trade and of the need for greater justice in world trade through Fair Trade. It advocates for the objectives and activities of Fair Trade according to the scope of the organization. The organization provides its customers with information about itself, the products it markets, and the producer organizations or members that make or harvest the products. Honest advertising and marketing techniques are always used.

Principle Ten: Respect for the Environment

Organizations which produce Fair Trade products maximise the use of raw materials from sustainably managed sources in their ranges, buying locally when possible. They use production technologies that seek to reduce energy consumption and where possible use renewable energy technologies that minimize greenhouse gas emissions. They seek to minimize the impact of their waste stream on the environment. Fair Trade agricultural commodity producers minimize their environmental impacts, by using organic or low pesticide use production methods wherever possible.

Buyers and importers of Fair Trade products give priority to buying products made from raw materials that originate from sustainably managed sources, and have the least overall impact on the environment.

All organizations use recycled or easily biodegradable materials for packing to the extent possible, and goods are dispatched by sea wherever possible.

Appendix 4
TIMELINE

1970s

1974 Richard Adams establishes Tearcraft – the trading arm of evangelical Christian relief organization, Tearfund

1976 Author starts work at Tearcraft

1977 Traidcraft starts its life as a shop based in Bristol

1979 Richard Adams leaves Tearcraft to establish Traidcraft in Newcastle-upon-Tyne on 2 July

Traidcraft Ltd commences trading, governed by the non-profit-making Traidcraft Trust

Traidcraft's public launch event is at the Greenbelt Festival in August

1980s

1980 WDM tea and Campaign Coffee launched

1981 Author joins Traidcraft, responsible for warehouse, distribution, and logistics

Traidcraft establishes the Traidcraft Educational Foundation

1982 Traidcraft introduces a range of wholefood products

1983 Traidcraft's turnover exceeds £1 million

First share issue launched

Traidcraft moves to its new HQ in Gateshead

Recycled paper products introduced

1984 Traidcraft Ltd becomes a public limited company (plc)

1985 Traidcraft's turnover exceeds £2 million

1986 Founding of Traidcraft Exchange – a new charity combining Traidcraft Educational Foundation and the Traidcraft Trust with

	Graham Young as first Director
	Launch of Traidcraft's second share issue
1987	Traidcraft launches its first range of clothing
1988	Richard Adams moves on from Traidcraft. Paul Johns takes over as Managing Director
1989	Traidcraft plc turnover exceeds £5 million
	Richard Adams convenes first steering group of what would become the Fairtrade Foundation
	IFAT (International Federation of Alternative Trade) is founded with Traidcraft as one of its original members (forerunner of WFTO, World Fair Trade Organization)

1990s

Early 1990s	Traidcraft Exchange establishes Overseas Business Development Service with partner organizations initially in the Philippines, India, South Africa, and Tanzania, and later in Zambia, Bangladesh, and Malawi
1990	Traidcraft Exchange instrumental to the establishment of Shared Interest
	EFTA (European Fair Trade Association) established with Traidcraft as one of its original members
1991	Philip Angier becomes Managing Director
	Traidcraft's third share issue
	Traidcraft joins Oxfam, Equal Exchange, and Twin Trading to establish Cafédirect
	Traidcraft Mascao becomes the UK's first Fair Trade chocolate bar
1992	The Fairtrade Foundation is formally established (following the initiative started in 1989), with Traidcraft Exchange as one of the leading founders
1993	Traidcraft plc publishes its first social sccounts (then called social audit), evaluating and measuring non-financial impact
1998	Traidcraft Exchange launches its Ethical Business Programme leading to the establishment of the Traidcraft Policy Unit based in London and the establishment of the Ethical Trading Initiative
	Teadirect launched, a product developed for Cafédirect by Traidcraft
1999	Traidcraft Exchange and Traidcraft plc come together under one unitary governance structure
	Philip Angier appointed as first Chief Executive Officer (CEO) of Traidcraft
	First unitary social accounts published
1999	Geobar launched with Waitrose

2000s

2001   Philip Angier leaves Traidcraft. Paul Chandler appointed CEO
Non-supermarket Traidcraft products which are eligible begin to carry the Fairtrade Mark

2002   Turnover exceeds £10 million
Start of a fruitful partnership with Co-op Retail jointly developing products which were not eligible to carry the Fairtrade Mark – initially wine, then barbeque charcoal and rubber gloves in later years

2003   Traidcraft's fourth share issue
Author appointed to Fairtrade International Standards Committee, serving for nine years

2005   Turnover exceeds £15 million
New approach to overseas programme work sees the establishment of permanent Traidcraft Exchange offices in Kenya and Bangladesh (India would be added in later years)

2006   Traidcraft plc enjoys its most profitable year
Author appointed to Traidcraft Board of Directors

2007   Traidcraft branded handmade cards launch in Marks & Spencer
Traidcraft awarded the Queen's Award for Enterprise in the Sustainable Development category

2008   Turnover peaks at just under £17 million signalling the beginning of a gradual decline

2010s

2010   Traidcraft sells its shares in Cafédirect

2011   Traidcraft plc's last year to turn a profit
Traidcraft plc decides to withdraw membership of WFTO leaving Traidcraft Exchange as an active member

2013   Paul Chandler leaves Traidcraft. Margaret Vaughan appointed CEO

2013   After years of campaigning by Traidcraft's Policy Unit, the first Grocery Code Adjudicator (supermarket watchdog) is appointed

2015   Created, formerly Tearcraft, closes down
Andy Biggs appointed interim CEO of Traidcraft

2016   Robin Roth appointed CEO of Traidcraft

2017   Traidcraft re-joins World Fair Trade Organization, process led by the author

2017   Author steps down from Traidcraft Board of Directors

2018   Announcement that Traidcraft is to cease trading. Traidcraft 2 emerges

2019   Author leaves Traidcraft
Traidcraft celebrates fortieth anniversary